AMC'S BEST DAY HIKES
CENTRAL
MASSACHUSETTS

**Four-Season Guide to 50 of the Best Trails,
from the Pioneer Valley to the Worcester Hills**

JOHN S. BURK

Appalachian Mountain Club Books
Boston, Massachusetts

AMC is a nonprofit organization, and sales of AMC Books fund our mission of protecting the Northeast outdoors. If you appreciate our efforts and would like to become a member or make a donation to AMC, visit outdoors.org, call 800-372-1758, or contact us at Appalachian Mountain Club, 10 City Square, Boston, MA 02129.

outdoors.org/books-maps

Distributed by National Book Network.

Front cover photograph of Mount Norwottuck © Steve Grossman
Back cover photographs (left to right) of Mount Sugarloaf State Reservation © John S. Burk
  and of Rock House Reservation © Peter Marotta
Interior photographs © John S. Burk except where noted
Maps by Ken Dumas © Appalachian Mountain Club
Book design by Abigail Coyle

Library of Congress Cataloging-in-Publication Data
Names: Burk, John S., author. | Appalachian Mountain Club.
Title: AMC's best day hikes in Central Massachusetts : four-season guide to
  50 of the best trails, from the Pioneer Valley to the Worcester Hills / by John S. Burk.
Other titles: Appalachian Mountain Club's best day hikes in Central
  Massachusetts
Description: Boston, Massachusetts : Appalachian Mountain Club Books, [2018]
  | "Distributed by National Book Network"--T.p. verso. | Includes index.
Identifiers: LCCN 2018022293 (print) | LCCN 2018024414 (ebook) | ISBN
  9781628420951 (ePub) | ISBN 9781628420968 (Mobi) | ISBN 9781628420944
  (paperback)
Subjects: LCSH: Hiking--Massachusetts--Guidebooks. |
  Hiking--Massachusetts--Franklin County--Guidebooks. |
  Hiking--Massachusetts--Hampshire County--Guidebooks. |
  Hiking--Massachusetts--Hampden County--Guidebooks. |
  Hiking--Massachusetts--Worcester County--Guidebooks. |
  Walking--Massachusetts--Guidebooks. | Walking--Massachusetts--Franklin
  County--Guidebooks. | Walking--Massachusetts--Hampshire
  County--Guidebooks. | Walking--Massachusetts--Hampden County--Guidebooks.
  | Walking--Massachusetts--Worcester County--Guidebooks. |
  Trails--Massachusetts--Guidebooks. | Outdoor
  recreation--Massachusetts--Guidebooks. | Massachusetts--Guidebooks.
Classification: LCC GV199.42.M4 (ebook) | LCC GV199.42.M4 A474 2018 (print) |
  DDC 796.5109744--dc23
LC record available at https://lccn.loc.gov/2018022293

The paper used in this publication meets the minimum requirements of the American National Standard for Information Sciences-Permanence of Paper for Printed Library Materials, ANSI Z39.48-1984. ∞

Outdoor recreation activities by their very nature are potentially hazardous. This book is not a substitute for good personal judgment and training in outdoor skills. Due to changes in conditions, use of the information in this book is at the sole risk of the user. The author and the Appalachian Mountain Club assume no liability for accidents happening to, or injuries sustained by, readers who engage in the activities described in this book.

Interior pages and cover are printed on responsibly harvested paper stock certified by The Forest Stewardship Council®, an independent auditor of responsible forestry practices. Printed in the United States of America, using vegetable-based inks.

10 9 8 7 6 5 4 3 2 1   18 19 20 21

MIX
Paper from
responsible sources
FSC® C005010
www.fsc.org

In memory of Chris Ellison and Elizabeth Farnsworth, gifted naturalists who were always helpful, encouraging, and willing to share their knowledge.

LOCATOR MAP

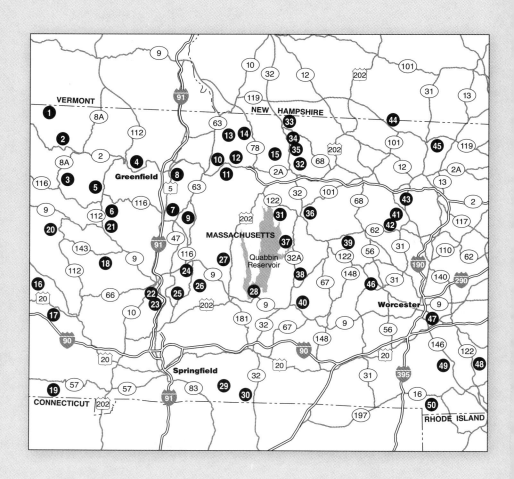

CONTENTS

NATURE AND HISTORY ESSAYS

AT-A-GLANCE TRIP PLANNER

TRIP NUMBER	TRIP NAME	LOCATION	DIFFICULTY	DISTANCE	ELEVATION GAIN
FRANKLIN COUNTY					
1	Monroe State Forest: Spruce Mountain	Monroe and Florida	Moderate	5.9 mi	1,150 ft
2	Mohawk Trail State Forest	Charlemont	Moderate-Strenuous	4.5 mi	1,240 ft
3	Kenneth Dubuque Memorial State Forest	Hawley and Plainfield	Moderate	5.5 mi	670 ft
4	High Ledges Wildlife Sanctuary	Shelburne	Moderate	3.1 mi	540 ft
5	Bear Swamp Reservation	Ashfield	Moderate	3 mi	450 ft
6	Two Bridges Trail	Ashfield	Moderate	4.2 mi	270 ft
7	Mount Sugarloaf State Reservation	Deerfield	Moderate	South Sugarloaf: 1.4 mi; North and South Sugarloaf: 4.2 mi	South Sugarloaf: 465 ft; North and South Sugarloaf: 1,465 ft
8	Rocky Mountain: Sachem Head and Poet's Seat	Greenfield	Moderate	Sachem Head Loop: 1.8 mi; Poet's Seat Loop: 1.9 mi	Sachem Head Loop: 450 ft; Poet's Seat Loop: 350 ft
9	Mount Toby	Sunderland and Leverett	Moderate-Strenuous	4.1 mi	940 ft
10	Northfield Mountain	Northfield	Moderate	3.9 mi	840 ft
11	Wendell State Forest	Wendell	Ruggles Pond Circuit: Easy; Lookout Trail Loop: Moderate	Ruggles Pond Circuit: 1.8 mi; Lookout Trail Loop: 3 mi	Ruggles Pond Circuit: 50 ft; Lookout Trail Loop: 575 ft
12	Hermit Mountain and Hermit's Castle	Erving	Easy-Moderate	4.8 mi	380 ft
13	Stratton Mountain	Northfield	Moderate-Strenuous	6.6 mi	850 ft
14	Mount Grace State Forest	Warwick	Moderate	4 mi	1,200 ft
15	Tully Mountain	Orange	Moderate	1.75 mi	470 ft

Estimated Time	Trip Highlights	Fee	Good for Kids	Dog-Friendly	X-C Skiing	Snowshoeing
3.25 hrs	Vistas, wildflowers, northern hardwood forest			✓	✓	✓
3 hrs	Ridgetop vista, old forests, river views	$		✓		✓
3.25 hrs	Cascading brook, old mill sites, scenic pond trail		✓	✓	✓	✓
2 hrs	Scenic vista, wildflowers, rocky stream		✓			✓
1.75 hrs	Pastoral views, wildflowers, ridges, beaver pond			✓		✓
3 hrs	Chapel Falls, Bullitt Farm meadows, cascading streams			✓	✓	✓
South Sugarloaf: 1.25 hrs; North and South Sugarloaf: 3.5 hrs	Spectacular view of Connecticut River/Pioneer Valley		✓	✓		✓
Sachem Head Loop: 1.25 hrs; Poet's Seat Loop: 1.25 hrs	Views from Sachem Head and Poet's Seat Tower		✓	✓		✓
2.75 hrs	Fire tower views, waterfall, wildflowers, pond			✓	✓	✓
2.75 hrs	Summit reservoir, Rose Ledge, winter trails			✓	✓	✓
Ruggles Pond Circuit: 1.25 hrs; Lookout Trail Loop: 1.75 hrs	Ruggles Pond, waterfalls, tornado site, ledges	$	✓	✓	✓	✓
3 hrs	Great view of Millers River valley, Hermit Castle site			✓	✓	✓
3.25 hrs	Scenic vista, remote valley and pond, AMC cabin			✓		
2.75 hrs	Three-state views from fire tower, old ski area site			✓	✓	✓
1.5 hrs	Scenic vista, talus slopes, meadow			✓		✓

HAMPSHIRE AND HAMPDEN COUNTIES

Trip #	Trip Name	Location	Difficulty	Distance	Elevation Gain
16	Keystone Arches Trail	Middlefield and Chester	Easy-Moderate	4.4 mi	260 ft
17	Chester-Blandford State Forest	Chester and Blandford	Circuit: Moderate-Strenuous; Sanderson Brook Falls only: Easy	Circuit: 4.3 mi; Sanderson Brook Falls only: 1.6 mi	Circuit: 1,080 ft; Sanderson Brook Falls only: 175 ft
18	Westfield River: East Branch Trail and Chesterfield Gorge	Chesterfield	Easy-Moderate	6 mi	150 ft
19	Granville State Forest	Granville and Tolland	Easy-Moderate	2 mi	250 ft
20	William Cullen Bryant Homestead	Cummington	Easy	1.8 mi	345 ft
21	Daughters of the American Revolution State Forest	Goshen	Moderate	3.7 mi	310 ft
22	Arcadia Wildlife Sanctuary	Easthampton and Northampton	Easy	1.9 mi	75 ft
23	Mount Tom State Reservation	Holyoke and Easthampton	Moderate-Strenuous	4.8 mi	1,150 ft
24	Silvio O. Conte National Fish and Wildlife Refuge: Fort River Division	Hadley	Easy	1.2 mi	25 ft
25	Mount Holyoke	South Hadley	Moderate	2.75 mi	850 ft
26	Mount Norwottuck, the Horse Caves, and Rattlesnake Knob	Amherst and Granby	Moderate-Strenuous	5.5 mi	1,185 ft
27	Mount Lincoln and Scarborough Brook Conservation Area	Belchertown and Pelham	Easy-Moderate	2.5 mi	500 ft
28	Quabbin Reservoir: Quabbin Park	Belchertown and Ware	Moderate	5.6 mi	700 ft
29	Laughing Brook Wildlife Sanctuary	Hampden	Easy-Moderate	4.2 mi	350 ft
30	Peaked Mountain	Monson	Moderate	2.6 mi	700 ft

WORCESTER COUNTY

Trip #	Trip Name	Location	Difficulty	Distance	Elevation Gain
31	Federated Women's Club State Forest and Soapstone Hill	Petersham and New Salem	Moderate	3.3 mi	450 ft
32	Bearsden Conservation Area	Athol	Moderate-Strenuous	3.6 mi	580 ft
33	Royalston Falls Reservation	Royalston	Moderate	1.6 mi	350 ft
34	Jacobs Hill Reservation	Royalston	Easy-Moderate	2.7 mi	480 ft

ESTIMATED TIME	TRIP HIGHLIGHTS	FEE	GOOD FOR KIDS	DOG-FRIENDLY	X-C SKIING	SNOWSHOEING
2.5 hrs	Historic railroad bridges, river views, waterfalls		✓	✓	✓	✓
Circuit: 3 hrs; Sanderson Brook Falls only: 1 hr	Sanderson Brook Falls, scenic vista			✓	✓	✓
3 hrs	Dramatic granite gorge, river views, historical sites	$	✓	✓	✓	✓
1 hr	Cascades, wildflowers, Hubbard River, beaver pond		✓	✓	✓	✓
1.25 hrs	Historical house and barn, old forest, country views		✓	✓	✓	✓
2.75 hrs	Views from fire tower, Highland Lake, beach	$		✓	✓	✓
1.25 hrs	Great birding, floodplain forest, viewing tower	$	✓		✓	✓
3 hrs	Outstanding ridge views, basalt cliffs, Lake Bray	$		✓		✓
45 mins	Universally accessible, elevated boardwalks, birding		✓			✓
2 hrs	Connecticut River views, Summit House			✓		✓
3.75 hrs	Scenic views, Horse Caves, old orchard			✓		✓
1.5 hrs	Views from fire tower, old mill pond, meadow		✓	✓	✓	✓
3 hrs	Views from Quabbin Hill and Enfield Lookout, wildlife					✓
2.25 hrs	East Brook, pleasant woods trail, stone walls		✓			✓
2 hrs	Vistas on summit ridge, old orchard		✓	✓		✓
2 hrs	Spectacular views, beaver pond, old quarry		✓			✓
2.5 hrs	Duck Pond, vistas at Sheep Rock and Round Top Hill			✓	✓	✓
1.25 hrs	Picturesque waterfall, natural pools and bridge		✓	✓		✓
2 hrs	Vistas at Jacobs Hill and the Ledges, Spirit Falls		✓	✓	✓	✓

TRIP NUMBER	TRIP NAME	LOCATION	DIFFICULTY	DISTANCE	ELEVATION GAIN
35	Tully Lake and Doane's Falls	Royalston and Athol	Easy-Moderate	4.5 mi	225 ft
36	Rutland Brook Wildlife Sanctuary	Petersham	Easy-Moderate	2.6 mi	500 ft
37	Quabbin Reservoir: Dana Common	Petersham	Easy	3.6 mi	75 ft
38	Mandell Hill Conservation Area	Hardwick	Easy	1.3 mi	100 ft
39	Ware River Watershed	Hubbardston, Barre, and Rutland	Easy-Moderate	5.8 mi	405 ft
40	Rock House Reservation	West Brookfield	Easy	2 mi	370 ft
41	Wachusett Mountain State Reservation	Princeton and Westminster	Moderate	3.4 mi	755 ft
42	Wachusett Meadow Wildlife Sanctuary	Princeton	Easy-Moderate	4 mi	350 ft
43	Leominster State Forest	Westminster and Leominster	Moderate	Crow Hill Loop: 1.2 mi; Rocky Pond-Ball Hill Loop: 4.9 mi	Crow Hill Loop: 355 ft; Rocky Pond-Ball Hill Loop: 675 ft
44	Mount Watatic	Ashburnham and Ashby	Moderate	2.8 mi	700 ft
45	Willard Brook State Forest	Ashby and Townsend	Easy-Moderate	3.3 mi	325 ft
46	Moore State Park	Paxton	Easy	2.1 mi	200 ft
47	Broad Meadow Brook Wildlife Sanctuary	Worcester	Easy-Moderate	3.25 mi	170 ft
48	Blackstone River and Canal Heritage State Park	Uxbridge	Easy	King Philip's Trail: 2.4 mi; Goat Hill to Plummer's Landing: 5 mi	King Philip's Trail: 100 ft; Goat Hill to Plummer's Landing: 65 ft
49	Purgatory Chasm State Reservation	Sutton	Easy-Moderate	2 mi	245 ft
50	Douglas State Forest	Douglas	Easy-Moderate	4.2 mi	200 ft

ESTIMATED TIME	TRIP HIGHLIGHTS	FEE	GOOD FOR KIDS	DOG-FRIENDLY	X-C SKIING	SNOWSHOEING
2.5 hrs	Scenic lake views, Doane's Falls, Tully Dam			🐕		🏂
1.75 hrs	Pond views, cascades, giant trees, rock ledges		🚶			🏂
2 hrs	Abandoned Quabbin town site, meadows, Pottapaug Pond		🚶			
1 hr	Pastoral views, grasslands, wildlife habitat		🚶		🎿	🏂
2.75 hrs	Outstanding wildlife habitat, Blood Swamp, meadows			🐕	🎿	🏂
1.5 hrs	Rock shelter and ledges, Carter Pond, butterfly garden		🚶	🐕	🎿	🏂
2.5 hrs	100+ mile view, old forests, Echo Lake, High Meadow			🐕		🏂
2.5 hrs	Brown Hill vista, meadows, wetlands, butterflies	$	🚶		🎿	🏂
Crow Hill Loop: 1 hr; Rocky Pond–Ball Hill Loop: 3 hrs	Scenic view, dramatic cliff, ponds, mountain laurel			🐕		🏂
2.25 hrs	Spectacular views, great hawk-watch site		🚶	🐕		🏂
2 hrs	Scenic brook trail, rare pitch pine forest	$	🚶	🐕	🎿	🏂
1.25 hrs	Colorful gardens, historic sawmill, waterfalls, Eames Pond		🚶	🐕	🎿	🏂
2.25 hrs	Urban sanctuary with diverse habitats and wetlands	$	🚶			🏂
King Philip's Trail: 1.5 hrs; Goat Hill to Plummer's Landing: 2.5 hrs	Vista, historical canal and lock, river views		🚶	🐕	🎿	🏂
2 hrs	Dramatic rocky chasm, Purgatory Brook	$	🚶	🐕	🎿	🏂
2.5 hrs	Rare cedar swamp, wetlands, Wallum Lake	$		🐕	🎿	🏂

ACKNOWLEDGMENTS

This guide, and the region's many recreational opportunities, would not have been possible without the efforts of many conservation organizations, public and private landowners, and trail groups. Thanks to Town of Amherst, Appalachian Mountain Club, Ashfield Trails, Town of Athol, Athol Bird and Nature Club, Town of Belchertown, East Quabbin Land Trust, Friends of the Keystone Arches, Town of Greenfield, Friends of the Wapack Trail, Kestrel Land Trust, Mass Audubon, Massachusetts Department of Conservation and Recreation, Massachusetts Division of Fisheries and Wildlife, MassGIS (the Massachusetts Bureau of Geographic Information), Midstate Trail Committee, Mount Grace Land Conservation Trust, National Park Service, New England Wildflower Society, North Quabbin Trails Association, Northfield Mountain Recreation and Environmental Center (FirstLight Power), Shelburne Trails, The Trustees of Reservations, University of Massachusetts, U.S. Army Corps of Engineers, U.S. Fish and Wildlife Service, and Wild and Scenic Westfield River Committee.

Individually, thanks to Vin Antil, Earle Baldwin, Beth Bazler, Paul Bissex, Kari Blood, Dan Bolton, Larry Buell, Jim Caffrey, Deborah Carey, Bob Clark, James Clune, Bobby Curley, Anthony D'Amato, Kristin DeBoer, Cindy Dunn, Chris Ellison, Elizabeth Farnsworth, John Foster, Curt Griffith, Cynthia Henshaw, Don Hoffes, Jonah Keane, Josh Knox, Dave Kotker, Dave Litterer, Jeff Mangum, Steve Manley, Joanne McGee, David Miller, Kathy Morris, John O'Keefe, Dave Orwig, Greg Parsons, Mauri Pelto, Tom Pirro, Phil Pless, Nathan Rudolph, Dave Small, Ron Wolanin, and Allen Young. For many helpful resources, thanks to the Athol Public Library, Erving Public Library, Harvard Forest, Phinehas S. Newton Library in Royalston, Petersham Memorial Library, and Woods Memorial Library in Barre. Thanks also to family, friends, and colleagues who accompanied me on hikes, shared sightings and trail updates, and offered encouragement.

Finally, thanks as always to the Appalachian Mountain Club for the opportunity to pursue this and other projects. Thanks to editor Shannon Smith, copyeditor Lenore Howard, editorial director Jennifer Wehunt, books intern Christina Sargent, mapmaker Ken Dumas, and production manager Abigail Coyle. Thanks also to Ryan Smith for contributing photos and to Kristen Sykes for feedback on the table of contents.

INTRODUCTION

With an abundance of protected land, diverse natural and historical features, and an extensive network of recreational trails, central Massachusetts is an explorer's paradise. Indeed, one of the biggest challenges in writing this guide was selecting 50 hikes out of the many possibilities. Whether you're looking for a family-friendly nature walk, a long-distance backcountry excursion, or a place to absorb abundant flora and fauna, there are a wealth of options to choose from in this book. Many large protected corridors have been established throughout the area, providing crucial habitats for wildlife and recreational opportunities in the heart of a heavily populated state.

The relatively compact geographic region, which stretches from the east slopes of the Berkshire Hills to the western edge of the southern New England coastal plain, boasts a long and rich natural and human history. The landscape is characterized by highly varied topography, numerous rivers and wetlands, and extensive forests. Mountain and hill elevations are modest, generally ranging between 600 to 2,000 feet, but many offer outstanding scenic views. Much of the land is within the watershed of the Connecticut River, New England's longest waterway. The Connecticut's major tributaries are the Deerfield and Westfield rivers in western Massachusetts and the Millers and Chicopee rivers in the central part of the state.

Other significant features include numerous waterfalls and cascades, Chesterfield Gorge, Purgatory Chasm, old-growth and floodplain forests, Atlantic white cedar and black gum swamps, and Quabbin Reservoir, southern New England's largest freshwater lake and conservation area. There are many historical sites to discover as well, such as the Keystone Arches railroad bridges, the abandoned town common of Dana, Mount Holyoke Summit House, Blackstone Canal, and old mill sites.

The summits and foothills of the eastern Berkshires, which are part of the northern Appalachian Mountains, were created by a series of continental collisions about 350 to 500 million years ago. The origins of the Connecticut River valley began with the Eastern Border Fault, a 130-mile fracture caused by earthquakes when the North American, African, and Eurasian continents divided as the supercontinent of Pangea broke apart some 200 million years ago. Lava from volcanoes associated with the fault formed the Metacomet Ridge, a long chain of mountains and ridges that includes Mount Tom, the Holyoke Range, and the Pocumtuck Ridge, which extends from Greenfield to Long Island Sound. Dinosaurs roamed the tropical valley, leaving behind well-preserved footprints that became significant discoveries for scientists, such as the noted geologist Edward Hitchcock in the nineteenth century. Wachusett Mountain, the highest peak east of the Berkshires, is one of several monadnocks (isolated mountains) in central New England that have resisted erosion to a greater degree than the surrounding countryside.

After the climate markedly cooled approximately 200 million years ago, a series of about twenty ice ages followed. Glaciers, formed by accumulating snow that compacted to ice, shaped the slopes of the mountains, ridges, and hills. They scoured deep valleys and deposited countless boulders and stones that made farming a considerable challenge for early Colonial settlers. (Much of the Northeast is forested now because many farmers abandoned the rocky, inhospitable land after the nineteenth century.) After the last ice age ended about 15,000 years ago, glacial Lake Hitchcock formed behind a debris dam near Rocky Hill, Connecticut, and extended along the valley for 200 miles to Saint Johnsbury, Vermont. After 4,000 years, the lake gradually drained, and the Connecticut River assumed its modern course, winding through sediment on the valley floor that has provided highly productive farmland for generations of inhabitants.

The first human beings arrived in the region about 12,000 years ago. Prominent tribes included the Pocumtuc, who established agricultural settlements along the Connecticut River in fertile areas (such as present-day Agawam, Northampton, and Deerfield), and the Nipmuck, who inhabited much of the adjacent uplands of central Massachusetts. European colonists arrived in the Connecticut Valley during the 1630s, drawn by the river's fertile farmlands and trade corridor, and gradually settled the surrounding uplands through the mid-eighteenth century.

When walking past a stone wall on a forest trail, try to imagine the same land as open countryside with long views to distant landmarks, such as Mount Monadnock or Wachusett Mountain. That's what most of the region looked like after the early Colonial settlers cleared an estimated three-quarters of the forests for agriculture. Only a few small sections of virgin forest remain today, sheltered in rugged areas such as the upper Deerfield River valley and the rocky slopes of Wachusett Mountain. The loss of woodland habitat also had adverse consequences for native wildlife, such as moose, black bears, white-tailed deer, beavers, wild turkeys, wood ducks, timber wolves, and mountain lions. By the mid-nineteenth century, however, the combination of poor soil and the start of the Industrial Revolution had prompted many farmers to abandon their land, and the forests gradually began to recover. Today places like Arcadia Wildlife Sanctuary, Dana Common, Wachusett Meadow Wildlife Sanctuary, and Mandell Hill maintain old fields as meadows and grasslands for wildlife.

With many high-energy rivers and streams fueled by abundant precipitation and varied topography, central Massachusetts was ideal for mills, which settlers established along waterways of all sizes from the mid-eighteenth century onward. Though an important part of the economy, the mills polluted and disrupted the flows of the waterways that powered them. The hilly terrain also led to the creation of two significant landmarks of railroad history: the Keystone Arches railroad bridges on Westfield River and the Hoosac Tunnel in the northern Berkshire Hills. Both opened up rail travel to important markets in New York and beyond.

In the early twentieth century, the lightly populated watersheds of the Swift, Ware, and Nashua rivers drew the interest of Massachusetts water supply planners, who had struggled for years to find adequate sources for the ever-growing metropolitan Boston region. In 1905, the Wachusett Reservoir, formed by an impoundment of the Nashua River in central Worcester County, opened as the world's largest artificial reservoir. It was followed in the 1930s by the much larger Quabbin Reservoir, which was built in the Swift River valley after four towns were abandoned and then flooded. A significant portion of the Ware River watershed was also added as a supplement to the reservoirs. In addition to providing millions of residents with drinking water, these protected areas have had great value for wildlife and recreational users. The water-supply projects were controversial, though, as thousands of residents lost their homes and properties. Some tensions still linger, as evidenced by the contentious debates over a state proposal in 2017 to establish a rattlesnake colony at Quabbin Reservoir.

Today forests and clean wetlands have reclaimed much of the landscape, and familiar wildlife species, such as moose, black bears, white-tailed deer, beavers, wood ducks, and bald eagles, have made remarkable recoveries in recent decades. That said, concerns remain, including development of forest and farmland, and the spread of forest pests and invasive plants. One of the first tree species to be impacted was the American chestnut, which was lost to the blight fungus during the early twentieth century. Eastern hemlock is now imperiled by the hemlock woolly adelgid (HWA), an introduced pest that arrived in central Massachusetts in the late twentieth century and has been gradually spreading throughout the state; Infested trees usually die within four to ten years. The loss of the evergreen cover has affected cold-water forest streams and deer wintering areas.

Thanks to the efforts of many conservation organizations, private landowners who have graciously allowed access to their land, and volunteer trail groups and maintainers, a considerable portion of the region is now permanently protected and open to the public for hiking and other recreational activities.

In addition to enjoying the trails, please support their efforts through donations, memberships, and volunteer work, and treat the land with respect.

HOW TO USE THIS BOOK

With 50 hikes to choose from, you may wonder how to decide where to go. The locator map at the front of this book will help you narrow down the trips by location, and the at-a-glance trip planner that follows the table of contents will provide more information to guide you toward a decision.

Once you settle on a destination and turn to a trip in this guide, you will find a series of icons that indicate whether fees are charged, the hike is good for kids, whether dogs are permitted, and whether cross-country skiing and snowshoeing are allowed.

Information on the basics follows: location, rating, distance, elevation gain, estimated time, and maps. The ratings are based on the author's perception and are estimates of what the average hiker will experience. You may find hikes to be easier or more difficult than stated. The estimated time is also based on the author's perception. Consider your own pace when planning a trip.

The elevation gain is calculated from measurements and information obtained from U.S. Geological Survey (USGS) topographic maps, landowner maps, and Google Earth. Each hike identifies the relevant USGS maps, if any, as well as where you can find additional trail maps. The boldface summary provides a basic overview of what you will see on your hike.

The directions explain how to reach the trailhead by car. GPS coordinates for parking lots are also included. Enter these coordinates into your own device for driving directions. Whether or not you own a GPS device, it is wise to consult an atlas before you leave home.

In the trail description, you will find instructions regarding where to hike, the trails on which to hike, and turn-by-turn directions. You will also learn about natural and human history along your hike, as well as information about flora, fauna, and any landmarks and objects you will encounter.

The trail maps that accompany each trip will guide you along your hike, but it would be wise to take an official trail map with you. They are often—but not always—available online, at the trailhead, or at the visitor center.

Each trip ends with a section titled "More Information" that provides details about restroom locations, access times and fees, the property's rules and regulations, and contact information for the place where you will be hiking. "Winter Activities" provides information on what kind of cold-weather activities are allowed or recommeneded for each location and the "Nearby" section provides useful information on other sights, hikes, and points of interests in the area.

TRIP PLANNING AND SAFETY

While elevations in and around central Massachusetts can be relatively low, and the hikes detailed in this guide aren't particularly dangerous, you'll still want to be prepared. Some of the walks traverse moderately rugged terrain along rocky hills, while others lead to ponds and fields where you'll have extended periods of sun exposure and slow walking. Many places in the region have complex trail networks, some of which are unmarked. Allow extra time in case you get lost.

You will be more likely to have an enjoyable, safe hike if you plan ahead and take proper precautions. Before heading out for your hike, consider the following:

- Select a hike that everyone in your group is comfortable taking. Match the hike to the abilities of the least capable person in the group. If anyone is uncomfortable with the weather or is tired, turn around and complete the hike another day.

- Plan to be back at the trailhead before dark. Before beginning your hike, determine a turnaround time. Don't diverge from it, even if you have not reached your intended destination.

- Check the weather. Spring and fall bring unstable air masses to the area; summer features late-afternoon thunderstorms. If you are planning a ridge or summit hike, start early so you will be off the exposed area before the afternoon hours, when thunderstorms most often strike. Temperatures at higher elevations are often significantly lower than they are in the cities and suburbs and tend to fall quickly after sunset. Storms are a potential hazard throughout the area. If rain is in the forecast, bring waterproof gear.

- Bring a pack with the following items:
  - ✓ Water: Two quarts per person is usually adequate, depending on the weather and the length of the trip.
  - ✓ Food: Even if you are planning a one-hour hike, bring some high-energy snacks, such as nuts, dried fruit, or snack bars. Pack a lunch for longer trips.
  - ✓ Map and compass: Be sure you know how to use them. A handheld GPS device may also be helpful but is not always reliable.
  - ✓ Headlamp or flashlight, with spare batteries
  - ✓ Extra clothing: rain gear, wool sweater or fleece, hat, and mittens
  - ✓ Sunscreen

- ✓ First-aid kit, including adhesive bandages, gauze, nonprescription pain-killers, and moleskin
- ✓ Pocketknife or multitool
- ✓ Waterproof matches and a lighter
- ✓ Trash bag
- ✓ Toilet paper
- ✓ Whistle
- ✓ Insect repellent
- ✓ Sunglasses
- ✓ Cell phone: Be aware that cell phone service is unreliable in rural areas. If you are receiving a signal, use the phone only for emergencies to avoid disturbing the backcountry experience for other hikers.
- ✓ Binoculars (optional)
- ✓ Camera (optional)

- Wear appropriate footwear and clothing. Wool or synthetic hiking socks will keep your feet dry and help prevent blisters. Comfortable, waterproof hiking boots will provide ankle support and good traction. Avoid wearing cotton clothing, which absorbs sweat and rain, contributing to an unpleasant hiking experience. Polypropylene, fleece, silk, and wool all wick moisture away from your body and keep you warm in wet or cold conditions. To help avoid bug bites, you may want to wear pants and a long-sleeved shirt.

- When you are ahead of the rest of your hiking group, wait at all trail junctions until the others catch up. This avoids confusion and keeps people from getting separated or lost.

- If you see downed wood that appears to be purposely covering a trail, it probably means the trail is closed due to overuse or hazardous conditions.

- If a trail is muddy, walk through the mud or on rocks, never on tree roots or plants. Waterproof boots will keep your feet comfortable. Staying in the center of the trail will keep it from eroding into a wide hiking highway.

- Leave your itinerary and the time you expect to return with someone you trust. If you see a logbook at a trailhead, be sure to sign in when you arrive and sign out when you finish your hike.

- Poison ivy is always a threat when hiking. To identify the plant, look for clusters of three leaves that shine in the sun but are dull in the shade. If you do come into contact with poison ivy, wash the affected area with soap as soon as possible.

- Snakes, common in many hiking areas, are cold-blooded. Their body temperature rises and falls with the ambient temperature, and they hibernate during cold months. In summer, snakes may bask on exposed rocks or on open trails, although you also may find them near stone walls, brush piles, or fallen logs. Snakes usually avoid confrontation and are not aggressive toward humans; when surprised or provoked, however, they may bite. Most snakes in the central Massachusetts region are harmless, but northern copperheads and timber rattlesnakes (which are very rare and restricted to a few isolated colonies) have venomous bites that can be painful or, in rare cases, fatal. To reduce the chance of an unpleasant encounter for both parties, use proper snake etiquette, especially when hiking around rocky areas in the warm seasons: Look before taking a step or reaching in between rocks; if you see a snake, leave it alone. If you are bitten by a snake, seek medical attention as quickly as possible.

- Wear blaze-orange items in hunting season. Hunting seasons vary. Check with state game commissions: mass.gov/hunting-in-the-parks.

- Ticks, which can carry diseases, are common in many wooded and grassy areas throughout the state though uncommon on mountain ridges, and are active year-round in Massachusetts. To reduce the chance of a tick bite, you may want to wear pants and a long-sleeved shirt. After you finish your hike, check for ticks on your clothes and body. The deer tick, which can carry Lyme disease, can be as small as a pinhead. Run a lint roller over your clothes. Take a shower when you get home and check for ticks again.

- Mosquitoes can be common in the woods and wet areas in summer and fall. Although some carry diseases, their bite is mostly annoying. As with ticks, you can reduce the chance of bites by wearing long sleeves and pants. A variety of options are available for dealing with bugs, ranging from sprays that include the active ingredient diethyl-meta-toluamide (commonly known as DEET), which potentially can cause skin or eye irritation, to more skin-friendly products. Head nets, often cheaper than a can of repellent, are useful in especially buggy conditions.

LEAVE NO TRACE

The Appalachian Mountain Club (AMC) is a national educational partner of Leave No Trace, a nonprofit organization
dedicated to promoting and inspiring responsible outdoor
recreation through education, research, and partnerships.

The Leave No Trace program seeks to develop wild land
ethics, or ways in which people think and act in the outdoors to minimize their
impact on the areas they visit and to protect our natural resources for future
enjoyment. Leave No Trace unites four federal land management agencies—the
U.S. Forest Service, National Park Service, Bureau of Land Management, and
U.S. Fish and Wildlife Service—with manufacturers, outdoor retailers, user
groups, educators, organizations such as AMC, and individuals.

The Leave No Trace ethic is guided by these seven principles:

1. **Plan ahead and prepare.** Know the terrain and any regulations applicable
   to the area you're planning to visit, and be prepared for extreme weather or
   other emergencies. This will enhance your enjoyment and ensure that
   you've chosen an appropriate destination. Small groups have less impact
   on resources and the experiences of other backcountry visitors.

2. **Travel and camp on durable aurfaces.** Travel and camp on established
   trails and campsites, rock, gravel, dry grasses, or snow. Good campsites
   are found, not made. Camp at least 200 feet from lakes and streams, and
   focus activities on areas where vegetation is absent. In pristine areas,
   disperse use to prevent the creation of campsites and trails.

3. **Dispose of waste properly.** Pack it in, pack it out. Inspect your camp for
   trash or food scraps. Deposit solid human waste in cat holes dug 6 to 8
   inches deep, at least 200 feet from water, camps, and trails. Pack out toilet
   paper and hygiene products. To wash yourself or your dishes, carry water
   200 feet from streams or lakes and use small amounts of biodegradable
   soap. Scatter strained dishwater.

4. **Leave what you find.** Cultural or historic artifacts, as well as natural
   objects such as plants and rocks, should be left as found.

5. **Minimize campfire impacts.** Cook on a stove. Use established fire rings,
   fire pans, or mound fires. If you build a campfire, keep it small and use
   dead sticks found on the ground.

6. **Respect wildlife.** Observe wildlife from a distance. Feeding animals alters their natural behavior. Protect wildlife from your food by storing rations and trash securely.

7. **Be considerate of other visitors.** Be courteous, respect the quality of other visitors' backcountry experiences, and let nature's sounds prevail.

AMC is a national provider of the Leave No Trace Master Educator course. AMC offers this five-day course, designed especially for outdoor professionals and land managers, as well as the shorter two-day Leave No Trace Trainer course at locations throughout the Northeast. For Leave No Trace information and materials, contact the Leave No Trace Center for Outdoor Ethics, PO Box 997, Boulder, CO 80306; 800-332-4100 or 302-442-8222; lnt.org. For information on AMC's Leave No Trace Master Educator training course, see outdoors .org/education/lnt.

FRANKLIN COUNTY

From the high summits and old-growth forests of the northern Berkshire Hills to the valleys of the Connecticut River and its tributaries, Franklin County is a place of diverse natural features and abundant protected land. Encompassing the northern portion of the Connecticut River watershed in Massachusetts, it is one of the state's most picturesque and lightly populated rural areas. The region is home to the Mohawk Trail Highway, one of New England's best-known scenic roads.

At the boundary between Franklin County and Berkshire County is the Hoosac Range, an extension of the southern Green Mountains that stretches from the Vermont state line to Savoy Mountain State Forest. One of the high peaks of the range is 2,730-foot Spruce Mountain, which rises above the valleys of Dunbar Brook and Deerfield River in the remote uplands of Monroe State Forest (Trip 1). Scattered throughout these rugged slopes and ridges are groves of old-growth forest, a rare and ecologically significant natural community in southern New England. On the east side of the range, Mohawk Trail State Forest (Trip 2), home of many of the state's largest and oldest trees, encompasses an area of steep ridges at the confluence of the Cold and Deerfield rivers.

The Vermont Piedmont ecoregion, nestled between the Berkshire highlands and the northwest corner of the Connecticut River valley, is compact and hilly, with elevations from about 400 to 1,500 feet. The calcium-rich bedrock and soils support rich mesic forest natural communities, which are characterized by

Facing page: Mohawk Trail State Forest is ablaze in color when fall foliage peaks in October.

abundant and diverse wildflowers and northern hardwood forests dominated by sugar maple, basswood, and ash. Characteristic wildflowers include red trillium, trout lily, dutchman's breeches, and spring beauty.

Deerfield River, one of the Connecticut River's largest tributaries, is abundant in scenery and human history. From its headwaters in the southern Green Mountains, it flows 76 miles past ridges and hills and farmland to its confluence with the Connecticut River at the Deerfield–Greenfield town line. In pre-Colonial times, the valley was part of a crucial American Indian travel route, used by the Mohawk and other tribes, between the Connecticut River and Hudson River. In the nineteenth century, the creation of the Hoosac Tunnel opened a key railroad line to Albany, New York. One of the finest perspectives of the valley is from the lookout at High Ledges Wildlife Sanctuary in Shelburne (Trip 4), where fertile soils support a wide variety of plant life, including colonies of colorful orchids.

In the uplands on the south side of the valley, the expansive Kenneth Dubuque Memorial State Forest (Trip 3) is a crucial link in a large conservation corridor that extends into adjacent northwest Hampshire County. In the nearby hills of Ashfield, the diverse habitats of Bear Swamp Reservation include rocky ridges with abundant wildflowers and hilltops with pastoral views across orchards to the Green Mountains. The Two Bridges Trail (Trip 6) connects several public and private conservation areas in another corridor of protected land in the South River watershed, including Bullitt Farm and the cascades of Chapel Falls.

The upper Connecticut River valley is a relatively narrow section of lowlands flanked by mountains and ridges at the north end of the Metacomet Ridge, which stretches south for roughly 100 miles to the Connecticut coast at Long Island Sound. On the west banks of the river, the Pocumtuck Ridge extends 15 miles, from Mount Sugarloaf in Deerfield to Rocky Mountain and Canada Hill in Greenfield. The south peak of Mount Sugarloaf (Trip 7) is well known for its spectacular views of the Connecticut River valley and surrounding hills, and the less-traveled north peak offers additional views to the Berkshire Hills. At the north end of the ridge, the twin rocky summits of Sachem Head and Poet's Seat (Trip 8) offer fine perspectives of Greenfield and the upper valley. On the east side of the river, Mount Toby (Trip 9) the highest point of the Connecticut Valley in Massachusetts at 1,269 feet, is home to a variety of natural features, including the cascades of Roaring Brook, Cranberry Pond, the Sunderland Caves, and rich wildflower habitat.

East of the Connecticut Valley are numerous low hills and wetlands on the western edge of the Worcester–Monadnock and Lower Worcester plateaus. Most of this land lies within the lower watershed of Millers River, the largest tributary of the Connecticut River in central Massachusetts. The river suffered heavily in the past from industrial pollution but has made a strong recovery in recent decades, thanks to cleanup efforts and protection of the watershed. On the south side of the river, Wendell State Forest (Trip 11), with its 7,000 acres of wooded ridges, rock outcroppings, cascading streams, and ponds, is part of an expanse of protected land along the New England National Scenic Trail corridor, from Lake Wyola to the New Hampshire state line.

In the uplands on the north side of Millers River, Northfield Mountain (Trip 10) is distinguished by its extensive recreational trail network; a large artificial summit reservoir; and Rose Ledge, a high sheer cliff favored by rock climbers. Hermit Mountain (Trip 12), Northfield Mountain's southeast shoulder, is the crest of a rugged ridge that rises dramatically above the riverbanks in Erving. The nearby Bald Hills are capped by Stratton Mountain (Trip 13), the site of a unique enclosed cabin built by AMC volunteers and a lookout with sweeping views across the upper New England Trail corridor. To the east sits Mount Grace (Trip 14), a monadnock, or isolated mountain, that is the highest point of the New England Trail, at 1,621 feet. The summit fire tower offers panoramic views across portions of three states.

Tully River, one of Millers River's largest tributaries, is the centerpiece of the North Quabbin Bioreserve, where public and private agencies and landowners protect more than 120,000 acres. The watershed's highest point is 1,168-foot Tully Mountain (Trip 15), where rock ledges offer views across ponds and unbroken forests to Wachusett Mountain and New Hampshire's Mount Monadnock. The mountain is one of the highlights of Tully Trail, a 22-mile loop that extends into adjacent northwest Worcester County.

In southeast Franklin County, the New England Trail passes through the northwest portion of the Swift River watershed. The river's west and middle branches are two of the main source waters for Quabbin Reservoir, which was built during the 1930s as the primary water supply for the greater Boston area. The reservoir, which supplies drinking water to millions of eastern Massachusetts residents, is southern New England's largest conservation area and offers crucial habitat for wildlife and a variety of recreational opportunities.

1

MONROE STATE FOREST: SPRUCE MOUNTAIN

Northern hardwood forests, abundant wildflowers, and scenic views of the Deerfield River valley are among the highlights of this excursion to Spruce Mountain and Hunt Hill in the Hoosac Range.

DIRECTIONS

From I-91 take Exit 26 in Greenfield and follow MA 2 west 28.3 miles to the junction with Whitcomb Hill Road in Florida (0.3 mile east of the Peace Elk statue at Whitcomb Summit). Turn right on Whitcomb Hill Road, take the first left on Monroe Road, and continue 2.3 miles (the latter portion of the road is dirt) to a three-way junction opposite Spruce Mountain Trail. Turn right and continue 0.2 mile to the parking area at a power-line clearing at the road's end. *GPS coordinates: 42° 41.560′ N, 72° 59.078′ W.*

TRAIL DESCRIPTION

With its rugged mountains, rocky streams, and remote location in the upper Deerfield River valley, Monroe State Forest offers a true backcountry experience. At 2,730 feet, Spruce Mountain is one of the highest peaks of the Hoosac Range, a southerly extension of Vermont's Green Mountains. In the valley below, Dunbar Brook cascades to its confluence with Deerfield River through a glacial ravine that shelters several tracts of old-growth forest.

This 5.9-mile outing combines a 5.3-mile loop on Spruce Mountain Trail and Raycroft Road (a dirt woods road) with a 0.3-mile side trip to Raycroft Lookout, which offers fine views of the Deerfield River valley. You can shorten the Spruce Mountain segment to 3.6 miles by backtracking to the trailhead from the summit.

At the parking area, the power-line clearing affords open views to two of New England's best-known peaks: Mount Greylock to the southwest and New Hampshire's

LOCATION
Monroe and Florida, MA

RATING
Moderate

DISTANCE
5.9 miles

ELEVATION GAIN
1,150 feet

ESTIMATED TIME
3.25 hours

MAPS
USGS Rowe and USGS North Adams; Massachusetts Department of Conservation and Recreation map: mass.gov/eea/docs/dcr/parks/trails/monroe.pdf

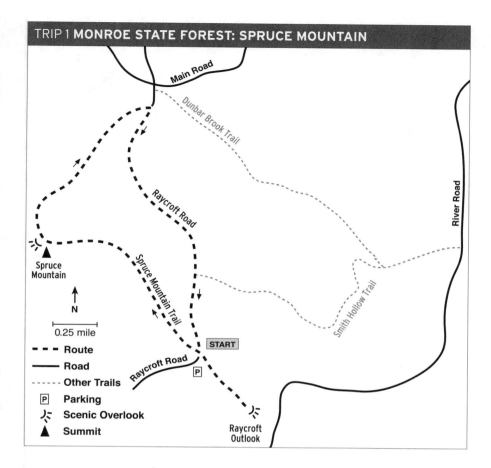

Mount Monadnock to the northeast. You can visit Raycroft Lookout before or after hiking Spruce Mountain. The trail to the lookout continues as an extension of the dirt road downhill along Hunt Hill's ridge. At 0.3 mile, reach a stone balcony built by the Civilian Conservation Corps during the 1930s. On the 1,900-foot overlook, there are fine views of the Deerfield River valley from roughly 1,000 feet above the river. After enjoying the sights, retrace your steps to the parking area. Elevation gain to the parking area is 175 feet.

To reach Spruce Mountain Trail, follow the dirt road to the parking area back to the junction with Raycroft Road. Cross Raycroft Road and begin an easy to moderately steep ascent on Spruce Mountain Trail through groves of birch, beech, and sugar maple. This forest community, known as northern hardwood, is characteristic of cool, high elevations, such as Vermont's Green Mountains, New Hampshire's White Mountains, and the highest summits of western Massachusetts. It is renowned for its vibrant fall foliage, from the bright orange and red hues of maples to the yellows of birches. Much of western Massachusetts lies within a transition forest zone that includes a mix of northern hardwoods and species that thrive in warmer environs, such as oak, hickory, and white pine.

Follow Spruce Mountain Trail across another power-line clearing with open views. This is a good place to stop and watch for wildlife, which benefit from "edges," or areas where different habitats overlap, providing food, cover, and travel corridors. In summer, you may see black bears foraging on blueberries or blackberries, or unintentionally flush ruffed grouse near the forest's edge. The sudden noise of flapping wings as the birds burst out of hiding has startled many hikers.

Like other mountains and hills in western Massachusetts, Spruce Mountain is an ideal habitat for wildflowers, due to nutrient-rich soils that sustain a wide variety of plants. One species that thrives here is trout lily, which is easily identified by its six yellow flower petals and narrow leaves with mottled brown markings. Other familiar spring ephemerals, or woodland wildflowers that emerge after the last snowmelt and before the trees fully leaf out, include spring beauty and red trillium; watch for the latter near brooks and other wet areas. Late April and May are the best times to see the wildflowers, before the deciduous trees fully unfurl their leaves and block light from reaching the forest floor.

Continue on Spruce Mountain Trail's easy to moderate ascent of the southeast slopes. On mild spring days, mourning cloak butterflies are common along the trail's edge, even at higher elevations. You can often find them basking on exposed rocks or perched on tree branches. On the middle slopes, you'll start to see a few red spruce trees, for which the mountain is named, growing amid the predominant hardwoods. Spruce is another characteristic species of northern hardwood forests, although it is mostly found in the uppermost portions of high mountains, where it thrives in conditions other species can't tolerate.

At 1.6 miles, cross Spruce Mountain's 2,592-foot lower summit, where there are partial views to the south. After a short descent, at 1.8 miles, make a quick, moderately steep climb to the nearby 2,730-foot summit, the ninth-highest peak in Massachusetts. An overlook just off the trail offers fine southerly views across a rocky clearing to the Deerfield River valley. The Bear Swamp Upper Reservoir (not to be confused with Bear Swamp in Ashfield) and a radio tower are visible to the left.

At this point you can either retrace your steps to the trailhead or continue the circuit by following Spruce Mountain Trail to its northern terminus on Raycroft Road. From the summit, Spruce Mountain Trail turns north and continues down the north slopes at a moderate grade through birch and beech groves and spruce saplings. The trail briefly levels at a junction with a woods road, marked with snowmobile trail signs, that branches to the right and offers an optional cutoff route to Raycroft Road. Spruce Mountain Trail turns briefly to the east (right) then bends northwest along the middle slopes. After passing a ledge, the trail continues downhill another 0.5 mile to its northern terminus on Raycroft Road, 1.3 miles from the summit and 3.1 miles from the start of the loop.

Facing page: Trout lilies thrive in the nutrient-rich soils of Spruce Mountain in western Franklin County.

Turn right on Raycroft Road, which is open seasonally to vehicles but lightly traveled. At 0.4 mile from the Spruce Mountain Trail junction, pass the lower junction with the aforementioned woods road, which comes down the slope on the right. Watch for wildflowers growing along brooks and wet areas near the road, which is lined by old sugar maples and groves of paper birch. After passing the intersection with Raycroft Extension Road on the left, continue past a gate and the junction with Smith Hollow Trail at the Monroe–Florida town line. Shortly after crossing the power-line clearing, complete the 1.9-mile segment on Raycroft Road and the loop at the junction with the dirt road, opposite Spruce Mountain Trail's southern trailhead. Turn left to return to the parking area.

DID YOU KNOW?

The highest point in Franklin County is 2,841-foot Crum Hill, west of Spruce Mountain and the state forest boundary in the highlands of Monroe. Most of the adjacent Hoosac Range is located in Berkshire County.

MORE INFORMATION

Open sunrise to sunset year-round, no fee. Three shelters are available. The property is unstaffed, with no other visitor facilities. Biking and dogs are allowed. Hunting is allowed in accordance with state laws. For more information visit mass.gov/locations/monroe-state-forest or call Mohawk Trail State Forest at 413-339-5504.

WINTER ACTIVITIES

Skiing and snowshoeing are allowed. Raycroft Road is wide, with gently rolling terrain; Spruce Mountain Trail is moderately steep, with some rocky sections.

NEARBY

For a different perspective of Monroe State Forest, Dunbar Brook Trail offers a 2.8-mile, one-way walk past rocky cascades and groves of old forests, including a giant white ash tree. To reach the trailhead, from MA 2 in Charlemont turn north on Zoar Road (which becomes River Road in Florida) and continue 11 miles to the marked trailhead at the Florida–Monroe town line. The closest places to eat are in North Adams, Charlemont, and Shelburne Falls.

2

MOHAWK TRAIL STATE FOREST

This moderately challenging circuit offers a fine sampling of the Mohawk Trail region, including old forests, meadows along Deerfield River, and the steep ridge of Todd Mountain, capped by a scenic overlook.

DIRECTIONS

From I-91 take Exit 26 in Greenfield and follow MA 2 west 17 miles to Charlemont. From the town center, continue on MA 2 west 4 miles to the entrance on the north side of the road. *GPS coordinates: 42° 38.206′ N, 72° 56.139′ W.*

TRAIL DESCRIPTION

Located at the confluence of the Deerfield and Cold rivers on the eastern slopes of the Berkshires, Mohawk Trail State Forest is a place of dramatic scenery and considerable ecological significance. The steep valley slopes shelter some of the Northeast's oldest and largest trees in groves that were never cut due to the rough topography. Two large meadows on the banks of Deerfield River add more diversity. The 6,400-acre state forest is part of a large conservation corridor that includes Monroe, Savoy Mountain, and Kenneth Dubuque Memorial state forests.

This hike combines several foot trails and a campground road in a moderately rugged circuit over Todd Mountain, one of the high points of the ridge on the north side of the valley. The outbound route follows a portion of Nature Trail, which is an easier loop past the meadows and a good option for wildlife watchers or those seeking a less strenuous outing. The descent includes a steep, rocky 0.3-mile segment of Indian Trail.

From the parking area near the ranger station, follow the paved campground road uphill along the north bank of Cold River beneath giant white pine trees, some of which are more than 140 feet tall. Cross under a power line

LOCATION
Charlemont, MA

RATING
Moderate to Strenuous

DISTANCE
4.5 miles

ELEVATION GAIN
1,240 feet

ESTIMATED TIME
3 hours

MAPS
USGS Rowe; Massachusetts Department of Conservation and Recreation map: mass.gov/eea/docs/dcr/parks/trails/mohawk.pdf

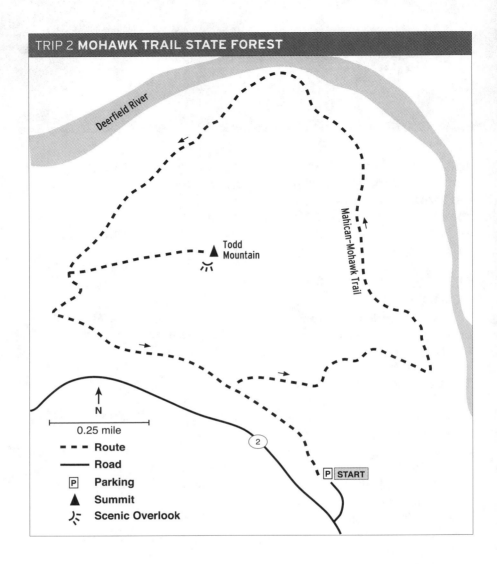

and bear right at a junction at 0.4 mile, following a sign for cabins. Pass a small grassy field then bear right onto a dirt road at a sign for Nature Trail and Thumper Mountain Trail. After passing the junction with Thumper Mountain Trail (a 0.5-mile loop with views of an old forest), follow the road left past a campsite to a brown gate and a sign for Nature Trail. From the gate, continue downhill at a moderate grade past two large boulders and an unmarked woods road on the left, to the start of the Nature Trail loop at a marked junction.

Turn left off the road and follow Nature Trail past a stone foundation at the site of a former sheep range. Although the rocky hills and slopes were largely inhospitable for agriculture in Colonial times, a few farms were established in the more fertile lowlands along Deerfield River. Watch and listen for a variety of

Little hikers enjoy Mohawk Trail State Forest's less strenuous trails. Photo by Massachusetts Office of Travel and Tourism, Creative Commons on Flickr.

migratory songbirds, including red-eyed vireos, ovenbirds, and chestnut-sided warblers. After 0.2 mile on Nature Trail, you'll reach the edge of a large meadow, at the base of the east slopes of Todd Mountain, which rises more than 1,000 feet above the valley. Here Nature Trail joins a portion of Mahican–Mohawk Trail, a long-distance route that follows a historical American Indian travel corridor from the Connecticut River valley to the Hudson River in upstate New York.

Follow the grass path across the meadow, which is home to a variety of wildlife, from songbirds, butterflies, and dragonflies to black bears and white-tailed deer. One of the characteristic migratory songbirds of open habitats is the indigo bunting, which arrives in the region to breed in late spring and summer. The males are known for their rich blue color that appears vibrant in muted light and darker in bright sunlight. Near the edge of the meadow is a marked junction where Nature Trail and Mahican–Mohawk Trail split. (Nature Trail continues to the right, to another meadow and the junction with Elder Grove Trail, then loops back along the banks of Deerfield River to the campground road.)

This hike continues straight on Mahican–Mohawk Trail, which initially leads north on a fairly easy, 0.6-mile ascent of the lower slopes of Todd Mountain then gradually curves left (southwest) and becomes increasingly steep as it approaches the top of the ridge. The wooded slopes are home to a thriving population of black bears, which are common in the hills of western Massachusetts. After being nearly eliminated by habitat loss and hunting in Colonial times, they have recovered strongly over the past half-century, thanks largely to the regrowth of mature woodlands, such as those at Mohawk Trail State Forest. Although sightings are unpredictable, claw marks on the smooth bark of beech trees reveal signs of the bears' presence.

At 1.3 miles from the meadow, reach a four-way junction in the saddle between Todd and Clark mountains on the crest of the ridge. (Indian Trail, the descent route, enters from the opposite side, and Mahican–Mohawk Trail on the right leads west toward Clark Mountain, which is wooded with no views.) Turn left here on the side trail to Todd Mountain and make an easy 0.4-mile amble along the ridge to a lookout near the 1,711-foot summit for a fine perspective of the steep, forested Cold River valley. The stunted oak trees that grow on the high ridge, where the soil is thin and vegetation is exposed to harsh weather, present a marked contrast with the large old trees on the sheltered lower slopes.

Backtrack to the four-way junction and turn left on Indian Trail to begin the descent to the trailhead. Take your time and carefully follow the rocky path 0.3 mile down the steep south side of the ridge. This portion of the route is especially colorful in June, when the mountain laurels are in bloom. At the base of the descent, turn left and complete the loop by following the paved campground road over a low knoll and along Cold River 0.7 mile to the parking area.

DID YOU KNOW?

Mohawk Trail State Forest is home to many of the Northeast's oldest and tallest trees. Researchers have documented more than 600 acres of old-growth forest, including many specimens between 200 and 500 years old. More than 120 white pines, which are mostly second growth, are at least 150 feet high.

MORE INFORMATION

Open sunrise to sunset year-round. A parking fee is charged from mid-May to mid-October ($8 MA residents, $15 out of state). The campground includes 47 seasonal sites and six year-round cabins. Biking and dogs are allowed. Hunting is allowed in accordance with state laws. For more information, visit mass.gov/locations/mohawk-trail-state-forest or call 413-339-5504.

WINTER ACTIVITIES

Skiing and snowshoeing are allowed. Nature Trail, which includes a moderately steep segment on a woods road and a level section along Deerfield River, and Elder Grove Trail are well suited to skiing. Indian Trail is very steep and rocky.

NEARBY

Several local businesses offer rafting and paddling tours on Deerfield River, including outfitters such as Zoar Outdoor (zaroutdoor.com), Berkshire Whitewater (berkshirewhitewater.com), and Crab Apple Whitewater (crabapplewhitewater.com). The Bissell Covered Bridge is on MA 8, just north of the junction with MA 2 (the Mohawk Trail Highway) in Charlemont. West of the state forest, MA 2 passes several scenic overlooks between Charlemont and North Adams. The closest places to eat are in Charlemont, Shelburne Falls, and North Adams.

A HOT SPOT OF BOTANICAL DIVERSITY

After a long New England winter ends, the blooms of spring ephemerals are a welcome sign of the changing seasons. Thanks to an ideal combination of geology and climate, western Massachusetts is a prime area for enjoying these colorful displays. In addition to brightening up the forests, the wildflowers and other plants also serve as indicators of soil types, landscape history, and, over the long term, our changing environment.

In western Massachusetts, the bedrock of the Appalachian Mountains, the Berkshire foothills, and the Metacomet Ridge yields abundant nutrients that support highly productive soils. In the eastern part of the state, the soils are more acidic, resulting in lower plant diversity. In rich mesic forest communities from the Connecticut River valley westward, dense colonies of wildflowers and ferns thrive in the understory of northern hardwood forests dominated by sugar maple, ash, and basswood. On some properties, botanists have documented more than 800 species.

The first hardy flowers usually emerge in early to mid-April at low elevations and gradually spread through the cooler uplands. (On the higher elevations of Mount Greylock, some can still be seen in late May.) Characteristic species of rich soils include bloodroot (a poppy with white flowers that emerge from a large protective leaf), dutchman's breeches, spring beauty, and trout lily. Red trillium (also known as "stinking Benjamin" due to its odor which attracts pollinating carrion flies), thrives in floodplains and on valley slopes. Rocky woods and hills, such as Mount Toby, the Holyoke Range, and the Swift River valley, are ideal habitats for round-lobed hepatica, identified by its light-blue or purple flowers. Trailing arbutus, the official state flower of Massachusetts, grows at forest edges and in disturbed areas, such as those near power lines.

As spring progresses, the early flowers are succeeded by a new round of species, including painted trillium, a photogenic lily found in moist deciduous and mixed forests; wild columbine, which thrives in rocky habitats; and fringed polygala, distinguished by its unique tubelike petals. Orchids emerge in late spring in forests and wetlands. Pink lady's slipper, a favorite of many wildflower enthusiasts, often grows in large colonies in mixed hardwood-conifer forests. (The much rarer yellow lady's slipper has suffered significantly from habitat loss and collecting and now occurs at only twelve sites in Massachusetts.)

As the last ephemerals fade from the shady woods, late spring and summer are peak times for viewing wildflowers in open habitats, such as wetlands and fields. Meadow flowers, including daisies, milkweeds, asters, and goldenrods, are crucial food sources for pollinating insects, many of which are declining worldwide. Boggy wetlands host many unique and rare species, such as northern pitcher plants, sundews, and bladderworts, which are well adapted to the acidic, largely inhospitable growing conditions. In mid to late summer, the colorful red blooms of cardinal flowers brighten many river and stream banks.

New England's native plants and wildflowers have faced many threats and disruptions over the past 400 years. According to the New England Wild Flower Society, nearly 600 species are now rare or likely extinct. In Colonial times, widespread land clearing had long-lasting effects on the region's natural communities and soils. While forests recovered strongly during the twentieth century, the land has been declining again in recent years due to development and fragmentation, resulting in a loss of plant habitats and dispersal corridors. Another significant concern is the increasing propagation of invasive species, such as Japanese barberry, garlic mustard, and purple loosestrife, which often compete with and displace native flora. Herds of white-tailed deer—which are thriving in the Northeast due to a lack of predators, as well as climate and habitat changes over the past century—have depleted forest vegetation in some areas.

In the long term, climate change may have a significant effect on New England's flora. In *State of New England's Native Plants*, a comprehensive report published by the New England Wild Flower Society in 2015, researchers speculate the region could have a climate similar to present-day North Carolina by the late 21st century if the current warming trend continues. This would likely cause plants and natural communities that favor cool environments to shift northward, lead to southern species migrating into the region, and increase the spread of invasive species and forest pests that thrive in mild environments and are already well established in many areas. Unusual weather can also disrupt flowering times and cause species to compete with each other. In the future, hikers may well observe natural communities that are entirely different from what we see on the trails today.

3

KENNETH DUBUQUE MEMORIAL STATE FOREST

In the remote highlands of Hawley, less-traveled trails and woods roads lead to northern hardwood forests, cascading brooks, old mill sites, and scenic Hallockville Pond.

LOCATION
Hawley and Plainfield, MA

RATING
Moderate

DIRECTIONS

From the north, at the junction of MA 2 and MA 8A in Charlemont, follow MA 8A (West Hawley Road) south 8.0 miles to the Hallockville Pond entrance, on the right, at the Hawley–Plainfield town line. From the south, at the junction of MA 116 and MA 8A in Plainfield, follow MA 8A north 1.0 mile to the entrance, on the left. *GPS coordinates:* 42° 33.118′ N, 72° 56.483′ W.

DISTANCE
5.5 miles

ELEVATION GAIN
670 feet

ESTIMATED TIME
3.25 hours

TRAIL DESCRIPTION

The 8,000-acre Kenneth Dubuque Memorial State Forest is part of a conservation corridor that also includes the Mohawk Trail and Savoy Mountain state forests and Mass Audubon's West Mountain Wildlife Sanctuary. Although the property is densely wooded today, old mill sites, stone walls, and a charcoal kiln offer evidence of past land uses. This hike, which begins at the Hallockville Pond entrance in the southern portion of the forest, combines a moderately rugged circuit on Hawley Pass Trail, Basin Brook Trail, and Hallockville Road with an easy 1.25-mile loop around Hallockville Pond on Pond Trail. You can walk either route individually; Pond Trail is excellent for families. Student Conservation Association AmeriCorps facilities (closed to the public) are adjacent to the parking area; information is available at the office when staff is present.

Begin the loop to Basin Brook at a trail sign on the entrance road. From the Hallockville Pond dam, follow the blue-blazed Hawley Pass Trail along King Brook to the extensive stone remains of an old mill site, including a large foundation at 0.1 mile. After crossing a footbridge,

MAPS
USGS Plainfield; Massachusetts Department of Conservation and Recreation map: mass.gov/eea/docs/dcr/parks/trails/dubuque.pdf

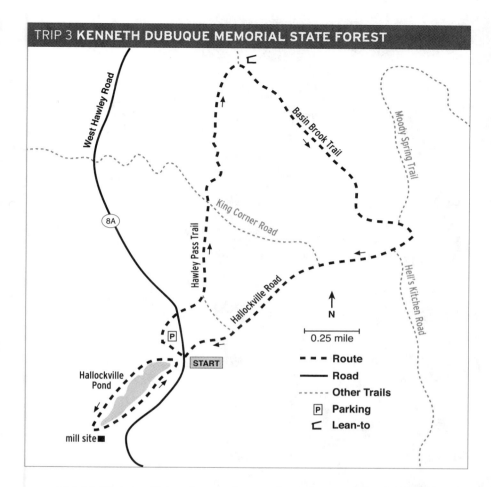

cross MA 8A (light traffic) and enter the woods on the east side of the road. Bear left and follow the blazed footpath north through mixed northern hardwood forests of beech, maple, birch, and hemlock that offer colorful foliage in autumn. Due to the relatively high elevations (between 1,500 and 1,800 feet), foliage peaks earlier here than in the lowlands of the Connecticut Valley. A character-istic wildflower of cool temperate forests is the bluebead lily, identified by bell-like yellow flowers that bloom in midspring, blue berries, and long, shiny leaves.

After crossing a series of log bridges, make a gentle descent along the base of a hill. At 0.8 miles, cross King Corner Road at a four-way junction. Carefully fol-low Hawley Pass Trail around a swampy area and over low knolls then begin a long descent into the ravine of Basin Brook along a hemlock-shaded stream. Follow the trail left along the base of a rock outcropping and continue downhill past a cluster of mossy glacial boulders. As the descent steepens, you can glimpse the valley hills through the trees to the right, especially when the branches are bare. Listen for the calls of common ravens soaring above the treetops. Black bears, bobcats, and other mammals are present, though rarely seen.

In June, the shores of Hallockville Pond are alive with the colorful blooms of mountain laurel.

At the base of the descent, cross a footbridge over Basin Brook and reach a marked three-way junction adjacent to a camping shelter at 1.7 miles. Turn right on Basin Brook Trail and begin an easy to moderate ascent along the bank of the cascading brook. A short distance beyond the shelter is the first of two crossings that are easy most times of the year but may be wet during high water periods. After a scenic segment along the south bank, cross the brook again and follow the blazed trail through a hemlock grove and along the edge of a small wetland ringed by conifers.

At a sign for Moody Spring, bear right and continue to the nearby junction with Hallockville Road, 1.3 miles from the shelter. Turn right and follow Hallockville Road, a woods road open seasonally to vehicles and snowmobiles, past the junction with Hell's Kitchen Road on the left and a spruce swamp on Basin Brook. Continue uphill past a bridge and the junction with King Corner Road on the right. Pass a red maple swamp and climb past an old log landing then descend to gate 2 at MA 8A, opposite the Hallockville Pond entrance. Cross the road and follow the driveway to the trailhead.

To make a counterclockwise circuit around Hallockville Pond, bear right from the pond's edge past the Student Conservation Association buildings and continue through groves of white pine, eastern hemlock, and red spruce on the west shore. The spruce, which thrives in cool upland settings, is an indicator of the pond's 1,600-foot elevation. In late May and June, pink lady's slippers grow in the acidic soil below the conifers.

At marker 3 near the pond's southwest corner, a small clearing offers a panoramic view across the water. In June the pink and white blooms of mountain laurel, a characteristic shrub of rocky hills and woods, make a colorful sight. Other shrubs include hobblebush, lowbush blueberry, and sheep laurel—distinguished by diminutive pink flowers that bloom in late spring,

Cross a footbridge over King Brook, one of several streams and brooks that converge in the valley, which made it an ideal site for a mill pond. After another brook crossing, follow Pond Trail as it curves left around the pond's narrow southern tip. At the next stream crossing is another old mill site where the stone remains include a large foundation, a dam, and a spillway.

Cross another footbridge and pass a marshy wetland that offers cover for waterfowl, such as black and mallard ducks. Continue along the east side of the pond to one of its prominent landmarks, a giant split glacial boulder that makes for a fun photo op and spot for children to explore. Beavers are active here, as evidenced by cut marks on trunks and mesh guards set up to protect some of the trees along the trail.

Follow the path over gently rolling terrain and through more groves of eastern hemlock and mountain laurel. In spring and summer, bumblebees and butterflies, such as tiger swallowtails and red-spotted purples, feed on the laurel and wildflowers, including the oxeye daisy and orange hawkweed that grows in grassy margins along the path. After crossing another cascading seasonal brook, complete the loop by crossing the large stone dam and a footbridge over the pond's outlet, where King Brook resumes its northerly course toward its confluence with Chickley River.

DID YOU KNOW?

The property, originally named Hawley State Forest, was formed by purchases of abandoned farmland. It was renamed in memory of Kenneth Dubuque, a former employee of the Department of Environmental Management (now the Department of Conservation and Recreation) who played a key role in the preservation of the land.

MORE INFORMATION

Open sunrise to sunset year-round, no fee. Biking and dogs are allowed. Hunting is allowed in accordance with state laws. Some of the state forest road gates may still be closed after damage from Tropical Storm Irene in 2011. For more information, visit mass.gov/locations/kenneth-dubuque-memorial-state-forest or call Mohawk Trail State Forest at 413-339-5504.

WINTER ACTIVITIES

The trail network includes 35 miles of multiuse trails (nearly all of which are unpaved roads) good for skiing. The Hallockville Pond parking area offers direct access to Klingholt Road and Hallockville Road on the east side of MA 8A.

Other parking areas are located at the junction of MA 8A and King Corner Road and at the junction of Plainfield Road and Kiln Road.

NEARBY

Hawley Bog, located on East Hawley Road 4 miles south of MA 2 in Charlemont, is a rare example of a northern bog in southern New England. A short boardwalk trail offers close-up views of the bog and its associated wetlands, wildlife, and flora, including carnivorous northern pitcher plants. Another interpretive trail offers an easy loop past historical sites at the former Hawley town common. The Nature Conservancy (nature.org, 413-229-0232) and Five Colleges Consortium manage Hawley Bog.

4

HIGH LEDGES WILDLIFE SANCTUARY

This loop follows Sanctuary Road past old fields and a spreading oak tree to an outstanding view of the Deerfield River valley then continues through the rocky, hemlock-shaded valley of Spring Brook and its associated habitats.

DIRECTIONS

From I-91 take Exit 26 in Greenfield and follow MA 2 west 5.8 miles to Shelburne. Turn right on Little Mohawk Road and continue uphill 1.4 miles to a sign for Patten District. Turn left on Patten Road, following signs for High Ledges. After 0.7 mile, follow Patten Road right at the junction with Tower Road then continue another 0.8 mile. Turn left and follow the dirt road past the overflow lot to the parking area on the left. *GPS coordinates: 42° 37.204′ N, 72° 42.338′ W.*

TRAIL DESCRIPTION

Named for its rocky outcroppings that offer panoramic views to the Berkshires, High Ledges Wildlife Sanctuary protects 700 acres in the uplands of the Deerfield River valley. Botanical diversity abounds here, thanks to nutrient-rich soils that sustain a wide variety of flora, including colorful orchids. Habitats include rocky streams and ravines, swamps, boggy wetlands, mixed forests, and old fields. Spring, when the wildflowers are in bloom and the forests are alive with migratory songbirds, is a great time to explore.

From the parking area, follow the dirt Sanctuary Road downhill to the entrance gate at a large sugar maple. In late spring, watch for the pink blooms of wild azalea at the forest edges, including the parking lot, fields, and the Ledges. From the information sign and trail map, follow

LOCATION
Shelburne, MA

RATING
Moderate

DISTANCE
3.1 miles

ELEVATION GAIN
540 feet

ESTIMATED TIME
2 hours

MAPS
USGS Shelburne Falls;
Mass Audubon map:
massaudubon.org/content/
download/8046/145176/file/
highledges_trails.pdf

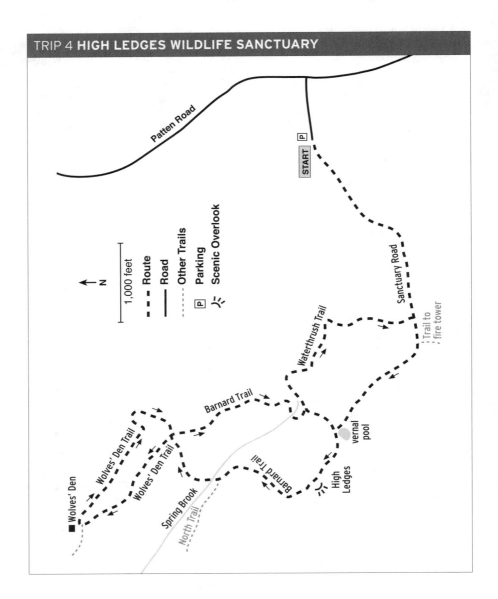

Sanctuary Road uphill past a small brushy field and nesting boxes on the left. Look for the tree swallows that arrive in early spring, making hunting rounds over the field in search of insects. Continue past a cluster of paper birches and a stone wall in the woods on the left. Eastern wood peewees and black-and-white warblers are among the many migratory songbirds that frequent these woods during spring and summer.

At 0.2 mile from the welcome sign on Sanctuary Road, reach another brushy field and the start of the loop at the junction with Waterthrush Trail, which enters from the right. In mid to late spring, colonies of pink lady's slipper bloom along the forest edge. Apple trees, holdovers from an old orchard, offer food for a variety of wildlife, including white-tailed deer, porcupines, black bears, and many birds and insects. Watch for tiger swallowtails and other butterflies feeding on the lilac bushes at the field edge in May.

On the southern side of the field, adjacent to the gate, is the junction with Ridge Trail (part of the Shelburne Trails community trail network), which links the sanctuary to the historic Shelburne fire tower on Mount Massaemett. From the sanctuary boundary, Ridge Trail leads uphill through a timber harvest on private land (please stay on the marked path) then continues along an access road to the distinctive stone tower, built in 1909. Small windows at the top of the enclosed structure offer views of Mount Monadnock and the Deerfield River valley. This optional side trip detour, which can be made now or at the end of the loop, adds about 20 to 25 minutes of walking each way.

From the gate, follow Sanctuary Road past more apple trees then continue downhill past a large white oak with broad, spreading branches. At the next junction, Sanctuary Road merges with a portion of the Dutch and Mary Barnard Trail, named for the family that donated the land to Mass Audubon in 1976.

At 1.1 miles from the trailhead (roughly 30 to 35 minutes), reach the Ledges and an old foundation and chimney marking the former site of the Barnards' rustic summer cabin. Red columbines, wildflowers that favor rugged environs, bloom around the foundation in May and June. The overlook offers a fine southwesterly perspective across the hills and ridges of the Deerfield River valley and Mohawk Trail corridor to Mount Greylock on the western horizon. Framing the view are red pine trees, which are uncommon in natural settings in southern New England.

From the Ledges, continue the loop on Barnard Trail, marked with a small green sign on the right. Pink lady's slipper orchids grow in abundance on this sunlit slope in late May and June. Less common are yellow lady's slippers, which grow locally in limestone hills and bogs in western New England. Follow the trail, now a narrow footpath marked with blue blazes, downhill through hemlock groves into the rocky valley of Spring Brook. At the base of the descent, bear right at the junction with North Trail (a rough 0.7-mile route that passes steep ledges along Spring Brook before connecting with the Wolves' Den Loop Trail) and continue to follow Barnard Trail across a brook and past a rock ledge. Round-lobed hepatica and red trillium are among the first species to bloom in this rich soil at the onset of the wildflower season in April.

At the next junction, bear left and follow Wolves' Den Loop Trail northwest through a remote, rocky part of the sanctuary. (You can shorten the walk 0.5 mile by continuing right on Barnard Trail.) At the three-way junction with North Trail, you'll see the source of this trail's name, an outcropping where the last wolf in Shelburne reputedly was killed. While predators, such as wolves and mountain lions, have been extirpated from New England since the nineteenth century, periodic reports of both are the subject of considerable intrigue and debate. Turn

Red pines and azaleas are among the diverse flora at High Ledges Wildlife Sanctuary, where an overlook offers panoramic views across the Deerfield River valley.

right at the junction to continue on Wolves' Den Loop Trail. A short side path leads to a small fen (a wetland with peaty soil) that's home to a colony of northern pitcher plants, another indicator of the sanctuary's botanical diversity.

At the close of the 0.5-mile loop, rejoin Barnard Trail and continue uphill through a mixed forest of oak, birch, maple, hemlock, and mountain laurel to Spring Swamp, a wetland where colorful marsh blue violets grow in spring. From the edge of the swamp follow Barnard Trail left, along the base of a rocky talus slope, to the junction with Waterthrush Trail.

Turn left and follow Waterthrush Trail uphill through hemlocks, along the upper portion of the aptly named Spring Brook, which is seasonal and may be dry by the onset of summer. After crossing the brook three times, continue through a growth of mountain laurel to Orchid Swamp, a wetland bordered by tall ferns, hobblebush shrubs, and bunchberry wildflowers. Pass a large gray birch tree at the edge of the swamp and continue to the end of the loop, at the junction with Sanctuary Road and the field. Turn left and retrace your steps along Sanctuary Road to the entrance gate and parking area.

DID YOU KNOW?

The Barnard family established a farm on the grounds in the late eighteenth century. Before donating the land to Mass Audubon, Ellsworth ("Dutch") and Mary Barnard built trails and cataloged the property's many plant and animal species. The foundation and chimney of their former cabin is still visible at the Ledges.

MORE INFORMATION

Open dawn to dusk year-round, no fee. The sanctuary is unstaffed and has no visitor facilities. Biking, dogs, and hunting are not allowed. Public programs are periodically offered through Arcadia Wildlife Sanctuary. For more information, visit massaudubon.org or call 978-464-2712. For information about Shelburne Trails, visit townofshelburne.com/documents/Shelburne_Trails_brochure.pdf.

WINTER ACTIVITIES

Skiing is not allowed; snowshoeing is allowed. Sanctuary Road is wide and follows gently rolling terrain; the other trails are narrow and rocky in places. Look for animal tracks around field edges on Sanctuary Road and along the interior forest trails.

NEARBY

The artisans' village of Shelburne Falls offers many attractions, including the popular Bridge of Flowers, a former trolley bridge over Deerfield River now planted with colorful garden flowers; the Glacial Potholes, an area of bedrock scoured by the river after the most recent ice age; and the Shelburne Falls Trolley Museum. There are also galleries, bookstores, antique shops, and places to eat.

5

BEAR SWAMP RESERVATION

This pleasant and less-traveled hike will lead you to wooded rocky ridges with abundant spring wildflowers, a beaver wetland, and hilltop overlooks with pastoral views across Ashfield's Apple Valley to the Green Mountains.

LOCATION
Ashfield, MA

RATING
Moderate

DISTANCE
3 miles

ELEVATION GAIN
450 feet

ESTIMATED TIME
1.75 hours

MAPS
USGS Ashfield; The Trustees of Reservations map: thetrustees.org/assets/ documents/places-to-visit/ trailmaps/BearSwamp_ TrailMap_2014.pdf

DIRECTIONS

From the south on I-91, take Exit 24 in Deerfield and follow US 5/MA 10 north 1.1 miles to the junction with MA 116. From the north on I-91, take Exit 25 and follow signs for MA 116. Drive 13.6 miles north on MA 116, through Conway and Ashfield center. At the four-way intersection with MA 112 and Hawley Road, continue straight on Hawley Road 1.7 miles to the roadside parking area. *GPS coordinates: 42° 32.940′ N, 72° 49.500′ W.*

TRAIL DESCRIPTION

Bear Swamp Reservation is a 312-acre mosaic of rocky ridges and wetlands set amid the rolling hills and orchards west of Ashfield's town center. Sweeping pastoral vistas from Orchard View and Apple Valley Overlook offer a glimpse into the landscape's past, when most of the forests were cleared for agriculture and timber. Today the revitalized woodlands are alive with colorful wildflowers in the spring and beautiful foliage in autumn. The reservation abuts the Brewer-Tatro Memorial Woods and is part of the Ashfield Trails community trail network. This hike combines Lookout, North–South, and Beaver Brook trails as a loop, with a side trip detour to Orchard View at the reservation's northwest boundary. A short route at the main entrance leads to Apple Valley Overlook.

From the information sign on the west side of Hawley Road (where maps are available), begin the loop by following a short connecting trail past a muddy area and rock ledge to the junction of Lookout Trail and Beaver Brook

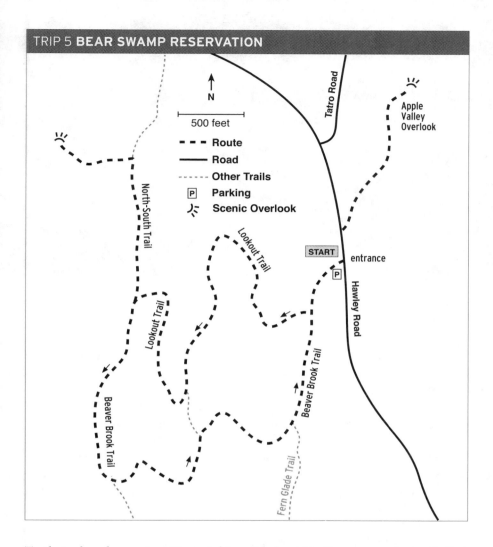

Trail at a brook crossing. Turn right on Lookout Trail, a narrow footpath that may be somewhat obscured in autumn by fallen leaves; watch for the orange blazes. After a few hundred feet, a marshy wetland comes into view on the left. The small pond it is associated with was originally built as a mill pond and today continues to be engineered by beavers; they've built a dam across the outlet. In spring, watch for the greater yellowlegs, a shorebird that periodically stops over in western Massachusetts during migrations. Look for these uncommon birds probing for food in the muddy soil along the wetland edge.

From the northern tip of the wetland, bear right and continue along the base of a rocky ridge. In spring, this portion of Lookout Trail is alive with colorful wildflowers that thrive in the nutrient-rich soil. One of the most distinctive is dutchman's breeches, so named for its row of white, pantaloon-shaped blossoms. Another characteristic species of the moist, rich woods is spring beauty,

Spring wildflowers such as red trillium are a sight to behold in late April and May.

which has five white or pinkish flowers with a maroon lining. Others include trout lily, red trillium, foamflower, and white and yellow violets. The best time to see the display is from late April to late May, before the deciduous trees fully leaf out and block light from the forest floor.

Continue to follow Lookout Trail left and uphill, to the top of the ridge through groves of maple and birch trees that offer vibrant foliage in early and mid-October. Continue south along the ridge to a partially open overlook above the wetland then turn right and make a short descent through a rocky area to a marked junction. Turn right again (the path on the left is a connecting trail to Beaver Brook Trail that offers a shorter loop) and follow Lookout Trail downhill then bear right through more groves of northern hardwood forest. The walking is easier here, on a wide path between the ledges.

After a sharp left turn, reach the junction with orange-blazed North–South Trail, the reservation's longest route, at 0.8 mile. To make the side trip to Orchard View, turn right and follow North–South Trail downhill 0.2 mile to a marked junction then turn left on the short path to the lookout. Here the trail continues on a right of way to a hilltop meadow on adjacent private land. (Please stay on the main trail.) The stone bench at the trail's end is a great spot to take a break and enjoy sweeping views of the adjacent orchards and surrounding countryside to the north.

Return to North–South Trail and retrace your steps uphill to the junction with Lookout Trail. Bear right to resume the loop on North–South Trail, which leads south along the reservation's western boundary over rolling, moderately rugged terrain. After passing a wetland, cross a low hill, then descend to a junction at a small seasonal waterfall. Turn left here on the upper end of white-blazed

Beaver Brook Trail and continue along the perimeter of a wetland, past a stone wall and a rocky brook crossing. Bear right at the junction with the aforementioned connecting trail and follow Beaver Brook Trail downhill along the brook to a small waterfall and pool, where you may see swirling fallen leaves in autumn.

Continue on Beaver Brook Trail through groves of birch and beech, along the perimeter of wetlands associated with the old mill pond. After passing an open outlook on the pond's east side, continue downhill to the end of the loop, at a footbridge that marks the three-way junction with Lookout Trail. Follow the connecting trail back to the trailhead and Hawley Road.

You can walk the path to Apple Valley Overlook either before or after the loop hike. From the trail sign on the east side of Hawley Road, a quick 0.3-mile climb along a woods road will bring you to the 1,544-foot hilltop in about 10 to 15 minutes. A brushy clearing offers northerly views across the nearby orchards and hills to the Deerfield River–Mohawk Trail corridor and the southern Green Mountains of Vermont, including Stratton Mountain on the horizon. In spring, violets, bluets, and wild strawberries bloom in the sunlit clearing. You may also see a bright-blue indigo bunting perched in the trees at the field edge in spring and summer.

DID YOU KNOW?

In spite of the rugged terrain and swampy wetlands, early Colonial settlers cleared the land in what is now Bear Swamp Reservation. In the mid-nineteenth century, approximately 75 percent of Massachusetts was similarly open, but today much of the land has reverted to forest.

MORE INFORMATION

Open sunrise to sunset year-round, no fee. A picnic area is located at Apple Valley Overlook; there are no restrooms. Dogs are allowed; biking is not allowed. Hunting is allowed in accordance with state laws. For more information, visit thetrustees.org or call 413-213-4751. For information about Ashfield Trails, a volunteer trail organization, visit facebook.com/AshfieldTrails.

WINTER ACTIVITIES

Skiing and snowshoeing are allowed. Portions of the trails are narrow and rocky, especially around the ridges.

NEARBY

Farms of Ashfield's Apple Valley include Clark Brothers Orchards, 580 Apple Valley Road, which grows many varieties of apples on 70 acres (fiveacrefarms.com/farmers/clark-brothers-orchards, 413-625-2940). Red Gate Farm, 4 Norman Road, is home to a farm school and summer camp (redgatefarm.com, 413-625-9503). Bear Swamp Orchard and Cidery, 1209B Hawley Road, offers seasonal apple picking and hard cider tasting (bearswamporchard.com, 413-625-2849).

6

TWO BRIDGES TRAIL

From the pastoral hilltop fields of Bullitt Reservation to the cascades of Chapel Falls, this recently established out-and-back trail offers a pleasant walk through a corridor of protected land in the hills of Ashfield.

LOCATION
Ashfield, MA

RATING
Moderate

DISTANCE
4.2 miles

ELEVATION GAIN
270 feet

ESTIMATED TIME
3 hours

MAPS
USGS Ashfield and USGS Goshen; The Trustees of Reservations map: thetrustees.org/assets/documents/places-to-visit/trailmaps/ChapelBrook_Bullitt_Trail_2012.pdf

DIRECTIONS

For the Bullitt Reservation trailhead: From the south on I-91, take Exit 24 in Deerfield and follow US 5/MA 10 to the junction with MA 116. From the north on I-91, take Exit 25 and follow signs for MA 116. Drive 10.5 miles north on MA 116 through Conway. Turn left on Bullitt Road and continue uphill 0.7 mile to the Bullitt Reservation entrance at the road's end. *GPS coordinates: 42° 30.135′ N, 72° 45.360′ W.*

For the Chapel Brook trailhead: From the junction of MA 116 and Bullitt Road, continue north 0.7 mile on MA 116 then turn left on Williamsburg Road and continue 2.2 miles to the roadside entrance and parking area. *GPS coordinates: 42° 28.920′ N, 72° 45.600′ W.*

TRAIL DESCRIPTION

Two Bridges Trail, which opened in 2013, is a footpath linking Bullitt Reservation and Chapel Brook, both of which are owned by The Trustees of Reservations. Along the way, the trail passes through portions of the Poland Brook Wildlife Management Area and adjacent private lands. These properties are part of a 3,000-acre public and private conservation corridor in the hills of Ashfield and Conway. Two Bridges Trail, named for twin wooden footbridges below Chapel Falls, runs generally north to south through the forested watershed of Poland Brook. The walking is mostly easy over gently rolling terrain, with a moderately steep segment near the ravine of Chapel Brook. The route described here starts from the north at

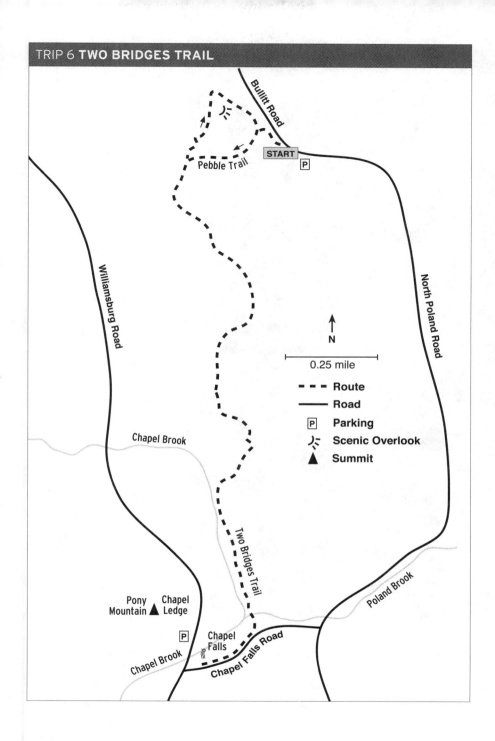

Chapel Brook's cascades, including the 20-foot lower falls, are at the south end of Two Bridges Trail.

Bullitt Reservation, but you can also start from the south at Chapel Brook.

The 265-acre Bullitt Reservation encompasses the grounds of a former farm, once the home of William C. Bullitt, the first U.S. ambassador to the Soviet Union. The meadows adjacent to the entrance are maintained for grassland birds and other wildlife. The former farmhouse, now a seasonally staffed visitor center, includes a well-designed garden with native plants for wildlife, berries, and grasses. A trail map is posted at the parking area, which is near a small beaver wetland.

From the trailhead at the edge of Bullitt Road, follow a grass path across the field on the left to the start of the yellow-blazed Pebble Trail loop, at the forest edge. This hike continues along the left fork of the loop, past groves of old sugar maple and oak trees, as well as a pine plantation. (The right fork, which leads to a meadow and vista, is the return route.) In late April, bloodroot and other wildflowers grow along the embankment. After passing a giant sugar maple on the right, continue uphill past more old maples to a three-way junction at the north end of Two Bridges Trail, 1.5 miles from Chapel Brook.

Turn left off Pebble Trail and follow Two Bridges Trail, well marked with light-blue blazes and directional signs, south through groves of tall hemlocks. Pass a small seasonal brook in a wet area then cross a stone wall and follow the path through mixed woods of hemlock, white pine, maple, birch, and other hardwoods. Cross another small stream and continue along a stone wall. Turn right at a gap in the wall and descend to signs at the reservation boundary. Here Two Bridges Trail continues through private property; please respect all posted areas and stay on the marked path. Cross a seasonal creek and continue up a gentle incline through unbroken forests that offer habitat for white-tailed deer, bobcats, black bears, and other mammals. These animals are often elusive, but you have a good chance of seeing wild turkeys, which are common in western Massachusetts. After being extirpated in the past due to hunting and forest clearing, turkeys were successfully reintroduced in the Berkshires during the 1970s, and there are now more than 25,000 statewide.

In 0.75 mile from the junction with Pebble Trail (about 45 to 50 minutes from the trailhead), reach the boundary of the Poland Brook Wildlife Management Area, managed by the Massachusetts Division of Fisheries and Wildlife. From the crest of a ridge, make a moderately steep descent to Chapel Brook on a series of switchbacks. After passing a swampy area at the base of the ridge bear left and continue downward on an old woods road parallel to a cascading brook. At the base of the descent, reach the boundary of Chapel Brook and the two wooden footbridges for which the trail is named. The second (westernmost) bridge spans Chapel Brook roughly a quarter-mile downstream from the main falls. From the bridges, Poland Brook flows generally north through portions of the wildlife management area and Bullitt Reservation to its confluence with South River, a major tributary of Deerfield River.

After crossing the bridges, bear right and continue upstream to the base of Chapel Falls. The largest of the three distinct cascades is the lower falls, where the brook drops 20 feet over a rock ledge and into a small pool. A short distance upstream is the 12-foot middle falls and the 10-foot upper falls, where the brook fans roughly 20 feet wide as it flows beneath the bridge on Williamsburg Road. Please stay on the marked trail, as a revegetation project is in progress. A sign near the upper falls marks the site of a former schoolhouse and chapel, part of a small community that included at least two gristmills.

The Chapel Brook entrance on Williamsburg Road is the north end of Two Bridges Trail and this out-and-back hike, although you have the option of exploring the trails on the western side of the road. Summit Trail offers a moderately steep 0.5-mile ascent past Chapel Ledge (a 100-foot vertical cliff) to the top of 1,420-foot Pony Mountain. Trout lilies, spring beauties, red trilliums, and violets bloom on the lower slopes during the spring. The 1.5-mile Chapel Brook to DAR State Forest Trail, part of the Ashfield Trails community trail network, connects Chapel Brook to Moose Run Trail in the Daughters of the American Revolution State Forest.

After exploring Chapel Brook, retrace your steps along Two Bridges Trail to Bullitt Reservation. You'll have about 20 to 25 minutes of moderately steep uphill walking after crossing the bridges, but after that the grade is easy. At the northern terminus of Two Bridges Trail, turn left to resume the Pebble Trail loop. A short climb will lead you to the source of the trail's name, a large glacial boulder (or "pebble") framed by trees. A short distance ahead, at the crest of a meadow, is an overlook with northeasterly views to the hills of the South River valley. Follow the grass path downhill and to the right to cross the field then bear left at the end of the Pebble Trail loop to return to the Bullitt Reservation entrance.

DID YOU KNOW?

In the nineteenth century, the land in Bullitt Reservation was part of the town's poor farm, where people performed chores for room and board. Renovation of the farmhouse uncovered old coins and other historical artifacts left by past occupants.

MORE INFORMATION

Open year-round sunrise to sunset, no fee. Portions of Two Bridges Trail are on private land; please stay on the marked path. At Chapel Brook, biking is not allowed, but bow hunting is allowed on portions of the property with written permission. Hunting is allowed at Bullitt Reservation and at Poland Brook Wildlife Management Area in accordance with state laws. For more information, visit thetrustees.org or call 413-213-4751. For information about Ashfield Trails, a volunteer trail organization, visit facebook.com/AshfieldTrails.

WINTER ACTIVITIES

Skiing and snowshoeing are allowed. The southern portion of Two Bridges Trail near Chapel Brook traverses moderately steep terrain; otherwise, grades are generally easy.

NEARBY

Belding Park, located on MA 116 (Main Street), just east of the junction with MA 112, includes picnic areas and a public boat launch on Ashfield Lake. The lake features a seasonal swimming beach with restrooms and is a popular paddling and fishing area. There are several places to eat in Ashfield on MA 116 and Buckland Road.

7

MOUNT SUGARLOAF STATE RESERVATION

Enjoy spectacular views of the Connecticut River and the surrounding countryside from the summit of South Sugarloaf. An optional rugged extension leads to more views atop less frequently traveled North Sugarloaf.

DIRECTIONS

From the south on I-91, take Exit 24 in Deerfield and follow US 5/MA 10 north to the junction with MA 116. From the north on I-91, take Exit 25 and follow signs for MA 116 south. Turn right on MA 116 south and continue 1.0 mile to the junction with Sugarloaf Street at the traffic light adjacent to the reservation entrance. Turn left on Sugarloaf Street then enter the parking area on the right. *GPS coordinates:* 42° 28.059′ N, 72° 35.690′ W.

TRAIL DESCRIPTION
South Sugarloaf

Mount Sugarloaf's south summit boasts arguably the best known and most scenic view of the Connecticut River valley, a perspective that has been featured in books, magazines, calendars, advertisements, and even movies. Although this overlook is just 650 feet high, it is ideally situated at the south end of the Pocumtuck Ridge above a picturesque bend in the river. The 791-foot north summit is higher and mostly wooded, although ledges offer westerly views across the valley.

This hike combines a portion of the long-distance Pocumtuck Ridge Trail (PRT) with Old Mountain Trail for a 1.4-mile loop over South Sugarloaf. An optional extension on PRT to North Sugarloaf adds 2.8 miles and about 1,000 feet of cumulative elevation gain. Walking the South Sugarloaf loop counterclockwise as detailed allows for a steep but fairly short climb to the summit and an easy return.

LOCATION
Deerfield, MA

SOUTH SUGARLOAF
RATING
Moderate

DISTANCE
1.4 miles

ELEVATION GAIN
465 feet

ESTIMATED TIME
1.25 hours

NORTH AND SOUTH
SUGARLOAF
RATING
Moderate

DISTANCE
4.2 miles

ELEVATION GAIN
1,465 feet

ESTIMATED TIME
3.5 hours

MAPS
USGS Mount Toby; Massachusetts Department of Conservation and Recreation map: mass.gov/eea/docs/dcr/parks/trails/sugarloaf.pdf

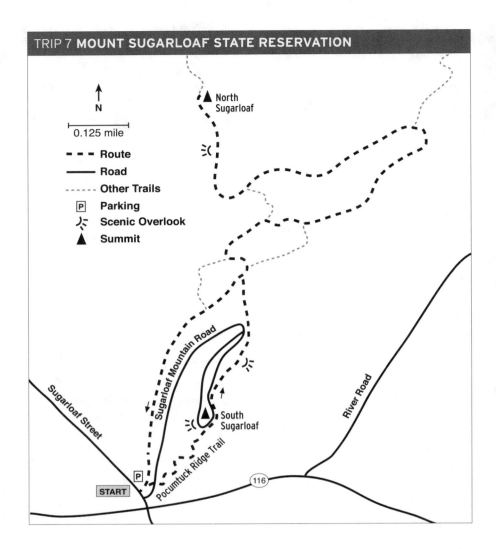

From the parking area, cross the auto road at the entrance gate and begin the loop on blue-blazed PRT. The trailhead is the southern terminus of PRT, which continues 15 miles along the Pocumtuck Ridge to Canada Hill, in Greenfield. Begin the ascent of the mountain's steep south cliff, which was shaped by glaciers as they passed over the end of the ridge. Mount Sugarloaf is composed of Arkose conglomerate sandstone rock, similar to Mount Toby on the east side of the valley. Follow PRT as it changes direction several times in a series of switchbacks, gaining roughly 465 feet of elevation in 0.4 mile. As you approach the summit, views across the Connecticut River valley unfold through gaps in the trees.

At the 650-foot summit, step across the cable fence at the edge of the auto road and enjoy the spectacular views from the grassy field and multilevel pavilion, where restrooms and water are available during the park's seasonal hours. To the south, the Connecticut River bends toward the ridges of Mount Tom and the Holyoke Range on the distant horizon. Across the valley, the town of Sunderland with its white church, nestled at the base of wooded hills, makes for a classic New England village scene. The long ridge of Mount Toby, capped by the fire tower atop its summit plateau, extends along the east side of the valley. Other points of interest include the Sunderland Bridge, the farm fields and neighborhoods of Deerfield and Hatfield to the south and west, and the University of Massachusetts Amherst campus in the distance.

The late afternoon and evening hours are ideal for photography, as the setting sun nicely lights the valley from the west. On clear evenings you may also catch the memorable sight of the moon rising above Sunderland and the valley hills to the east. Fall foliage peaks in mid to late October, later than in the surrounding hills due to the low elevation and milder climate of the Connecticut River valley.

While enjoying the views, keep an eye out for red-tailed hawks, peregrine falcons, and other birds of prey, which often use the summit trees and cliffs as lookouts for hunting forays into the fields at the base of the mountain. You may also see large flocks of Canada geese flying along the valley between their feeding or resting grounds. These flights make a striking spectacle when they happen around sunset. Watch for tiger swallowtails and other butterflies feeding on the planted flowers around the pavilion.

From the pavilion, continue past the picnic area and summit parking lots. Reenter the woods at a blue-blazed PRT marker on the right and continue to another overlook and wood bench with a fine easterly view of Sunderland, the Connecticut River, and the valley hills. PRT then zigzags down a steep slope and briefly rejoins the auto road at a sharp hairpin turn. (In low light or bad weather, the road offers a direct route to the parking area with good footing.) From the edge of the road, continue downhill on PRT to a marked junction in the saddle between North and South Sugarloaf.

North and South Sugarloaf
Here you have the option of completing the South Sugarloaf loop with a 0.6-mile walk on red-blazed Old Mountain Trail or continuing on PRT 1.4 miles (one-way) to North Sugarloaf.

For the North Sugarloaf side trip, follow PRT uphill to the base of an outcropping then make a steep descent to the east side of the gap. At the base of the descent, near the reservation boundary, bear left and follow PRT on a moderately steep ascent of the east side of the ridge. As you near the top of the ridge, the grade eases, and there are partial views of South Sugarloaf and the Connecticut River through the trees. Continue to the crest of the ridge and North Sugarloaf's summit, where there are westerly views of South Deerfield and the valley hills. Retrace your steps along PRT to the junction with Old Mountain Trail.

Complete the hike by following red-blazed Old Mountain Trail on an easy descent along an extension of Mountain Road to the base of the lower west slopes.

Mount Sugarloaf offers the finest view of the Connecticut River along its 410-mile course.

Bear left at the end of the paved portion of Mountain Road (at the reservation boundary) and continue along an old bridle path. A telephone line corridor and auto road will be on your left, with privately owned fields and residences on your right. Look for eastern coyotes, red and gray foxes, white-tailed deer, and wild turkeys near the forest edge. After passing a ball field on the right, complete the circuit at the parking area, 1.1 miles from South Sugarloaf's summit.

DID YOU KNOW?

According to Algonquian lore, Mount Sugarloaf and the Pocumtuck Ridge are remnants of a giant beaver that once lived in a lake in the Connecticut River basin. After the last ice age ended more than 10,000 years ago, a large postglacial lake (Lake Hitchcock) extended along the valley for 150 miles. Fossils tell us that *Casteroides,* a prehistoric beaver species that lived in this region, grew as large as 6 to 7 feet and weighed 200 to 275 pounds.

MORE INFORMATION

Open 9 A.M. to sunset year-round. No fee for hikers; a parking fee ($5 MA residents, $10 out of state) is charged at the summit. The auto road is open to vehicles from May to October and to pedestrians year-round. Dogs and biking are allowed. Hunting is allowed in accordance with state laws. For more information, visit mass.gov/locations/mount-sugarloaf-state-reservation or call 413-665-2928.

WINTER ACTIVITIES

Snowshoeing is allowed. Pocumtuck Ridge Trail on South Sugarloaf is not well suited for skiing because it is steep and rough, and there is heavy foot traffic. The portion of the trail on North Sugarloaf, best for advanced skiers, has moderate to steep grades.

NEARBY

Historic Deerfield, at 84B Old Main Street off US 5 in Deerfield, is dedicated to the history of Deerfield, the Connecticut River valley, and New England villages. Attractions include museums, a visitor center, an inn, and eleven well-preserved buildings in the village of Old Deerfield—a National Historic Landmark. For more information, visit historic-deerfield.org or call 413-774-5581. There are several places to eat in South Deerfield and Sunderland.

CONSERVING THE CONNECTICUT RIVER

The Connecticut River, New England's largest and best-known river, is a crucial natural resource with a long and rich history. The 11,000-square-mile watershed provided productive farmland and a vital trade and travel corridor for American Indians and early Colonial settlers, abundant hydropower during the Industrial Revolution, drinking water for millions of residents, and habitat for a wide variety of flora and fauna, including ten endangered species. With these benefits have come a variety of conservation challenges over the past 400 years.

The Connecticut Valley's human history began after the end of the last ice age, more than 10,000 years ago, when the first human beings arrived in the region. (The name Connecticut is derived from *Quinnehtukqut*, a Monhegan word meaning "long tidal river.") The prominent tribes in Massachusetts included the Pocumtuc, which inhabited the land at the confluence of the Connecticut and Deerfield rivers and the fertile meadows north of Springfield, and the Norwottuck, who lived in present-day Northampton–Hadley.

European colonists arrived in the valley during the 1630s and rapidly transformed the landscape by clearing an estimated 80 percent of the forests. The abrupt deforestation and soil erosion adversely affected water quality and wildlife habitat, and species such as moose, black bears, white-tailed deer, beavers, and wild turkeys were extirpated from much of the area.

In the nineteenth century, the Connecticut River and its tributaries were at the forefront of the Industrial Revolution. Although the mills brought financial prosperity over the years, with them came the unwelcome effects of industrial pollution and dams blocking fish runs. As the decades passed, the contamination continued. Longtime residents of the Millers River valley remember when the color of the river would change regularly when chemicals and dyes were dumped by factories. The Connecticut River was a mess of industrial waste, sewage, and agricultural pesticides, such as DDT, which contaminated the food chain. In the 1965 documentary *The Long Tidal River*, the actor Katharine Hepburn famously described the Connecticut River as "the world's most beautifully landscaped cesspool," an oft-repeated phrase that inspired early restoration efforts.

The watershed's fortunes changed for the better during the late twentieth century, an era of increased environmental awareness. After the federal Clean Water Act of 1972, sewage treatment facilities were constructed as part of a multimillion-dollar cleanup project. A controversial proposal by state water supply planners to divert a portion of the Connecticut River to Quabbin Reservoir via the Northfield Mountain pumping station, which could have affected the river's ecology, met with considerable local opposition during the 1970s and 1980s and was never enacted. While pollution effects still linger in some places, the region's waterways are now significantly cleaner. Herring and shad returned to the Connecticut River after fish passageways were built at old industrial dams, restoring migratory routes. Another welcome sign of progress occurred in 1989, when bald eagles—indicators of clean waterways—established a nest on the Connecticut River at Barton Cove. In 2012, the river was designated as America's first National Blueway and cited by Secretary of the Interior Ken Salazar as a model for restoration and conservation efforts.

While the ecological health of the Connecticut River and its tributaries has greatly improved in recent decades, many challenges remain. Nearly 90 percent of the watershed is currently undeveloped, but most of this land is not permanently protected. Many planners believe the watershed is vulnerable to future development and sprawl due to the region's relatively affordable land values, high quality of living, and densely populated areas. A significant amount of farmland has already been lost to development, and pollution remains a concern in places with aging industrial facilities. Many hemlock forests are being devastated by the hemlock woolly adelgid, an introduced pest. All of this leads to deteriorating water quality and a loss of habitat for brook trout and other cold-water fish.

Fortunately, many organizations—including federal and state agencies, land trusts, and regional nonprofits, such as Mass Audubon and The Trustees of Reservations—are working collectively to protect the watershed. Under the recently launched Connect the Connecticut initiative, more than 30 partners are developing a coordinated long-term conservation plan. Connecticut River Greenway State Park and Silvio O. Conte National Fish and Wildlife Refuge are examples of successful collaborations between state agencies and local groups, such as the Kestrel Land Trust, which has protected more than 25,000 acres in the Connecticut Valley. In the words of Kestrel's executive director, Kristin DeBoer, "These collaborations and the public support from people who live and recreate here are critical to ensure that this unique, important, and beautiful landscape endures for future generations."

8

ROCKY MOUNTAIN: SACHEM HEAD AND POET'S SEAT

Two loop trails, which can be walked individually or combined, lead to fine views from Sachem Head and Poet's Seat atop a narrow ridge, at the north end of the Pocumtuck Range.

DIRECTIONS

From I-91 take Exit 26 and follow MA 2A east 1.7 miles through downtown Greenfield. Turn right on Maple Street (which becomes Mountain Road) at a sign for Poet's Seat Tower and continue uphill 0.4 mile to the parking area at the base of the Poet Seat Tower auto road. *GPS coordinates: 42° 35.329′ N, 72° 35.242′ W.*

TRAIL DESCRIPTION

Rocky Mountain, a narrow basalt ridge that rises abruptly between the Connecticut River and downtown Greenfield, lies at the north end of the Pocumtuck Range, which extends 15 miles to Mount Sugarloaf. The southern portion, known as Temple Woods, is capped by Sachem Head, an open rocky summit with fine views. The northern portion is home to the popular Poet's Seat Tower, one of Greenfield's best-known landmarks, atop the 492-foot peak of the ridge. Mountain Road, where the main parking area and trail access are located, roughly divides the two segments. Loop hikes for both—easily combined for a longer outing, if desired—are detailed in this trail description. (*Caution:* There are precipitous dropoffs near cliff edges.) You can shorten the Poet's Seat Tower outing by making a direct walk to the tower on the auto road.

Sachem Head Loop

Carefully cross Mountain Road (visibility is limited) and enter the forest on the combined Pocumtuck Ridge Trail (PRT, blue blazes) and Red Trail (red blazes). At a junction

LOCATION
Greenfield, MA

SACHEM HEAD LOOP
RATING
Moderate

DISTANCE
1.8 miles

ELEVATION GAIN
450 feet

ESTIMATED TIME
1.25 hours

POET'S SEAT LOOP
RATING
Moderate

DISTANCE
1.9 miles

ELEVATION GAIN
350 feet

ESTIMATED TIME
1.25 hours

MAPS
USGS Greenfield; Greenfield Recreation Department map: greenfieldrecreation.com/pdfs/trails.pdf

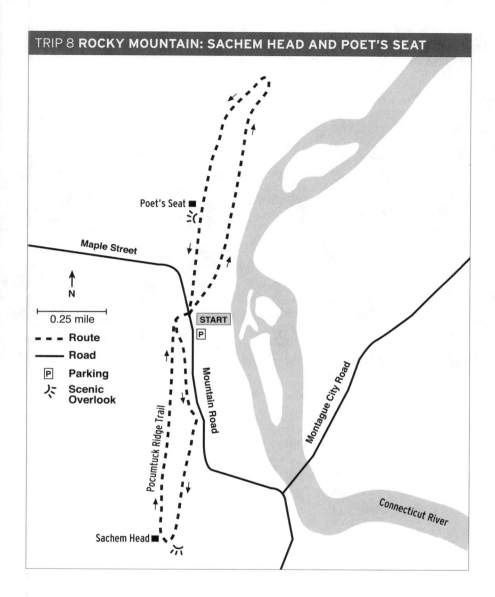

where the trails split off, begin the loop by bearing left on Red Trail, which follows a narrow footpath along the slope above Mountain Road. A familiar shrub that grows along the trail is maple-leaf viburnum, distinguished by its broad three-lobed leaves, similar in shape but much larger than those on maple trees. Continue along a contour parallel to Mountain Road then follow Red Trail right and uphill past the junction with a white-blazed trail that connects with the PRT near Sachem Head.

Bear left and follow Red Trail on a short, steep descent past the upper junction with a connecting trail (marked with yellow blazes as of this writing) to a fire road gate on Mountain Road. Turn right onto Bear's Den Lane, a wide unpaved

Sachem Head offers outstanding views across the upper Pocumtuck Ridge.

road, and begin an easy ascent along the base of the east side of the ridge. Wild geranium, easily identified by its five pink or purple petals and relatively tall height of 20 inches, grows along the margins of the road in mid to late spring. Pass the lower junction with the connecting trail and continue uphill to the southern junction with PRT at the base of Sachem Head, 0.5 mile from the gate.

Turn right on blue-blazed PRT and make a steep ascent, capped by a short scramble over exposed rock (use caution when wet or icy), to 452-foot Sachem Head at the crest of the ridge. A wide, square observation platform, built by Greenfield Center School students in 2009, offers fine views that include the central portion of the Pocumtuck Range to the south and the wooded foothills and ridges of the Connecticut River valley to the west. (*Caution:* Cliff edges here are steep 100-foot dropoffs.)

To continue the loop, carefully walk across the exposed rocks and follow PRT north through a hemlock grove to another partially open outlook. Rocky Mountain serves as an oasis of forest amid the farmland and development of the upper Connecticut River valley. Among the migratory songbirds that use these woods for breeding and resting are several state-listed species, including northern parulas and mourning warblers. A conspicuous year-round resident is the pileated woodpecker, easily distinguished by its red crest, large size, and loud laughing call.

Continue to follow PRT north along the ridge over rolling terrain. Pass junctions with the aforementioned white-blazed connecting trail and several unmarked or overgrown paths on the right. To the left are more glimpses of the valley through the trees. As you approach the north end of the ridge, the buildings and roads near downtown Greenfield come into view at the base of the steep, wooded hillside. At approximately 0.9 mile from Sachem Head, complete the loop at the northern junction with Red Trail. Continue straight on PRT to return to Mountain Road and the parking area.

Poet's Seat Loop

At the auto road gate, pass a red-blazed trail that leads down the slope on the right (an optional 2.2-mile loop). At the next junction, bear right off the road onto the white-blazed trail and continue along a contour below the crest of the ridge, which rises above to the left. On this pleasant woodland path, listen for a variety of songbirds during spring and summer. Also watch for tiny spring peepers, well camouflaged amid fallen leaves when not moving.

Continue north over gently rolling terrain past a rocky talus slope and a grove of hemlock trees that have suffered significantly from hemlock woolly adelgid infestation. At 0.4 mile, pass below the high point of the ridge and reach a junction at a stone wall with a yellow-blazed connecting trail that leads directly to Poet's Seat Tower (an option for a shorter loop). Continue straight on the white-blazed trail, which offers an easy walk through the wooded north end of the ridge.

At 0.8 mile, reach a three-way junction with blue-blazed PRT on the left and the red-blazed trail, which comes up the slope on the right. Turn left and follow PRT uphill through a hemlock grove then begin an easy to moderate ascent, heading south along the crest of the ridge past several outlooks on the right. Watch for spicebush swallowtail butterflies, which favor open woods, basking on sunlit leaves near the trail edge during late spring and summer.

Shortly after passing the upper junction with the yellow-blazed trail, PRT meets the auto road on the north side of Poet's Seat Tower. The sandstone structure, built in 1912, got its name for the poets, including the local writer Frederick Goddard Tuckerman, who once frequented the hilltop. The 360-degree view includes the Beacon Park baseball field at the base of the ridge, Pocumtuck Ridge to the south, and a glimpse of the Connecticut River to the east. The grassy clearing on the north side of the tower has several benches where you can relax and enjoy westerly views to the Berkshire Hills. Complete the loop by following PRT downhill along the auto road 0.3 mile to the parking area.

DID YOU KNOW?

The diverse habitats of the Pocumtuck Ridge, which include exposed cliffs and talus slopes, support many different plant and wildlife species. Nearly 40 species of ferns have been documented.

MORE INFORMATION

Open dawn to dusk year-round, no fee. Biking and dogs are allowed. For more information, visit greenfieldrecreation.com or call 413-772-1553. For information on Pocumtuck Ridge Trail, visit pocumtuck.org.

WINTER ACTIVITIES

Most trails are suitable for skiing. Pocumtuck Ridge Trail follows rolling, rocky terrain along the ridge; use caution near trail edges, at Sachem Head, and around steep dropoffs. Snowshoeing is allowed on all trails.

NEARBY

Energy Park, a newly established community park at 50 Miles Street in downtown Greenfield, includes sustainability exhibits, an arboretum with native New England plants, and a caboose now used as a museum. The park hosts weekly concerts and frequent events. Visit greenfieldrecreation.com for details. There are many places to eat in downtown Greenfield.

9

MOUNT TOBY

From Cranberry Pond, an old carriage road offers a moderately steep ascent past rich wildflower habitat and the cascades of Roaring Brook en route to the fire tower atop Mount Toby, the highest point of the Connecticut River valley.

DIRECTIONS

From the south, on I-91 take Exit 24 in Deerfield and follow US 5/MA 10 north to the junction with MA 116. (From the north take Exit 25.) Follow MA 116 south 1.8 miles to the junction with MA 47 in Sunderland. Turn left on MA 47 and, after 3.9 miles, turn right and follow Reservation Road 0.5 mile to a parking area and kiosk. Continue another 0.5 mile to the parking area at Cranberry Pond. *GPS coordinates: 42° 30.198′ N, 72° 31.514′ W.*

TRAIL DESCRIPTION

Mount Toby, a broad massif with several peaks and a long summit plateau, rises high above the eastern banks of the Connecticut River in Sunderland and Leverett, opposite Mount Sugarloaf and the Pocumtuck Ridge. Although the 1,269-foot summit, the highest point of the Connecticut River valley, is wooded, a fire tower offers sweeping 360-degree views across the region. The mountain is also renowned for its diverse natural communities, including Cranberry Pond and the cascades of Roaring Brook. The University of Massachusetts manages the 755-acre Mount Toby Demonstration Forest for research and education.

This circuit hike begins at Cranberry Pond, at the base of the northeast slopes, and follows Tower Road and a portion of the long-distance Robert Frost Trail (RFT) to the summit. An optional short detour leads to Roaring Falls and a series of interesting rocky outcroppings. The descent follows RFT and other footpaths through mixed forests on

LOCATION
Sunderland and Leverett, MA

RATING
Moderate to Strenuous

DISTANCE
4.1 miles

ELEVATION GAIN
940 feet

ESTIMATED TIME
2.75 hours

MAPS
USGS Mount Toby; University of Massachusetts Amherst Department of Environmental Conservation map: eco.umass.edu/ wp-content/uploads/ 2011/09/Mt.-Toby.pdf

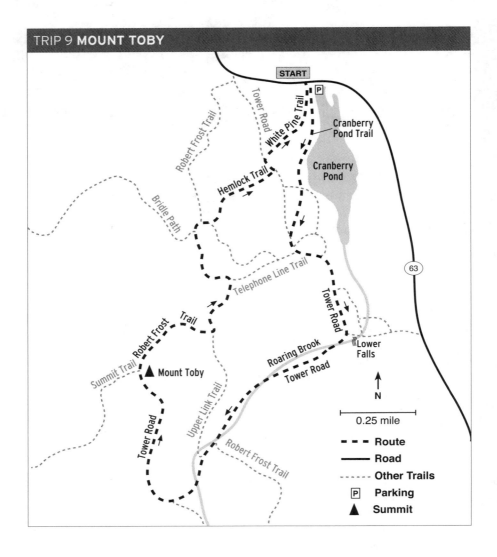

the north slopes. Seasonal attractions include abundant wildflowers in mid to late spring and colorful fall foliage in October.

From the Cranberry Pond parking area, follow blue-blazed Cranberry Pond Trail (restricted to foot travel only to prevent erosion) into the woods along the west shores of the pond. This scenic glacial kettle pond, stocked with trout in spring, is a good place to watch for familiar waterfowl, such as mallard ducks and Canada geese. Beavers are present here too, as evidenced by a few cut trees along the path; the animals are most active and visible during the early morning and evening hours.

At 0.1 mile, pass the unmarked junction with White Pine Trail, the return route for this hike, on the right. Make a short descent to the water's edge and continue through tall oaks, pines, and hemlock saplings then bear right and head southwest, away from the pond, to the junction with Tower Road (also known as Summit Road), a historical carriage road that was originally built to provide access for a hotel at Mount Toby's summit. The hotel, constructed during the nineteenth century, was destroyed by fire after a year and was never rebuilt. Turn left at the end of Cranberry Pond Trail and follow Tower Road past a power-line corridor and the junction with Telephone Line Trail (a steep, direct route to the summit) on the right.

Continue to the nearby junction with Roaring Falls Bypass Trail on the left, marked by a blue directional blaze. Here you have the option of leaving Tower Road and making an easy 10-minute walk to the distinctive waterfall and rocky ravine where Roaring Brook drops nearly 20 feet over a ledge before funneling through a jumble of giant mossy boulders. In spring, red trillium, bloodroot, round-lobed hepatica, and other wildflowers grow in abundance around the falls and along Tower Road. You can rejoin Tower Road via Roaring Falls Trail, a short, rugged path that winds over rock ledges, or you can backtrack on the bypass trail.

From the upper junction with Roaring Falls Trail near a mossy rock ledge, follow Tower Road uphill on an easy to moderate ascent along Roaring Brook. The top of Roaring Mountain, a 1,195-foot shoulder of Mount Toby, is visible above the trees on the left. In late April and early May, dense colonies of red trillium bloom along the edge of the brook. After crossing Roaring Brook several times, reach the junction with orange-blazed RFT on the left, 0.7 mile from Roaring Falls Trail. Follow Tower Road and RFT past the junction with Upper Link Trail near the confluence of two brooks. After passing the junction with Robert Frost Bypass Trail on the left, bear right and follow Tower Road and RFT on a last climb to the south end of Mount Toby's long summit plateau.

Continue along the wooded ridge crest to the summit, where the fire tower offers panoramic views of the Connecticut River, Mount Monadnock, and the southern Green Mountains of Vermont to the north; Mount Sugarloaf and the Pocumtuck Ridge across the valley to the west; and the Holyoke Range and Mount Tom to the south. The tower is part of a forest fire control network that includes lookouts atop Mount Grace, in Warwick, and Moore Hill, at the Daughters of the American Revolution State Forest in Conway.

Begin your return trip by following RFT on a steep descent along the power-line corridor. The wide clearing affords a bird's-eye glimpse of Cranberry Pond, your starting point, in the valley far below. After passing the second junction with Upper Link Trail on the right, continue to follow RFT downhill to the junction with Telephone Line Trail, 0.6 mile from the summit. Turn right, leaving the clearing, and follow RFT through an old pine plantation and groves of oak, birch, and beech to a rock ledge at the University of Massachusetts property boundary.

At the next junction, turn right on Hemlock Trail, which connects RFT and Tower Road and leads downhill at a moderately steep grade through

hemlock-hardwood forest. At the base of the descent, turn left on Tower Road for a few hundred feet then turn right on White Pine Trail at the next junction. Follow this aptly named path through groves of tall white pines to the junction with Cranberry Pond Trail to complete the loop. Turn left on Cranberry Pond Trail to return to the parking area.

DID YOU KNOW?

The fire tower replaced an observation tower that was built at the summit during the 1870s. Visitors took carriages or trains to the top of the mountain to enjoy the views and escape the increasing congestion and pollution of nearby mill towns such as Springfield, Holyoke, and Chicopee.

MORE INFORMATION

Open year-round, no fee. Biking on designated trails only, dogs are allowed. Hunting is allowed in accordance with state laws. Trail maps have been available at the kiosk on Reservation Road in the past, but hikers are advised to print their own copies before visiting. For more information, including the map, visit eco.umass.edu.

WINTER ACTIVITIES

According to the trail map, skiing is listed as an authorized use on Tower Road, Paddy Farms Trail, Roaring Falls Bypass Trail, Robert Frost Bypass Trail, South Mountain Road, Sugar Farms Trail, Timber Management Trail, Upper Link Trail, and White Pine Trail. Snowshoeing is allowed on all hiking trails.

NEARBY

The Montague Bookmill, at 440 Greenfield Road in Montague, offers a wide variety of used books in a nineteenth-century mill on the Sawmill River. Open 10 A.M. to 6 P.M. daily; for more information, visit montaguebookmill.com or call 413-367-9206. The closest places to eat are along MA 116 in Sunderland and US 5/MA 10 in Deerfield.

Facing page: Roaring Brook is picturesque during spring high water or after a soaking rain.

10

NORTHFIELD MOUNTAIN

The wooded slopes of Northfield Mountain include a historical quarry site, a unique summit reservoir with views to Vermont's Green Mountains, and the dramatic Rose Ledge. The mountain is also an excellent winter recreation destination.

DIRECTIONS

From I-91 take Exit 27 in Greenfield and follow MA 2 east 7.0 miles to the junction with MA 63 in Millers Falls, a village of Montague. Turn north on MA 63 and continue 2.1 miles to the visitor center driveway on the right (99 Millers Falls Road). *GPS coordinates:* 42° 36.619′ N, 72° 28.316′ W.

TRAIL DESCRIPTION

Northfield Mountain, the northernmost significant eminence of the Connecticut River valley in Massachusetts, rises high above the east banks of the Connecticut River and the nearby French King Gorge. The mountain's broad summit plateau is capped by several peaks, including Hermit Mountain (Trip 12), and a 300-acre artificial reservoir used to store water from the Connecticut River for hydroelectric power. On the southeast slopes is Rose Ledge, a long rock cliff with views across the upper Connecticut Valley.

The Northfield Mountain Recreation and Environmental Center, operated by the utility company FirstLight Power, maintains an extensive network of footpaths (open to hiking and snowshoeing) and multiuse trails (open seasonally for skiing, horseback riding, biking, and hiking). Nearly all of the hike described here is on foot trails marked with red diamond blazes. The multiuse trails, which follow old carriage roads, offer outstanding cross-country skiing in winter, with more than 25 miles of

LOCATION
Northfield, MA

RATING
Moderate

DISTANCE
3.9 miles

ELEVATION GAIN
840 feet

ESTIMATED TIME
2.75 hours

MAPS
USGS Millers Falls; FirstLight Power map: h2opower.ca/wp-content/ uploads/2017/01/ Northfield-Map-2016 -Update-Shaded-Relief -Rev08.pdf

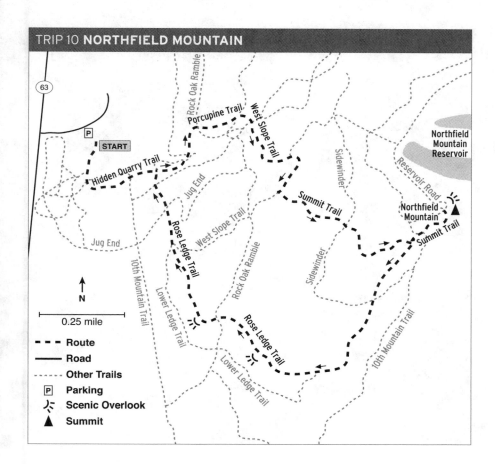

groomed classic and freestyle routes. See "Winter Activities" at the end of this trail description for seasonal information and winter hours.

From the visitor center, where maps are available, follow signs for Hidden Quarry and Rose Ledge trails. Watch for bullfrogs, rose-breasted grosbeaks, and other wildlife at the small pond near the trailhead. Continue along the field edge to the start of Hidden Quarry Trail (adjacent to the 10th Mountain Trail). Enter the woods and follow Hidden Quarry Trail through a pine grove, where pink lady's slippers bloom in late May. Cross a power-line clearing that offers habitat for indigo buntings, chestnut-sided warblers, and common yellowthroats, along with skippers and other butterflies. These species all favor brushy fields, and the clearing offers similar conditions.

Continue uphill past the hemlock forest interpretive station to a marked junction; here, Rose Ledge Trail, the return route, branches to the right. Begin the loop by continuing straight on Hidden Quarry Trail, past an area of exposed bedrock and a stone wall, to the former quarry site, where granite rocks were extracted for building foundations and railroads. From the quarry, bear left and

Northfield Mountain offers habitat for migratory songbirds, such as the rose-breasted grosbeak.

continue on Porcupine Trail, so named because the nearby boulders offer denning habitat for porcupines, as well as fishers and other animals. Follow Porcupine Trail as it levels and winds through hemlock-hardwood forest then cross Rock Oak Ramble, a multiuse trail, and continue uphill at a gentle grade past the Chocolate Pot shelter (where visitors can purchase hot chocolate and enjoy an outdoor fire in winter) in a sunlit clearing.

At a junction above the shelter, bear right on the upper portion of West Slope Trail, the mountain's longest hiking trail. Descend past a seasonal stream and follow the winding path on a pleasant, mostly level stretch. Check smooth-barked beech trees for claw marks made by black bears. Pass the junction with Bobcat Trail then bear right and continue past a grove of hemlock trees (now infested with hemlock woolly adelgid, look for tiny white egg sacs on the evergreen needles) and a stream crossing. At the next junction, turn left on Summit Trail to begin the 0.7-mile ascent to the top of the mountain. After a short, moderately steep segment, cross Sidewinder Trail and continue through groves of mature forest, including tall oaks and a giant hemlock.

At the junction with the upper end of Rose Ledge Trail, turn left and continue to follow Summit Trail another 0.3 mile to the 1,100-foot summit of Northfield Mountain. Shortly after crossing another multiuse trail, reach the paved Reservoir Road. A short path on the right leads to a wooden observation deck with fine views across the summit reservoir to Stratton Mountain and Mount Snow in the southern Green Mountains of Vermont, Mount Pisgah in southern New Hampshire, and the peaks of nearby Crag and Hermit mountains to the northeast. The reservoir, which has a capacity of 5.6 billion gallons, is fed by water pumped up 800 feet from the Connecticut River. The facility began operating in 1972 and is one of the largest power-generating stations in New England.

Begin the descent by retracing your steps along Summit Trail to the Rose Ledge Trail junction, following the red blazes at the road and trail crossings. Continue straight on Rose Ledge Trail past the junction with Hill 'N Dale Trail at marker 29. After a gentle descent, the trail curves south along the forested southeast shoulder of the mountain, with partial views when the trees are bare.

At marker 33, pass the upper junction with Lower Ledge Trail, which leads to the base of Rose Ledge (an optional detour for those interested in a close-up perspective of the cliffs). Rose Ledge Trail continues through the woods along the perimeter of the 0.3-mile long gneiss ledge, a popular destination for rock climbers. Side paths lead to southwesterly views across the upper Connecticut Valley from the top of the ledge: Mount Sugarloaf, the Pocumtuck Ridge, and the village of Millers Falls. Use caution near steep dropoffs.

From Rose Ledge, continue downhill past a series of low, shelflike gneiss outcroppings and blueberry bushes. After crossing Rock Oak Ramble again in Yellow Jacket Pass, follow Rose Ledge Trail as it bends to the west and passes successive junctions with West Slope Trail and Lower Ledge Trail. One of the many migratory songbirds that nests in these woods is the scarlet tanager, so named for the male's brilliant red color. Listen for the raspy *cheerio, cheer-up* call, which bird-watchers often describe as sounding like a hoarse robin. This portion of the trail is another good place to watch for pink lady's slippers and other wildflowers.

Follow the lower portion of Rose Ledge Trail across a seasonal stream in a ravine then cross a larger cascading stream on a footbridge. After crossing Hemlock Hill Trail near the power line, complete the loop at the junction with Hidden Quarry Trail, 1.9 miles from the summit. Turn left on Hidden Quarry Trail and retrace your steps downhill to the fields at the base of the mountain then turn right and walk along the field edge to go back to the visitor center and parking area.

DID YOU KNOW?

As the result of a prolonged drought in the 1960s, state water supply planners drafted a proposal to divert portions of the Connecticut River to Quabbin

Reservoir via the Northfield Mountain summit reservoir. The project never happened due to local opposition, the end of the drought, and the adoption of water conservation measures in eastern Massachusetts.

MORE INFORMATION
During the warm months, the trails are open seven days a week for hiking (no fee). Trails are closed from the last snowmelt to the end of mud season, generally mid-April to early May, depending on the year. Biking (on designated trails) and leashed dogs are allowed. Hunting is allowed in accordance with state laws. For more information, visit h2opower.ca/recreation/northfield-mountain-recreation-and-environmental-center, call 800-859-2960, or check the Northfield Mountain Recreation and Environmental Center Facebook page for updated conditions.

WINTER ACTIVITIES
Northfield Mountain Recreation and Environmental Center maintains an extensive network of cross-country ski trails (on multiuse trails) and snowshoe trails (on blazed hiking trails). In winter, the trails are open Wednesday to Sunday, 9 A.M. to 4:30 P.M. There is no fee for snowshoeing, but a free pass is required. Fees for skiing: adults, $12 ($10 after 1:30 P.M.); seniors, ages 62 to 69, $11 ($9 after 1:30); children, ages 8 to 14, $8 ($6 after 1:30). No fee for seniors older than 70 and children younger than 8. Skis and snowshoes are available for rent.

NEARBY
Northfield Mountain Recreation and Environmental Center offers scenic tours of French King Gorge, the Connecticut River, and Barton Cove on the *Quinnetukut II* riverboat. Contact the center for seasonal hours. Facilities at Barton Cove include a boat launch, canoe and kayak rentals, a campground, and a 1.1-mile nature trail with views of the cove and distinctive rocky outcroppings. Restaurants are located on Main Street (MA 10) in Northfield and in Greenfield.

11

WENDELL STATE FOREST

The New England Trail offers several options for exploring the diverse features of Wendell State Forest, including an easy loop around Ruggles Pond and a longer, more challenging excursion to Hidden Valley and giant rock outcroppings.

DIRECTIONS

From the junction of MA 2 and MA 63 in Erving, follow MA 63 south to the junction with Wendell Road at the four-way intersection in the center of Millers Falls. Continue straight on Wendell Road (which becomes Montague Road) 3.1 miles to the forest headquarters and entrance on the left. If the gate is closed, park at the headquarters and walk downhill along the paved road 0.2 mile to Ruggles Pond. *GPS coordinates: 42° 33.006′ N, 72° 27.159′ W.*

TRAIL DESCRIPTION

The 7,550-acre Wendell State Forest is part of a large conservation corridor that extends from the Millers River valley to Warwick. The 1.8-mile trail around Ruggles Pond, which is excellent for families, is a pleasant, easy walk with fine views of the 10-acre pond and its associated habitats. On the north side of the pond, a more rugged circuit leads to cascading streams in Hidden Valley, a ridge with two overlooks, and dramatic rocky outcroppings. These loops, which begin at the Ruggles Pond day-use area, may be walked individually or combined as a 4.6-mile outing.

Ruggles Pond Circuit

Carefully cross the footbridge over Lyons Brook at the Ruggles Pond dam and follow the white-blazed New England Trail (NET) south along the western shores, past a pavilion and field. The 10-acre artificial pond is a popular

LOCATION
Wendell, MA

RUGGLES POND CIRCUIT RATING
Easy

DISTANCE
1.8 miles

ELEVATION GAIN
50 feet

ESTIMATED TIME
1.25 hours

LOOKOUT TRAIL LOOP RATING
Moderate

DISTANCE
3 miles

ELEVATION GAIN
575 feet

ESTIMATED TIME
1.75 hours

MAPS
USGS Millers Falls;
Massachusetts Department of Conservation and Recreation map:
mass.gov/eea/docs/dcr/parks/trails/wendell.pdf

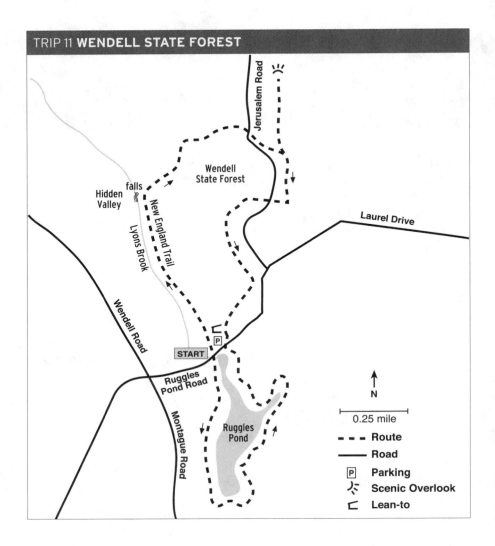

fishing and swimming area. On the left is a good view of a large, abandoned beaver lodge. Beavers usually leave a wetland when their supply of desirable trees, usually hardwoods, has been depleted. Freshly cut branches and logs on top of a lodge indicate that it is still in use.

Continue through the pond's forest buffer, where fringed polygala, bluebead lily, mayflower, pink lady's slipper, and painted trillium bloom in spring. The trillium's three white petals surround a bright red center that looks like a splotch of paint. Black-and-white warblers, with a call that sounds like a squeaking wheel, are among the many migratory songbirds nesting here in the spring. You may also hear the cheerful whistles of northern orioles echoing across the water.

At the southern end of the pond, follow the NET through a rocky area and over boardwalk bridges at the inlet, where a large colony of jack-in-the pulpit blooms in spring. Some of the common damselflies, which can be distinguished from dragonflies by their smaller size and practice of perching with wings folded, include eastern forktails and several species of bluets. At a marked junction, turn left to continue on blue-blazed Pond Loop Trail, leaving the NET, which branches to the right at an M–M Trail sign. Scan the marshy areas for the colorful wood ducks that use wetland edges for cover. They are often quite skittish, so walk quietly to increase your odds of finding one. Their takeoff is often accompanied by a loud *ooo-eek* call.

Cross a footbridge over another brook and follow Pond Loop Trail as it swings north to an outlook at the wetland edge. Here you'll enter a different type of forest habitat, a shady hemlock-pine grove. Note the lack of understory vegetation compared with the trail on the east side, the result of the dense evergreens blocking light from reaching the forest floor. Although botanical diversity is limited, these groves offer crucial habitat for porcupines, red squirrels, and blackburnian warblers. White-tailed deer often use hemlock forests, which offer shelter from heavy snow and cold temperatures, as wintering areas.

After crossing a low knoll, descend to follow the perimeter of a swamp at the pond's northeastern arm. Bear left through a rocky section at the wetland's outlet (you may hear water gurgling beneath the rocks) then continue straight where another trail enters from the right. Trek through the woods above the perimeter of the wetland then return to the pond's edge. Follow the footpath through a growth of mountain laurel at the pond's northern tip to the beach and the end of the loop.

Lookout Trail Loop

Follow the NET across the Ruggles Pond parking lot then enter the woods and begin the descent into Hidden Valley along the banks of Lyons Brook. A short distance from the trailhead is a wooden camping shelter that accommodates six to eight people (reservations not required; visit newenglandtrail.org for availability and to register). Continue through a forest grove that was damaged by a short-lived but powerful tornado that passed through Wendell in July 2006. The forest has gradually been regenerating over the past decade, but the tornado's path is still clearly discernible.

The NET heads downhill through a growth of mountain laurel to the base of the ravine (0.5 mile from the parking area), where Lyons Brook meets another cascading brook at Lynne's Falls, a 25-foot-high seasonal waterfall that is picturesque during high water but dries up quickly during the summer. Watch for green frogs along the banks of the brooks during the warm months. Bear right and follow the NET uphill along Lynne's Falls to the boundary of the Hidden Valley Conservation Area, a 66-acre inholding managed by the Mount Grace Land Conservation Trust. Here the NET follows Lynne's Falls Trail along the brook then turns right on a woods road and passes a large exposed outcropping.

After reentering the state forest, turn right onto Jerusalem Road and continue the moderately steep ascent to the base of another large outcropping. Turn left off the road and follow the NET on a short, steep climb to the top of the ledge,

where blue-blazed Lookout Trail, the return route for this hike, enters from the right. Continue to follow the NET along the top of the ridge through more mountain laurel to two marked overlooks with westerly views to Mount Greylock and the Berkshires. At this point you've gained 470 feet in elevation from the base of the valley and hiked 1.5 miles from Ruggles Pond.

From the second lookout, retrace your steps on the NET to the junction with Lookout Trail, bearing left on Lookout Trail and descending to Jerusalem Road. Turn left on the road for a short distance then turn right at the next junction and follow Lookout Trail into the woods on the western side of the road. For the next 0.6 mile, follow Lookout Trail over rolling terrain and past more rock ledges and hemlock-hardwood forests. After the last descent, pass the base of another impressive outcropping on the left. The parking area is a short distance ahead.

DID YOU KNOW?

Massachusetts averages just three to four tornadoes annually, a relatively low number given New England's cool climate and northern location, but it has the nation's highest tornado fatality per area ratio due to its small size and high population density.

MORE INFORMATION

Open year-round. A seasonal parking fee ($8 MA residents, $15 out of state) is charged at the Ruggles Pond day-use area, which is open in summer from 9:30 A.M. to 5:30 P.M. weekdays and 9:30 A.M. to 7:30 P.M. weekends. (The access road is gated; do not park at this lot after hours.) Biking and dogs are allowed. Hunting is allowed in accordance with state laws. A boat launch is available at Wickett Pond. For more information, visit mass.gov/locations/wendell-state-forest or call 413-659-3797.

WINTER ACTIVITIES

Skiing and snowshoeing are allowed. The trail network includes many wide dirt roads with gentle to moderate elevation gain. The NET and other hiking trails are narrow and rougher, with several steep and rocky sections around ridges. The Ruggles Pond day-use area is closed in winter, but parking is available at the headquarters on Montague Road.

NEARBY

Food, coffee, ice cream, and other goods are available at the Wendell Country Store, at 57 Lockes Village Road. It's open Monday to Saturday, 7 A.M. to 9 P.M., and Sunday, 8 A.M. to 8 P.M. Call 978-544-8646 for more information.

Facing page: Lynne's Falls is one of two cascading streams that converge in Hidden Valley.

12

HERMIT MOUNTAIN AND HERMIT'S CASTLE

This mostly easy outing, with a more rugged side loop, leads to the unique Hermit's Castle historical site and a ledge with arguably the finest scenic view of Millers River valley.

DIRECTIONS

From I-91 take Exit 27 in Greenfield and follow MA 2 east 12.4 miles to Erving. Turn left on Mountain Road and continue uphill 1.8 miles to the parking area, on the left side of the road, at the New England Trail crossing. From the east, follow MA 2 west 0.5 mile from Erving center then turn right on Mountain Road. *GPS coordinates:* 42° 37.619′ N, 72° 25.062′ W.

TRAIL DESCRIPTION

The rugged ledges of Hermit Mountain, which form the southeast slope of the Northfield Mountain massif, rise sharply above Millers River valley in Erving. Nearly hidden within this dramatic scenery of rock ledges, caves, and sheer cliffs is Hermit's Castle, a rock cave so named because it was once the home of the legendary local recluse John Smith. Below Hermit Mountain's 1,206-foot summit, the highest of Northfield Mountain's several distinct peaks, is a lookout with an outstanding panoramic view of the valley.

This hike follows a portion of the New England Trail (NET) from uplands on Mountain Road to a side loop trail to Hermit's Castle. The trailhead is the highest point of the trip at 1,108 feet, and the walking is mostly easy along the NET, with a gradual descent on the outbound leg and a climb on the return. The Hermit's Castle side trail is more rugged, as it travels steeper slopes below the ridge. You can bypass the cave loop by following the NET directly to the overlook for a 1.4-mile one-way walk. Most of the route is within the western portion of Erving State Forest.

LOCATION
Erving, MA

RATING
Easy to Moderate

DISTANCE
4.8 miles

ELEVATION GAIN
380 feet

ESTIMATED TIME
3 hours

MAPS
AMC Massachusetts Trail Map 4; USGS Millers Falls; New England Trail map: newenglandtrail.org/ get-on-the-trail/ma-net -section-16-metacomet -monadnock-trail

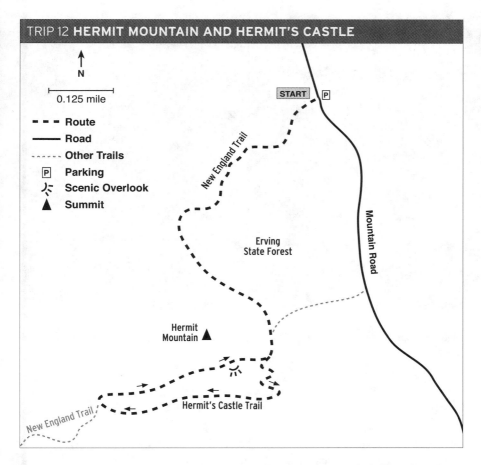

From the trailhead on the western side of Mountain Road, follow the white-blazed NET south into the woods, past a brook crossing. Continue left through a hemlock grove and over a low knoll. Descend past a small swamp in a ravine on the right then follow the well-marked NET on an easy walk through hardwood-conifer forests and mountain laurel shrubs characteristic of central New England's uplands. A few American chestnut saplings, which sprouted from trees killed by the chestnut blight outbreak of the early twentieth century, grow along the trail's edge. A common late-season wildflower is the white wood aster, a member of the daisy family, that blooms from July to October.

These unbroken forests form a crucial buffer that helps maintain the water quality of Millers River, the largest tributary of the Connecticut River in central Massachusetts. The river suffered heavily from industrial pollution but is recovering, thanks to cleanup efforts in recent decades and protection of the surrounding watershed. Keep an eye out for black bears, increasingly common on the east side of the Connecticut River valley. Moose also periodically visit these woods, although sightings are unpredictable. During the autumn mating season (known as the "rut"), females make high-pitched wailing calls that may be audible through the trees.

Panoramic views of the forested Millers River valley unfold from this New England Trail lookout above Hermit's Castle.

Follow the NET left at a junction with an overgrown trail on the right then continue past a state forest boundary marker on an old woods road. After roughly 0.7 mile, pass through a hemlock grove and continue the gradual descent past another unmarked path on the left. In 1.4 miles (roughly 35 to 45 minutes) from the trailhead, reach the ledges above the Millers River valley and the marked upper junction with Hermit's Castle Trail, where the loop begins. (To bypass the trail to Hermit's Castle and go directly to the overlook, turn right and follow the white-blazed NET along the crest of the ridge 0.2 mile.)

This hike continues left on blue-blazed Hermit's Castle Trail, which snakes down the moderately steep valley slope then bends to the right and runs along a contour below the top of the ridge. At 0.5 mile from the junction, reach Hermit's Castle, which was John Smith's home for three decades. According to a biography compiled by the naturalist John Foster, Smith, a Scotsman who worked briefly as an actor before immigrating to America, settled at the cave in 1867 before the land was subdivided by the town. After the location of his unusual home became publicly known, local residents and tourists alike flocked to the "castle." One newspaper reported that Smith had entertained more than 15,000 guests by 1874. He was an avid gardener, and the rock walls in front of the cave likely are old flower beds. Following a dispute with another settler (whose cellar hole is also visible nearby), Smith moved to a cabin a quarter-mile away then left the area shortly before his death in 1899. The site was rediscovered in the late 1990s by Foster, who created Hermit's Castle Trail.

From the cave, continue on Hermit's Castle Trail up the valley slope to the lower junction with the NET. Turn right and follow the white-blazed NET north along the ridge, with partial views of the valley through the trees to the south. You'll soon reach the rock ledge and scenic overlook, which offers 180-degree views across the densely forested Millers River valley. The Erving Paper Mill and town cemetery are visible in the distance to the east, and you may see a freight train on the railroad tracks that parallel the river. Across the valley to the south are the wooded slopes of Bear Mountain in Wendell State Forest. The lookout is an excellent place for enjoying and photographing fall foliage, which usually peaks around the third week of October and lasts into early November, when the last of the oaks drop their leaves. Bright yellow false foxglove wildflowers bloom along the ridge in late summer.

From the overlook, continue along the ridge another 0.2 mile to the end of the loop, at the upper junction with Hermit's Castle Trail. Turn left and retrace your steps along the NET on a gradual, mostly easy ascent back to the Mountain Road trailhead.

DID YOU KNOW?

During the late nineteenth century, nature retreats became increasingly popular in America, due in part to the influence of writers such as John Burroughs, John Muir, and Walt Whitman.

MORE INFORMATION

Open year-round, no fee. No visitor facilities. Biking and dogs are allowed. Hunting is allowed in accordance with state laws. For more information, visit newenglandtrail.org/get-on-the-trail/hermits-castle-trail-0. The Erving State Forest main tract includes a swimming beach and campground at Laurel Lake (entrance at 122 Long Pond Road in Warwick; mass.gov/locations/erving -state-forest, 978-544-3939).

WINTER ACTIVITIES

Skiing and snowshoeing are allowed. The Hermit's Castle side loop trail and portions of the New England Trail along the ridge are steep and rocky. The Erving State Forest main tract at Laurel Lake includes a network of woods roads and trails that are ideal for skiing.

NEARBY

At Laurel Lake, the 0.7-mile Laurel Trail offers an easy ascent through a growth of mountain laurels to a ridge with views of the surrounding hills and Mount Monadnock. Another nature trail offers a short walk to an observation area at a beaver pond, at the western end of the lake. The famous French King Bridge, located on MA 2 at the Erving–Gill town line, offers spectacular views of the Connecticut River and French King Gorge from 135 feet above the river. There are several places to eat on MA 2 and MA 2A in Erving and Orange.

13

STRATTON MOUNTAIN

In the Upper Bald Hills of Northfield, this quiet segment of the New England Trail offers a moderately rugged trek through beech groves, rolling terrain, and a hidden valley to outstanding views atop Stratton Mountain.

DIRECTIONS

From I-91 take Exit 27 in Greenfield and follow MA 2 east 12.7 miles to Erving. Turn left on North Street, which becomes Gulf Road, and continue 4.4 miles to the roadside parking area adjacent to the Brush Mountain Conservation Area. *GPS coordinates:* 42° 39.603′ N, 72° 25.153′ W.

TRAIL DESCRIPTION

At 1,289 feet, Stratton Mountain is a high point of the ridge of the Upper Bald Hills, a chain of rolling hills on the east side of the Connecticut River valley in Northfield. The summit offers panoramic easterly views to several of central New England's well-known peaks, including Mount Monadnock, Wachusett Mountain, and nearby Mount Grace. Another attraction for hikers is the enclosed Richardson-Zlogar Cabin, recently built by AMC volunteers.

This 3.3-mile, one-way outing follows the New England Trail (NET) from the Gulf Road trailhead to the summit of Stratton Mountain. The route passes through a deep valley on the east side of the ridge and thus requires a moderately steep ascent on both the outbound and return trips. There are several opportunities to explore other trails, including Bald Hills Loop, which connects with the NET at two junctions near the trailhead.

At the NET crossing on Gulf Road, the welcome sign on the western side of the road includes information and maps for local sites, including the adjacent Northfield

LOCATION
Northfield, MA

RATING
Moderate to Strenuous

DISTANCE
6.6 miles

ELEVATION GAIN
850 feet

ESTIMATED TIME
3.25 hours

MAPS
AMC Massachusetts Trail Map 4; USGS Northfield; New England Trail map: newenglandtrail.org/ get-on-the-trail/ma-net -section-17-metacomet -monadnock-trail

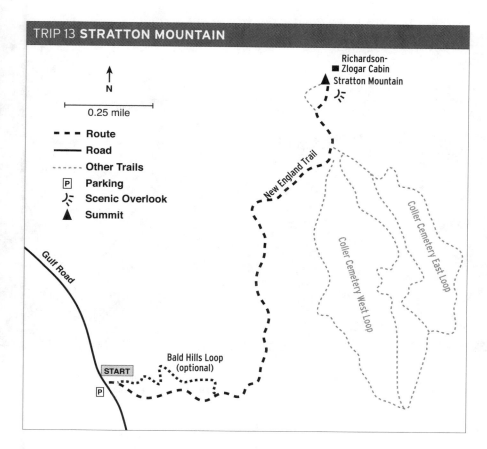

Town Forest and Brush Mountain Conservation Area. From the trailhead on the east side of the road, follow the white-blazed NET uphill into the woods for a few hundred feet to the western junction with blue-blazed Bald Hills Loop Trail. Appropriately marked as the "Over the Top Route" on the trail sign, Bald Hills Loop is an optional side path that crosses the top of the ridge above Gulf Road then rejoins the NET at the eastern junction. It is somewhat rugged, with 360 feet of elevation gain over rolling terrain. There are no open views, but Mount Grace and the surrounding hills can be glimpsed through the trees when the leaves have fallen. Walk the loop trail on the way out or on the way back, or bypass it entirely by continuing on the NET.

From the junction, the NET continues to the right over gently rolling terrain on a shoulder of the ridge. Make a quick climb around a rock outcropping to the eastern junction with Bald Hills Loop, which enters from the high point of the ridge to the left. Begin a moderate to steep descent of the east side of the ridge into the ravine of Hidden Pond, Great Swamp, and Keyup Brook on a series of switchbacks. Along the way you'll pass through groves of American beech trees, easily identified by their smooth bark. Beeches thrive in valley ravines and

At Stratton Mountain, an overlook adjacent to AMC's Richardson-Zlogar Cabin offers views to Mount Grace (right) and Mount Monadnock, two of central New England's prominent landmarks.

bottomlands with moist, rich soil. Early settlers often used the trees' presence to identify prime farming areas.

These woodlands are an excellent example of a transition forest, one of New England's significant natural communities. Transition forests, which occur in areas with varied topography, are logically named because they contain species characteristic of both mild lowland and cool upland settings, including oak, birch, beech, sugar maple, eastern hemlock, and white pine. Stratton Mountain and the Bald Hills lie in the heart of New England's transition forest region, which stretches from the hills of northwestern Connecticut and western Massachusetts to south-central New Hampshire and southern Maine.

At the base of the descent, enter a shady hemlock grove along the perimeter of the wetlands in the valley lowlands. Here the NET bends to the left and continues north over generally level terrain along the base of the crescent-shaped ridge. Pass a cluster of large boulders deposited by glaciers at the end of the most recent ice age, more than 10,000 years ago. Blue markings on trees indicate the Northfield State Forest boundary. At 1.2 miles, continue along the western side of the appropriately named Hidden Pond; a short path on the right leads to the edge of this less-visited wetland. At the north end of the pond, pass the junction with a green-blazed trail that connects to the Coller Cemetery trails of North-field State Forest.

From the north end of the ravine, begin the easy to moderate ascent back up the ridge to Stratton Mountain's summit. On the upper slopes, pass several NET signs and the junction with the Coller Cemetery trails (a network of well-marked but lightly maintained trails). Turn left at a sign for the Alexander Street trailhead and follow the NET along an old woods road then bear right and pass the junction with Asa Stratton Trail. At the summit, a short side path on the left leads to an overlook with westerly views. The large clearing near the Richardson-Zlogar Cabin offers a fine 180-degree perspective of the north end of the NET/Metacomet-Monadnock trail corridor, including a close-up view of the western slopes of nearby Mount Grace in Warwick (the third-highest summit in central Massachusetts) and Mount Monadnock to the northwest. Also visible in the distance are Mount Ascutney in the Connecticut River val-ley of central Vermont (on the far left), Wachusett Mountain on the eastern horizon, and a portion of Mount Watatic and the Wapack Mountains behind Mount Grace.

Barbara and Sam Richardson, longtime trail maintainers who own the sur-rounding land, built the cabin in 2011 with Mike Zlogar and a team of AMC Berkshire Chapter volunteers. The cabin is available for overnight guests for a nominal donation (reservations required; see "More Information" below). The fully enclosed structure includes mattresses and a kitchen table and counter. Outdoor facilities include two tent platforms, a posted trail map, a portable toi-let, a picnic area, and a fire ring. Visitors who stay here are often treated to col-orful sunrises or views of the moon above the countryside.

From the summit, retrace your steps on the NET back to the eastern junction with Bald Hills Loop Trail. Here you can go right for the more rugged route over the crest of the ridge on blue-blazed Bald Hills Loop or left for an easier walk on the NET. Follow either trail to the western junction and the Gulf Road trailhead.

DID YOU KNOW?

The summit of Stratton Mountain is protected, thanks to the efforts of landown-ers and New England Trail stewards Sam and Barbara Richardson, who donated a 38-acre conservation restriction to the town of Northfield in 2011.

MORE INFORMATION

Open year-round, no fee. Hunting is allowed in accordance with state laws. For more information, visit newenglandtrail.org. (There is currently no official web-site or map for Northfield State Forest.) The Richardson-Zlogar Cabin is avail-able by reservation for a $3 per person donation. Visits are limited to two consecutive nights; see newenglandtrail.org/facilities/richardson-zlogar-cabin. Information about Northfield trails, Bald Hills Loop, Coller Cemetery trails, and Brush Mountain is available at northfieldmasstrails.org.

WINTER ACTIVITIES

Skiing and snowshoeing are allowed. The New England Trail is mostly a narrow footpath with moderate to steep segments, some rough areas, and a level section below the ridge of the Bald Hills. A network of hiking/ski trails is located on Alexander Hill north of Stratton Mountain. For the most direct access, from the junction of Main and Maple streets in Northfield, follow Maple Street east 1.0 mile then follow Alexander Hill Road to the trailhead at the road's end.

NEARBY

At Brush Mountain Conservation Area, a 1.1-mile trail leads to a view of Mount Monadnock and Mount Grace and a rare black gum swamp. The nearby summit of Brush Mountain (also known as Crag Mountain) is privately owned and currently closed to the public. The adjacent Northfield Town Forest offers a 2.2-mile loop trail to an interesting section of cliffs. Both trails begin on the western side of Gulf Road opposite the Stratton Mountain trailhead.

14

MOUNT GRACE STATE FOREST

Mount Grace boasts striking, 360-degree, tristate views despite its modest 1,621-foot elevation. Other attractions on this eastern slopes circuit include hemlock-lined streams, northern hardwood forests, an old ski area, and a camping shelter.

DIRECTIONS

From the junction of MA 2 and MA 2A at the Erving–Orange town line, follow MA 2A east 2.0 miles to the junction with MA 78. Turn left and follow MA 78 north 6.8 miles to the parking area at Oscar Ohlson Memorial Field on the left, 0.4 mile north of Warwick center. *GPS coordinates:* 42° 41.420′ N, 72° 20.471′ W.

TRAIL DESCRIPTION

The 1,621-foot summit of Mount Grace has the distinction of being the highest point of the 230-mile New England Trail and the third-highest peak in Massachusetts east of the Berkshires, after Wachusett Mountain and Mount Watatic. At the wooded summit, a fire tower offers 360-degree views across central New England. Like Wachusett Mountain and Mount Monadnock, Mount Grace is an example of a monadnock, an isolated mountain that has resisted erosion to a greater degree than the surrounding landscape. The 1,458-acre Mount Grace State Forest is part of a large area of protected land on the New England Trail corridor that extends south to the Millers River valley.

This circuit combines the New England Trail (NET) and several state forest trails as a moderately difficult 4-mile loop. Hiking the route counterclockwise allows for a quick descent from the summit without elevation gain on the return segment. The mountain is an excellent destination

LOCATION
Warwick, MA

RATING
Moderate

DISTANCE
4 miles

ELEVATION GAIN
1,200 feet

ESTIMATED TIME
2.75 hours

MAPS
AMC Massachusetts Trail Map 4; USGS Mount Grace; Massachusetts Department of Conservation and Recreation map: mass.gov/eea/docs/dcr/parks/trails/mgrace.pdf

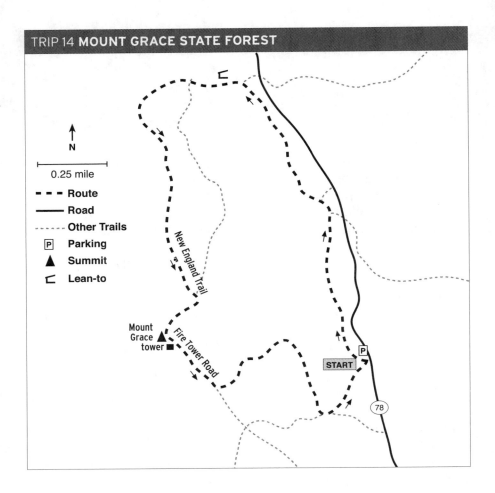

Legend:
- - - Route
—— Road
- - - - Other Trails
P Parking
▲ Summit
⊏ Lean-to

N

0.25 mile

New England Trail

Fire Tower Road

Mount Grace tower ▲■

START

P

78

for viewing fall foliage in early to mid October, and the trails are ideal for snow-shoeing and cross-country skiing in winter.

From the parking area, walk north (to the right when facing away from the road) to the northwest corner of Ohlson Memorial Field, which offers habitat diversity amid the mountain's densely forested slopes. Tiny bluets, wildflowers that often form large patches, bloom in the sunlit field in spring. Another familiar flower that benefits from open areas is buttercup. Look for red fox and wild turkey tracks near the forest edge. Enter the woods on Round-the-Mountain Trail, marked with periodic blue blazes, and continue north over rolling terrain on the lower eastern slopes, roughly parallel to Route 78. Cross a brook on a wood bridge then follow the trail as it bends left along Mountain Brook, which flows along the base of the slopes, at 1.0 mile. Watch for red trillium wildflowers at the edge of the brook in late April and early May.

Shortly before reaching the junction with the NET, look for an old rope tow wheel and cable poles from a former ski area that operated on the mountain during the mid-twentieth century. The site, which included several trails created by the Civilian Conservation Corps in the late 1930s, was described in a 1950 guide to Massachusetts ski areas as a "championship racing course with excellent novice open slopes." It ceased operations in the early 1960s due to insufficient facilities and the mountain's remote location.

At 1.4 miles from Ohlson Field, reach the junction with the white-blazed NET near MA 78. Turn left and begin ascending Mount Grace's north slopes on the combined NET and Round-the-Mountain Trail. About 0.25 mile from the junction is a wooden Adirondack-style camping shelter with space for six to eight guests and access to water at a stream crossing (reservations are not required; visit newenglandtrail.org for availability and to register).

Continue the ascent, steady but not steep, past another stream crossing. The waterways on the north slopes drain into the Ashuelot River watershed in southern New Hampshire, while those on the southern side ultimately discharge into Millers River in central Massachusetts. At 0.3 mile from the shelter, follow the NET straight at a junction where Round-the-Mountain Trail branches to the right. The northern hardwood forest community, which includes sugar maple, American beech, and paper and gray birch, is characteristic of New England's cool high elevations.

After climbing 1.4 miles on the NET and gaining roughly 1,000 feet in elevation, reach the junction with Fire Tower Road. Continue right on the NET for a few hundred feet to the summit, where the fire tower rises above a small grassy clearing. The 68-foot structure, listed on the National Historic Lookout Register, was built in 1939 to replace the first fire tower, which was erected in 1911 and destroyed by the 1938 hurricane (see "A Terrible Trio," page 189). The sweeping views from the tower include the densely forested surrounding countryside; Mount Monadnock to the north; the southern Green Mountains of Vermont to the northwest; and the distant, isolated, pyramid-shaped profile of Mount Ascutney in the Connecticut River valley, 75 miles to the north. A portion of Quabbin Reservoir is visible amid the hills of the Swift River valley and central Massachusetts to the southeast. To the west are Northfield Mountain, Mount Toby, and Mount Tom in the Connecticut River valley, and Mount Greylock and the Berkshire Hills on the distant horizon.

The sunlit clearing, which includes a picnic area, is a great place to relax after the long climb. During spring and summer, watch for dragonflies, such as chalk-fronted corporals (a common early-season species), swarming around the exposed rocks, and tiger swallowtails and other butterflies fluttering along the forest edge. Turkey vultures, which have expanded their range to central New England from the south in recent decades, are often visible soaring overhead.

Begin the relatively quick return to the trailhead by following Fire Tower Road downhill 0.4 mile to a posted junction. Turn left on a blue-blazed footpath, which will lead you on a moderately steep 0.4-mile descent of the southeast slopes. At the base of the descent, turn left at the next marked junction and

The fire tower atop Mount Grace, the highest point of the New England Trail, offers 360-degree views across portions of three states. Photo by Ryan Smith.

complete the loop with an easy 0.25-mile walk to Ohlson Memorial Field and the parking area.

DID YOU KNOW?

Mount Grace is named for Grace Rowlandson, an infant who died after she and her mother Mary were captured by the Narragansett during King Philip's War in 1676. She was reportedly buried at the base of the mountain.

MORE INFORMATION

Open year-round, no fee. Biking and dogs are allowed. Hunting is allowed in accordance with state laws. The property is unstaffed; for more information, visit mass.gov/locations/mount-grace-state-forest or call Erving State Forest at 978-544-3939.

WINTER ACTIVITIES

Skiing and snowshoeing are allowed. The majority of the NET from MA 78 to the summit is moderately steep. Round-the-Mountain Trail follows gently rolling terrain on the lower slopes. Fire Tower Road is wide, rocky, and moderately steep. Snowmobilers also use the trails.

NEARBY

The Arthur Iversen Conservation Area, a property of Mount Grace Land Conservation Trust, protects 500 acres of forests and wetlands along Gale Road near Warwick. The 1.5-mile Devil's Washbowl Trail offers a moderately difficult walk that leads to a beaver wetland and a seasonal waterfall in a steep ravine. Another trail offers a short walk to fine views of a wetland on Rum Brook. For more information, visit mountgrace.org. Nearby restaurants include Copper Angel Pizzeria (24 Athol Road, Warwick) and Johnson's Farm (210 Wheeler Avenue, Orange).

15

TULLY MOUNTAIN

Outstanding views of north-central Massachusetts and Mount Monadnock highlight this relatively short loop over Tully Mountain.

DIRECTIONS

From the west, on MA 2 take Exit 16 in Orange and continue north on Daniel Shays Highway (follow signs for Athol) 2.3 miles to the junction with MA 2A. Turn right and follow MA 2A east 1.6 miles to the traffic light in downtown Athol. Turn left on Exchange Street and, in 0.3 mile, turn left on Pinedale Avenue (which becomes Tully Road in Orange) and continue 3.2 miles. Turn right on Mountain Road at Tully Pond then bear left at a fork and continue on Mountain Road 0.5 mile to the parking area at the road's end.

From the east, on MA 2 take Exit 18 in Athol and follow MA 2A west 3.1 miles to the junction with Exchange Street. Turn right on Exchange Street and follow directions above. *GPS coordinates:* 42° 38.779′ N, 72° 14.706′ W.

TRAIL DESCRIPTION

Tully Mountain, the highest point on the 22-mile Tully Trail, offers one of the finest views in north-central Massachusetts for a modest effort: a panoramic perspective across ponds and forested countryside to Mount Monadnock and Wachusett Mountain. The 1,187-acre Tully Mountain Wildlife Management Area is part of the North Quabbin Bioreserve, one of only five designated bioreserves in Massachusetts.

This hike follows the mountain's 1.75-mile loop trail, which is marked with light-blue blazes and is generally easy to moderate, with a short, steep segment below the summit. The trail coincides with a portion of yellow-blazed Tully Trail from the summit to a junction near Mountain Road. A detailed map of the entire Tully Trail is available

LOCATION
Orange, MA

RATING
Moderate

DISTANCE
1.75 miles

ELEVATION GAIN
470 feet

ESTIMATED TIME
1.5 hours

MAPS
AMC Massachusetts Trail Map 4; USGS Mount Grace and USGS Royalston; The Trustees of Reservations map: thetrustees.org/assets/documents/places-to-visit/trailmaps/Tully-Trail-Map.pdf

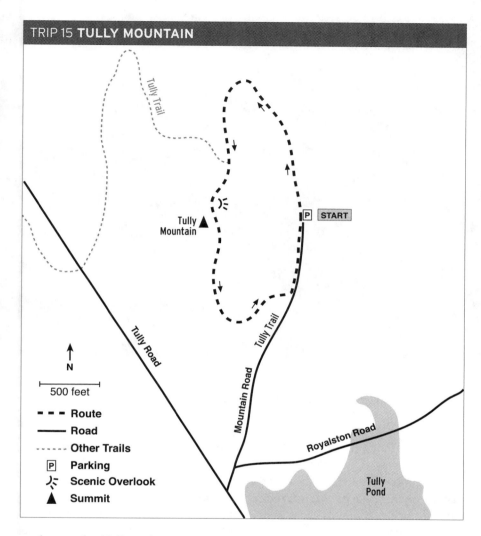

at the nearby Tully Lake Recreation Area on MA 32 at the Athol–Royalston town line.

At the parking area, the grassy meadow offers habitat for a variety of wildlife, including white-tailed deer, butterflies, dragonflies, wild turkeys, American woodcocks, and nonnative ring-necked pheasants, which are stocked for hunting. From a brown sign and a rock marked with blue paint blazes, follow the grass path to a stone wall at the edge of the woods to the left. Continue on a short connecting trail to the start of the loop at a marked junction. Turn right to begin the counterclockwise 1.25-mile walk to the summit. (The left fork of the loop, your return leg for this hike, is a more direct but steeper 0.5-mile route to the top.)

Follow the blue-blazed trail north through hemlock-hardwood forest at the base of the rocky eastern slopes. During spring and summer, these woodlands

The summit ledges of Tully Mountain, the highest point of Tully Trail, offer sweeping views across the hills, ponds, and forests of north-central Massachusetts.

offer habitat for a variety of songbirds, including roughly ten species of warblers. Continue past a tall white pine tree and a jumble of boulders on a talus slope. This is a good spot to look for the tracks and signs of porcupines, bobcats, and eastern coyotes, which use such rocky places for dens. Black bears are occasionally seen in these woods; chances of sighting one may be best in spring, when mothers are active with newborn cubs and displaced juveniles are dispersing to new territories.

After passing through a forest grove damaged by a storm, reach the junction with an old cart road (a former route of Tully Trail), which enters from the right. Turn left to begin the ascent to the summit, which is steady but generally easy to moderate. Watch for trailing arbutus, eastern starflower, and mayflower along the trail edge in midspring. You may hear the trilling call of a red squirrel scolding you for venturing into its territory. Red squirrels, which favor conifer forests, are much more territorial than gray squirrels.

Near the summit, at a junction marked with red blazes, the loop trail merges with yellow-blazed Tully Trail, which enters from the western side of the mountain. Follow the combined trails on a steep but quick 0.1-mile ascent to the rocky ledges on the east side of the 1,163-foot summit. The 180-degree views include the familiar profile of Mount Monadnock to the north, the long ridge of Mount Watatic and the Wapack Mountains to the northeast, and Wachusett Mountain on the eastern horizon. Also visible are Tully Lake, the valley ledges and white church steeple in Royalston, the hills of the Millers River valley, and Tully Pond and Packard Pond at the base of the mountain. The blueberry bushes that grow along the ridge offer delectable snacks during the summer and turn brilliant crimson at the onset of autumn.

Begin your return trip by carefully following the combined trails over and around the rocky edge of the ledges. Bear left and make a steep descent of the mountain's partially exposed south slope, which was scoured by ice when glaciers passed over the top of the mountain. Take your time and watch your footing, especially in wet or icy conditions. In spite of the rugged, rocky terrain, even this part of the mountain was once cleared for agriculture, as evidenced by a stone wall at the base of the descent.

Shortly after the grade levels, reach the lower junction of the loop trail and Tully Trail. Turn left to continue on the blue-blazed trail. (Tully Trail runs along Mountain Road to Royalston Road and Tully Lake.) Follow the narrow route along the lower eastern slopes past several discontinued or overgrown paths. At 0.5 mile from the summit, complete the loop at the junction with the connecting trail. Turn right to return to the meadow and parking area.

DID YOU KNOW?

Geologists consider Tully Mountain a *roche moutonnée*, or a rock hill with a smooth back and an abrupt, steep slope shaped by glaciers. The French term relates to sheep, which have similar smooth, rounded backs.

MORE INFORMATION

Open year-round, no fee. No visitor facilities. Biking and dogs are allowed. Hunting is allowed in accordance with state laws. For information about Division of Fisheries and Wildlife lands, visit mass.gov/orgs/department-of -fish-and-game. For information about Tully Trail, visit thetrustees.org/places -to-visit/places-to-stay/tully-lake-campground/tully-trail.html.

WINTER ACTIVITIES

Skiing and snowshoeing are allowed. The loop trail is rough in places and has a rocky, steep section below the summit.

NEARBY

Trailhead Outfitters and General Store, at the junction of MA 2A and MA 122 (1 South Main Street) in Orange, offers outdoor gear, camping supplies, and maps and guides. Open Monday to Saturday, 9 A.M. to 6 P.M. (until 8 P.M. on Thursday). For information, visit trailhead.biz or call 978-249-8500. Miller's River Cafe is located inside the store; for hours, visit millersrivercafe.com.

HAMPSHIRE AND HAMPDEN COUNTIES

Although the lower Connecticut Valley is more populated and developed than the regions to the north, there are still many trails and places to explore. With hilly uplands divided by the Connecticut River, the area is topographically similar to Franklin County, although the slightly lower elevations and milder climate yield subtle variations. The New England Trail corridor extends from the Metacomet Ridge in the heart of the valley to the hills on the west side of the Quabbin Reservoir watershed.

Named for its location between the eastern slopes of the Berkshire Hills and the Connecticut Valley, the Berkshire Transition ecoregion consists of rolling hills, steep valleys, and largely unfragmented woodlands. The highest elevations, which generally range between 1,000 and 1,700 feet, are somewhat lower than in the adjacent Vermont Piedmont region to the north. The forests thus include a mix of northern and southern species, such as oak, hickory, maple, beech, and eastern hemlock. The highest summit is 2,125-foot West Mountain in Plainfield, which rises along the three-way boundary of Hampshire, Franklin, and Berkshire counties.

Westfield River, composed of three branches that converge to form the main flowage in Huntington, is the largest tributary of the Connecticut River in Massachusetts. Approximately 80 miles of its watershed have been designated as a National Wild and Scenic River. In the remote valley of the West Branch in Middlefield and Chester, Keystone Arches Trail (Trip 16) leads to a series of

Facing page: Westfield River cuts a stunning path through Chesterfield Gorge.

striking historical stone arch railroad bridges originally built as part of America's first mountain railway in the mid-nineteenth century. Downstream is Chester-Blandford State Forest (Trip 17), where cascading streams and rugged eminences, such as Observation Hill, offer a fine sampling of the watershed's landscape. The East Branch's signature attraction is Chesterfield Gorge (Trip 18), a rare example of a granite gorge in New England. In the uplands above the East Branch, the former estate of the acclaimed poet William Cullen Bryant (Trip 20) includes an enchanting forest of giant trees nourished by rich soil in the ravine of Rivulet Brook.

The Connecticut Valley runs through the center of the region, forming a bottle-shaped lowland corridor in Hampshire and Hampden counties. Elevations are as low as 50 feet in the Longmeadow Flats, a wildlife-rich floodplain near the Connecticut state line. Due to the milder temperatures, wildflowers emerge earlier in spring; fall foliage peaks later; and there is less snowfall than in the surrounding uplands. Oak-hickory forests, along with transition northern hardwoods, are predominant. Along the riverbanks, floodplain forests are dominated by silver maple, cottonwood, and American sycamore. In recent years, many of the hemlock forests have suffered significantly from infestation by the hemlock woolly adelgid, an introduced insect pest that became established in the valley during the 1990s.

In pre-Colonial times, the Pocumtuc and Norwottuck established settlements along the river in areas including present-day Springfield, Northampton, and Deerfield, where the fertile soils were ideal for agriculture, and fish and game abounded. The valley was the first section of interior Massachusetts to be settled by European colonists, who arrived during the 1630s. During the Industrial Revolution in the nineteenth century, large mill complexes were established at Holyoke, Springfield, and South Hadley. In the early twentieth century, several significant storms, including the flood of March 1936 and the 1938 hurricane, caused widespread damage throughout the valley and prompted the establishment of an extensive flood-control network (see "A Terrible Trio," page 189).

The Connecticut Valley's most prominent geographic landmarks are the traprock summits and ridges of the central Metacomet Ridge, which were formed by volcanoes about 200 million years ago. When the lava cooled, it formed basalt rock that has resisted erosion to a greater degree than the surrounding landscape. The dramatic sheer cliffs and unique basalt towers of Mount Tom's summit ridge (Trip 23), which rises steeply above the west banks of the Connecticut River in Holyoke and Easthampton, are excellent examples of these geologic processes.

On the east side of the valley, the Holyoke Range, distinguished by its unusual east-to-west orientation, stretches from the riverbanks in South Hadley to Long Mountain in Belchertown. The scenic views from Mount Holyoke (Trip 25) have attracted visitors since the early nineteenth century. The Summit House, now used as a state park visitor center, is the only remaining example of the elaborate hotels built atop many of the region's mountains in the late eighteenth century. On the east side of the Notch, a low gap in the range near Amherst, Mount Norwottuck (Trip 26) is known for its fine views and the distinctive Horse Caves, giant sandstone ledges that were reputedly used as a hideout by western Massachusetts farmers during Shays' Rebellion in 1787.

The valley's wetlands offer crucial habitat for wildlife and a glimpse of the region's distant geologic past, when it was a land of tropical swamps roamed by dinosaurs (see "When Dinosaurs Roamed New England," page 124). Arcadia Wildlife Sanctuary (Trip 22) protects several uncommon natural communities at the confluence of the Mill River and Oxbow Lake, including a floodplain forest and expansive grasslands where rare birds are regularly seen. At the Fort River Division of the Silvio O. Conte National Fish and Wildlife Refuge (Trip 24), a unique universally accessible boardwalk trail winds through a mosaic of habitats on the banks of the Fort River, Hampshire County's largest undammed waterway.

East of the Connecticut Valley are the hills and valleys at the western edge of the Lower Worcester Plateau, which extends across south-central Massachusetts. The Pelham Hills, which divide the watersheds of the Connecticut River and Quabbin Reservoir, are capped by 1,240-foot Mount Lincoln (Trip 27), the site of a University of Massachusetts Amherst research forest and a fire tower with sweeping views. The adjacent Swift River watershed forms a natural bowl that has been filled since the 1940s by Quabbin Reservoir, the primary water supply for eastern Massachusetts. At the reservoir's south end, the many attractions of Quabbin Park (Trip 28) include Quabbin Hill (the watershed's highest point), Enfield Lookout, meadows, historic sites, Winsor Dam, and Goodnough Dike. The reservation's abundant wildlife includes moose, common loons, and bald eagles, which were successfully reintroduced to Massachusetts on one of the islands in the 1980s.

Downstream from Quabbin Reservoir, the main stem of the Swift River merges with the Ware and Quaboag rivers in Palmer to form the Chicopee River, the Connecticut River's largest drainage basin in Massachusetts. One of the Chicopee's numerous tributaries is East Brook in Hampden, the centerpiece of Mass Audubon's Laughing Brook Wildlife Sanctuary (Trip 29). The summit of nearby Peaked Mountain (Trip 30), the highest point of a ridge that extends into northern Connecticut, offers several fine perspectives across this lesser-heralded region.

16

KEYSTONE ARCHES TRAIL

This unique out-and-back trail offers a combination of history and backcountry scenery, including the distinctive Keystone Arches bridges, views of the unspoiled Westfield River, and cascading streams.

DIRECTIONS

From the Massachusetts Turnpike (I-90) take Exit 3 and follow MA 10/US 202 south 1.5 miles to downtown West-field. Turn right on US 20 west and continue 17.8 miles through Russell and Huntington to Chester center. Turn right on Middlefield Road and continue 2.6 miles to the parking area at the junction with Herbert Cross Road on the left. *GPS coordinates: 42° 18.692′ N, 72° 59.573′ W.*

TRAIL DESCRIPTION

During the 1840s, the remote, rugged valley of the West Branch of Westfield River was chosen as the site of the Western Railroad, America's first mountain railway. In spite of the many engineering challenges presented by the steep, rocky terrain, the valley offered the most feasible route across the Berkshire Hills to the crucial markets of New York State and beyond. The construction of the rail line included a series of giant stone arch bridges known as the Keystone Arches. The railway was a transportation landmark, and designer George Washington Whistler was subsequently commissioned by the czar of Russia to build the Trans-Siberian Railroad.

The Keystone Arches Trail was built by the Friends of the Keystone Arches, an organization committed to the preservation of these unique structures. The trail crosses over two of the bridges. (*Note:* The path is wide and safe, but there are no railings on the bridges.) The trail, marked

LOCATION
Middlefield and Chester, MA

RATING
Easy to Moderate

DISTANCE
4.4 miles

ELEVATION GAIN
260 feet

ESTIMATED TIME
2.5 hours

MAPS
USGS Chester and USGS Becket; Keystone Arches website map:
keystonearches.com

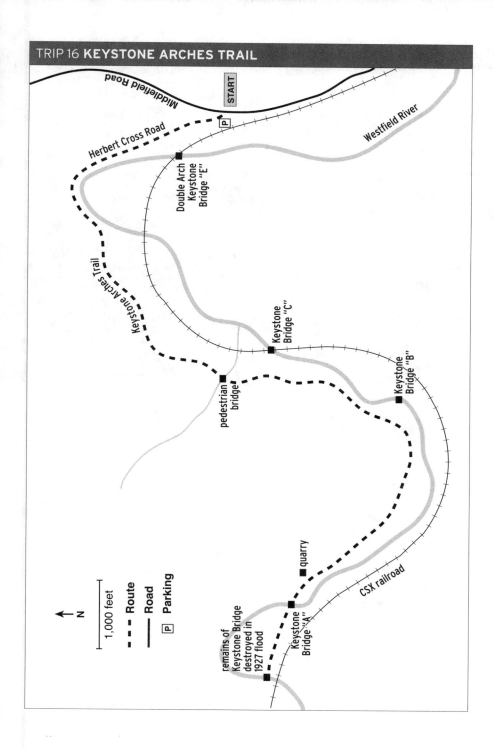

Middlefield Road

START

Herbert Cross Road

P

Westfield River

Double Arch
Keystone
Bridge "E"

Keystone Arches Trail

Keystone
Bridge "C"

Keystone
Bridge "B"

pedestrian
bridge

quarry

CSX railroad

remains of
Keystone Bridge
destroyed in
1927 flood

Keystone
Bridge "A"

N

1,000 feet

- - - Route
—— Road
P Parking

The venerable Keystone Arches railroad bridges were built in the mid-nineteenth century as part of the Western Railroad, America's first mountain railway.

with blue blazes and trail markers, follows rolling terrain along the north banks of Westfield River. Interpretive signs provide information about the natural and human history of the railroad and watershed. Most of the route passes through the Walnut Hill Wildlife Management Area, which is managed by the Massachusetts Division of Fisheries and Wildlife. In addition to the bridges, there are many natural attractions, including cascading streams, songbirds and wildflowers in spring and summer, and colorful foliage in autumn.

From the interpretive sign and map at the trailhead, follow the dirt Herbert Cross Road downhill to a stream crossing, where there's a good view of a rocky cascade on the right. After the crossing, turn left on a short footpath that leads to the riverbank and a good view of Bridge E, the easternmost of the stone bridges. It is distinguished by its double arches, which were necessary for the width of the river here. You may see freight and passenger trains traveling over the stout structure, as it is part of an active rail line currently used by CSX Railways and Amtrak.

Continue on Keystone Arches Trail along the winding north banks of the river. In spring and summer, the valley's extensive unbroken forests offer habitat for many species of migratory songbirds, including scarlet tanagers, chestnut-sided warblers, eastern phoebes, ovenbirds, and veeries. The latter, a member of the thrush family, is named for and easily recognized by its almost eerie *veer-ur, veer-ur, ve-ry* song. Watch for tiger swallowtail butterflies along margins of the road and the riverbanks, where they sometimes congregate in large communal feeding groups.

At a 90-degree bend in the river, look for a small seasonal cascade on the rocky slope to the right. Then, at a marked junction at 0.6 mile, turn right and follow the trail uphill, heading away from the river and the dirt road. Shortly after passing a large stone foundation on the left, you'll reach an interpretive sign with details about the watershed and its wildlife. Follow the narrow path along the hillside, bearing left at an arrow marker and cross a footbridge with a view of another cascading stream in a steep ravine. Look carefully and you may see water striders in the pool at the base of the cascade.

Descend the embankment through a grove of beech trees then turn right at a junction on the riverbank, onto a portion of the old Pontoosic Turnpike, a former stagecoach road to Albany, New York. Make a short climb to Bridge B at 1.4 miles, where a portion of the original rail line, which was rerouted across the valley in 1912 to bypass a dangerous curve and accommodate faster trains, enters from the left. At the interpretive sign, make a short detour left to the top of the 65-foot-high arch bridge, where there are fine open views of the forested valley hills, Westfield River, and a portion of the active rail line on the opposite bank. Use caution around the edges, as there is no railing. Red columbines, which thrive in rocky habitats, grow along the edge of the trail and the bridge stonework in late spring.

From Bridge B, follow Keystone Arches Trail along the abandoned rail line, past a retaining wall and through a dramatic, steep-walled rock cut that was blasted during the creation of the railroad. Portions of the trail may be seasonally wet or muddy here. Cross over the top of Bridge A, where there are more open views, including valley hills to the left and a narrow river gorge to the right. This scenery is especially colorful during the peak of the fall foliage in October. (Again, use caution near the bridge edges.)

Near the western end of the trail, pass through a small tract of land abutting the wildlife management area. In spring, red trilliums grow in abundance in the woods here, along with yellow violets, foamflowers, and other wildflowers. At 2.2 miles from the trailhead, reach the trail's western terminus at the remains of a stone arch bridge that was washed out by floodwaters from a hurricane in 1927 (see "A Terrible Trio," page 189). The interpretive sign includes driving directions to Bancroft Bridge on Town Hill Road in Middlefield, the only one of the Keystone Arches that can be reached by car. (It is not accessible via Keystone Arches Trail.) Retrace your steps to the trailhead, following markers at junctions.

DID YOU KNOW?

The construction of the Western Railroad was motivated by a desire to connect Boston to markets in New York State and beyond and to stave off a proposed railroad to New York City that would have bypassed the Springfield area. When the Western Railroad opened in 1841, it was the highest (peak elevation: 1,460 feet) and longest (150 miles) railway in existence. Visitors to the Keystone Arches included Charles Dickens, Abraham Lincoln, and Harry Truman.

MORE INFORMATION

Open year-round, no fee. Biking and dogs are allowed. Hunting is allowed in season in accordance with state laws. Trespassing on the active railroad tracks is prohibited. For information about the Keystone Arches and the trail, including a map, visit the Friends of the Keystone Arches website at keystonearches.com. For information on MassWildlife lands, visit mass.gov/eea/agencies/dfg.

WINTER ACTIVITIES

Skiing and snowshoeing are allowed. Keystone Arches Trail mostly follows wide dirt roads and a portion of the former railroad line, with a short segment on a narrower foot trail.

NEARBY

Railroad enthusiasts will also enjoy the Chester Railway Station and Museum on 10 Prospect Street in Chester. It's open Wednesdays, Thursdays, or by appointment; for hours and information, visit chesterrailwaystation.net or call 413-354-7878. Glendale Falls, one of the largest waterfalls in Massachusetts, is the centerpiece of a 60-acre property (owned by The Trustees of Reservations) on Clark Wright Road, off River Road in Middlefield. A quarter-mile trail leads to the base of the 160-foot cascade. For more information, visit thetrustees.org. The closest restaurant is Chester Common Table on Main Street in Chester.

17

CHESTER-BLANDFORD STATE FOREST

This hike offers two options: a challenging trek to Observation Hill and a lookout on the slopes of the Westfield River valley, or an easy out-and-back walk to Sanderson Brook Falls.

DIRECTIONS

From the Massachusetts Turnpike (I-90) take Exit 3 and follow MA 10/US 202 south 1.5 miles to downtown West-field. Turn right on US 20 west and continue 16 miles through Russell and Huntington to the parking area for the state forest and Sanderson Brook Falls on the left (south) side of the highway. *GPS coordinates: 42° 15.366′ N, 72° 56.813′ W.*

TRAIL DESCRIPTION

In the heart of the remote and scenic valley of the West Branch of Westfield River, the Chester-Blandford State Forest encompasses nearly 2,500 acres of rugged hills, cascading streams, and unbroken forests. Its best-known attraction is Sanderson Brook Falls, a 60-foot cascade on Sanderson Brook. Atop aptly named Observation Hill, one of the steep hills that characterizes the watershed, an overlook offers an outstanding view of the Westfield River valley.

This fairly challenging 4.3-mile circuit includes an easy climb to Sanderson Brook Falls on a woods road, followed by a steeper ascent to the upland plateau. The final leg follows the H. Newman Marsh Trail to the overlook on Observation Hill then concludes with a steep descent to the trailhead. You can take an out-and-back walk to the falls alone for an easy 1.6-mile round-trip.

Begin on Sanderson Brook Road, a wide gravel road that parallels Sanderson Brook to the cascade. In April and May, watch for early spring wildflowers, including red tril-lium, along the banks of the brook before the hardwood

LOCATION
Chester and Blandford, MA

CIRCUIT
RATING
Moderate to Strenuous

DISTANCE
4.3 miles

ELEVATION GAIN
1,080 feet

ESTIMATED TIME
3 hours

SANDERSON BROOK FALLS ONLY
RATING
Easy

DISTANCE
1.6 miles

ELEVATION GAIN
175 feet

ESTIMATED TIME
1 hour

MAPS
USGS Blandford and USGS Chester; Massachusetts Department of Conservation and Recreation map: mass.gov/eea/docs/dcr/parks/trails/chester.pdf

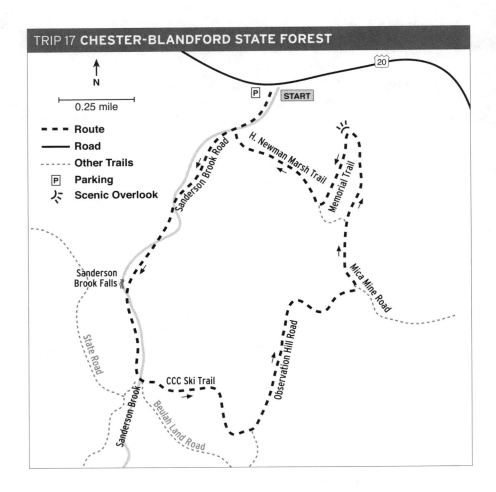

trees leaf out. After a few minutes, pass a gate and cross the first of three bridges over Sanderson Brook. At 0.2 mile, pass the junction with H. Newman Marsh Memorial Trail, your return route of the loop, at the base of Observation Hill on the left.

Follow Sanderson Brook Road on a pleasant walk along the water, with views of a series of pools and cascades to the right. Native brook trout frequent the pools, which fluctuate with seasonal changes in water flow. After crossing two metal bridges, continue uphill along the ravine above the brook. At 0.8 mile from the trailhead, turn right on a side trail that leads downhill to the boulders and pools at the base of Sanderson Brook Falls (about a five-minute walk). The area around the falls may be littered with fallen trees, but if you walk to the left, there are good views of the 60-foot cascade.

Return to Sanderson Brook Road and turn right to resume the loop or turn left to retrace your steps to the trailhead, if visiting the falls only. From the junction, Sanderson Brook Road continues uphill at a moderately steep grade away from the ravine. Look to the right through a subtle gap in the forest for a long-distance glimpse of the falls and watch for more wildflowers along the trail edge, especially near wet areas. After passing the Blandford town line, continue to a cascading stream and a gate at the junction with a woods road on the right, about 0.5 mile from Sanderson Brook Falls. Walk around the gate and turn left onto the 0.6-mile CCC Ski Trail; the trail is unmarked as of this writing. Make a moderate to steep ascent along the eastern banks of the stream then bear right away from the ravine, continuing uphill through mixed forests that include groves of aspen, beech, and mountain laurel, which blooms in June.

At the upper end of CCC Ski Trail, at the crest of the climb, turn left at an unmarked junction and begin a much easier 0.8-mile segment on Observation Hill Road heading north through the valley uplands. After a level stretch, descend past the edge of a swamp. During or after spring and summer rains, you'll likely see many tiny red efts, or juvenile red-spotted newts, scampering across the forest floor. After spending one to three years in the woods, they return to their native ponds and streams as adults.

Pass another stream on the left and follow Observation Hill Road as it bends to the right then curves sharply left around the base of a rock ledge at the descent's low point. Cross the stream and turn left at an unmarked T junction on Mica Mine Road. Follow Mica Mine Road for 0.25 mile to a circular turnout at the road's end and the junction with the upper portion of blue-blazed H. Newman Marsh Memorial Trail, which loops around the top of Observation Hill.

Bear right to follow the eastern fork of the Marsh Memorial Trail over the elongated northern shoulder of Observation Hill. Pass a closed trail on the left and continue past the first of two mostly overgrown lookouts, where trees largely obscure the views. Carefully follow the narrow path downhill past the second lookout then continue west along the ridge to an open area. After seeing numerous fleeting glimpses through the trees, you'll finally enjoy a fine unobstructed perspective here of the Westfield River valley and its densely wooded ridges and rolling hills. Visible in the base of the valley is a portion of Westfield River, paralleled by US 20 and railroad tracks. You may see trains coming from or going to the Keystone Arches railroad bridges, which are a short distance west of the state forest.

From the overlook, follow blue-blazed Marsh Memorial Trail on a brief ascent through mountain laurel, hemlock, and white pine then continue over rolling terrain to the junction with the west fork of the loop at a cascading stream. Turn right and begin a steep 0.5-mile descent to the base of the valley. Bear left to cross the stream then continue through a rocky section along the southern bank. Take your time and watch your footing around the tree roots, rocks, and steep segments; many injuries occur late in hikes due to fatigue and inattentiveness.

After leaving the stream, continue downhill through the woods past a cascading seasonal brook. One last steep descent through a hemlock grove completes the loop at the junction with Sanderson Brook Road. Turn right and retrace your steps past the first bridge and gate to the trailhead.

Below the cascades of Sanderson Brook Falls, Sanderson Brook flows past cold-water pools favored by trout before emptying into Westfield River.

DID YOU KNOW?

The names of features in Chester-Blandford State Forest, such as Gold Mine Brook, Mica Mine Road, and Mica Mine Trail, are a legacy of the Westfield River valley's mining heritage. Chester was an active mining center from the mid-nineteenth century until after World War II and was the first place in America where emery, a dark granular rock used in abrasive powders, pavement, and flooring, was discovered.

MORE INFORMATION

Open sunrise to sunset year-round, no fee. Biking and dogs are allowed. Hunting is allowed in season in accordance with state laws. For more information, visit mass.gov/locations/chester-blandford-state-forest or call 413-534-6347 (summer) or 413-269-6002 (winter). Boulder Park, on US 20, 2.0 miles east of the Sanderson Brook Falls entrance, includes an easy universally accessible trail.

WINTER ACTIVITIES

Skiing and snowshoeing are allowed. Sanderson Brook Road follows an easy to moderate grade past Sanderson Brook Falls, and there are several other wide dirt roads. H. Newman Marsh Memorial Trail and CCC Ski Trail are narrow and rougher, with steep sections.

NEARBY

C. M. Gardner State Park, on MA 112 south of the junction with MA 66 in Huntington, offers picnic areas, a boat launch, and trails along Westfield River (mass .gov/locations/cm-gardner-state-park, 413-354-6347). Nearby Littleville Lake, a flood-control impoundment of Westfield River, includes a picnic area, boat ramp, and views from the 1,500-foot dam (www.nae.usace.army.mil/Missions/ Recreation/Littleville-Lake). There are several places to eat in Huntington on US 20 and MA 112.

18

WESTFIELD RIVER: EAST BRANCH TRAIL AND CHESTERFIELD GORGE

From the dramatic granite cliffs of Chesterfield Gorge, this outing follows East Branch Trail past scenic outlooks and historical sites along the banks of Westfield River. There are options for both shorter and longer walks.

DIRECTIONS

From the south, on I-91 in Northampton, take Exit 19 and continue straight at the end of the ramp on Damon Road 1.1 miles to the junction with US 5/MA 10. (From the north, on I-91, take Exit 20 for US 5/MA 10 then take the first right on Bridge Road.) Continue straight on Bridge Road 2.3 miles then turn right on MA 9 west and continue 5.1 miles to the junction with MA 143 in Williamsburg. Turn left on MA 143 west and continue 8.2 miles through Chesterfield. Turn left on Ireland Street, and after 0.8 mile, turn left on River Road and continue 0.1 mile to the Chesterfield Gorge Reservation entrance. Parking is also usually available at the private Chesterfield Four Seasons Club, adjacent to Chesterfield Gorge. *GPS coordinates:* 42° 23.580′ N, 72° 52.800′ W.

TRAIL DESCRIPTION

The East Branch of Westfield River, a portion of which is a designated National Wild and Scenic River, is rich in natural resources, scenery, and history. Arguably its best-known and most dramatic feature is Chesterfield Gorge, a rocky, high-walled canyon scoured by the water's relentless cutting power over millions of years. Downstream are picturesque views and natural habitats interspersed with several historical sites.

This hike begins at Chesterfield Gorge, managed by The Trustees of Reservations, and continues downstream along the western banks of the river on East Branch Trail and River Road. The walking is easy, with only a few gentle

LOCATION
Chesterfield, MA

RATING
Easy to Moderate

DISTANCE
6 miles (other options available)

ELEVATION GAIN
150 feet

ESTIMATED TIME
3 hours

MAPS
USGS Windsor, USGS Goshen, and USGS Westhampton; The Trustees of Reservations map: thetrustees.org/assets/documents/places-to-visit/trailmaps/Chesterfield Gorge_TrailMap.pdf

Wild & Scenic Westfield River Committee map: westfieldriverwildscenic.org/documents/EastBranch TrailBrochure.pdf

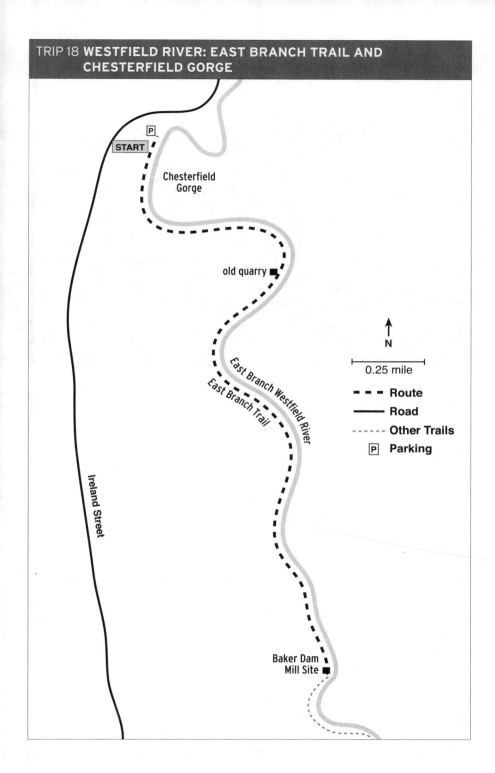

The granite cliffs of Chesterfield Gorge are a prominent landmark of the East Branch of Westfield River, a designated National Wild and Scenic River.

ups and downs. You can choose to return from the Baker Mill site at mile marker 3 for a 6-mile round-trip. For a shorter walk, double back at any point. (The state forest gate, at 1.4 miles, is an option for a round-trip of roughly 3 miles.) Alternatively, you could continue south along the river to the designated trail's end at 6.6 miles or the Knightville Dam at 9.4 miles.

At the Chesterfield Gorge parking area, a welcome sign includes information about the watershed and East Branch Trail, including mileage to the various points of interest. In late April and early May, large colonies of bloodroot wildflowers grow around the old stone foundations across the road from the entrance. Adjacent to the upper end of the gorge is a hefty stone abutment that once supported the High Bridge, part of the former Old Post Road that once connected Boston to Albany, New York. The bridge, which British soldiers crossed during the American Revolution, was washed out by a flood in 1835.

Begin on the unnamed 0.5-mile footpath along the western rim of the gorge, where there are fine views of Westfield River and the 70-foot granite walls. Gorges are relatively uncommon in the Northeast; they are more frequent in the western states, where the drier climate is more conducive to soil erosion.

At the southern end of the gorge trail, pass through a gate and turn left to follow East Branch Trail along River Road, heading downstream along the west banks of Westfield River. At the lower end of Chesterfield Gorge is a popular catch-and-release fishing area where short paths offer the opportunity to explore the river's edge. Roughly 0.3 mile south of the gorge, the trail curves right to follow a 90-degree bend in the river. Here you'll pass Whitside Brook, one of many tributary waterways that drain the steep slopes, and a large rocky out-cropping in a grove of dying hemlocks. Diminutive yellow violets are among the first wildflowers that grow along the riverbanks in spring, followed later by wild geraniums, daisies, and eastern starflowers.

Continue straight at a junction with a woods road marked with snowmobile trail signs. At 0.7 mile from Chesterfield Gorge, reach the boundary of Gilbert Bliss State Forest, a 2,500-acre preserve that is part of East Branch Forest Reserve, a designated area where forests are allowed to mature with minimal management. The woodlands along the river corridor—which include maple, beech, birch, oak, ash, and hemlock—help ensure high water quality. Unfortunately, the hemlocks are suffering significantly from hemlock woolly adelgid infestation, and ash trees are threatened by the imminent arrival of the emerald ash borer, an insect that has rapidly spread across the eastern United States and recently has been confirmed in Massachusetts. An understory shrub that thrives here is mountain laurel, which grows along both sides of the trail. The reserve offers habitat for mammals, such as moose, black bears, and bobcats, and for migratory songbirds, such as eastern wood peewees and scarlet tanagers.

At mile marker 1 on East Branch Trail is a former quarry site where rocks were once extracted from the riverbanks. At 1.4 miles, reach a gate where the portion of River Road open to vehicles ends. A cascading stream flows into the river here; watch for twin waterfalls when water levels are high. Walk around the gate and continue along the river, past a section of small rapids and pools. After a brief descent, follow the road close to the water's edge and pass mile marker 2. Check the muddy soil along the riverbank for tracks of raccoons, mink, river otters, and white-tailed deer. Continue on a level segment past a footpath to the river's edge then cross another tributary stream at the junction with a woods road on the right.

You'll soon reach a broad quiet-water area that is an excellent place to watch for wildlife and enjoy picturesque views. Here the river divides to flow around a small island. Watch for common mergansers and other waterfowl. Belted king-fishers hunt from the trees along the riverbanks. These birds, which make hunt-ing dives from perches on wetland edges, are a familiar sight along the region's waterways during the warm months, and they periodically linger during the winter around open water. Beavers are also active along this portion of the trail, as evidenced by trees with fresh cut marks at their base.

Shortly after the trail curves to the right, reach mile marker 3 and the stone foundation of an old sawmill at the historical site of Baker Mill, near a section of rocky rapids. The mill, built by Lemuel Baker in 1848, operated for twenty years before being washed out by a flood in 1869.

From the mill site, East Branch Trail continues south to Inner Gorge at 3.5 miles, Indian Hollow and the Dead Branch at 5.0 miles, and a gate and parking area at the trail's southern end at 6.6 miles. River Road then continues from the south parking area to Knightville Dam at 9.4 miles.

This walk returns from the mill site for a 6-mile round-trip. On the way back you'll enjoy a different perspective of Westfield River, now looking upstream. There is an elevation gain of roughly 145 feet from mile marker 3 to Chesterfield Gorge, but it's very gradual, especially below the gorge. You can bypass the trail along the gorge by continuing straight on River Road to the parking area.

DID YOU KNOW?

In 1993, a 78-mile segment of Westfield River was designated as Massachusetts's first National Wild and Scenic River. These waterways are selected for notable natural resources, scenery, recreational opportunities, historical sites, and other qualities. The designation restricts the construction of dams and other development.

MORE INFORMATION

Chesterfield Gorge is open from 8 A.M. to sunset from April 1 to December 1. There is a $2.50 admission fee for adults who are not members of The Trustees of Reservations. Restrooms are available seasonally. Biking (on River Road only) and dogs are allowed; swimming and rock climbing are not allowed. Hunting is allowed in accordance with state laws. For more information about Chesterfield Gorge, visit thetrustees.org or call 413-532-1631. The Chesterfield Four Seasons Club parking lot is open year-round, but availability is dependent on club events (small fee, donation box at the lot entrance). For more information about Westfield River, visit westfieldriverwildscenic.org.

WINTER ACTIVITIES

Chesterfield Gorge is open from April 1 to December 1 only due to potentially dangerous ice conditions in winter. East Branch Trail is open to skiing and snowshoeing in winter. The trail is wide with gentle grades and is also used by snowmobilers. Parking is usually available at the Chesterfield Four Seasons Club lot adjacent to the gorge.

NEARBY

Knightville Dam, a flood-control dam on Westfield River, offers a picnic and recreation area, trails, and scenic views. The entrance is off MA 112 north of the junction with MA 66 in Huntington (www.nae.usace.army.mil/Missions/Recreation/Knightville-Dam). Mass Audubon's Road's End Wildlife Sanctuary, at the end of Corbett Road off MA 143 near Chesterfield Gorge, offers easy loop trails through an old farm site (massaudubon.org). The closest places to eat are in Williamsburg and Goshen.

19

GRANVILLE STATE FOREST

A moderately steep descent into the valley of scenic Hubbard River leads to views of cascades and spring wildflowers in the wooded ravine of Halfway Brook. A short loop near the trailhead offers views of an old beaver wetland at the crest of the valley.

DIRECTIONS

From I-91 take Exit 3 in Springfield and follow MA 57 west 23.1 miles through Southwick and Granville. Turn left on East Hartland Road, 4.9 miles west of Granville, and drive 0.6 mile to the state forest boundary. Continue 2.0 miles to the Halfway Brook parking area on the right, opposite the campground. Maps are available at the headquarters, which is 0.4 mile north of the Halfway Brook parking area on East Hartland Road. *GPS coordinates:* 42° 03.026′ N, 72° 58.260′ W.

TRAIL DESCRIPTION

Situated in the scenic, remote highlands along the Connecticut border in southern Hampden County, Granville State Forest protects 2,426 acres of unbroken northern hardwood and hemlock forests, cascading brooks, waterfalls, and pools in the Hubbard River watershed. The property abuts 9,150-acre Tunxis State Forest in Connecticut, forming an expansive corridor of nearly 12,000 acres of protected land.

This walk combines the Halfway Brook, Camp, and Beaver Pond Loop trails in a 2.0-mile circuit. There is also the option to extend the outing on the trails along Hubbard River. Midspring is a great time for a visit, when hobblebush, trillium, and other wildflowers and shrubs are in bloom, and the cascades of Halfway Brook and Hubbard

LOCATION
Granville and Tolland, MA

RATING
Easy to Moderate

DISTANCE
2 miles

ELEVATION GAIN
250 feet

ESTIMATED TIME
1 hour

MAPS
USGS West Granville; Massachusetts Department of Conservation and Recreation map: mass.gov/eea/docs/dcr/parks/trails/granville.pdf

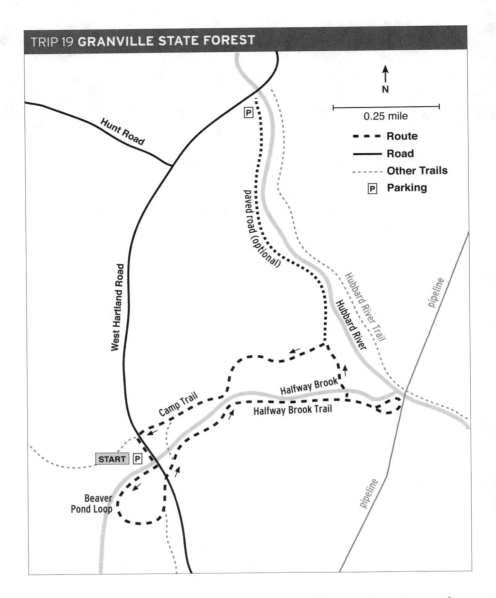

N

0.25 mile

- - - **Route**
—— **Road**
------ **Other Trails**
P **Parking**

Hunt Road

West Hartland Road

paved road (optional)

Hubbard River Trail

Hubbard River

pipeline

Camp Trail

Halfway Brook

Halfway Brook Trail

START P

Beaver
Pond Loop

pipeline

River are alive with a high volume. Maps are posted at some junctions and are available at the forest headquarters.

From the trailhead on the east side of West Hartland Road, opposite the parking area, begin by following Halfway Brook Trail past a footbridge that connects to the campground and a small pond at the confluence of Halfway Brook and Small Brook. Enter the woods and begin the moderately steep descent along the southern banks of Halfway Brook. In May, this portion of the trail comes alive with the white blossoms of hobblebush (also known as witch-hobble or moosebush), a shrub of the viburnum family that grows along stream banks and in moist woods. "Hobble" refers to the rooted lower branches that often form tangles—the bane of people trying to bushwhack through the woods.

The ravine is also an ideal habitat for painted trilliums, which flower in abundance here in May. During peak blooms, you may see large colonies growing out of the acidic soil along the embankment. Also watch for sessile bellworts (commonly known as wild oats), identified by small bell-shaped white or pale yellow flowers that bloom from April to June. Once the domain of American Indians of the Tunxis tribe, the hemlock-hardwood forests were cleared for agriculture by Colonial settlers who arrived in the mid-eighteenth century. Not surprisingly, farmers soon abandoned the rocky land in favor of more fertile areas in the Midwest.

At 0.5 mile from the trailhead, reach a marked junction adjacent to a footbridge over Halfway Brook, which is part of your return route. Continue straight here along the lower portion of Halfway Brook Trail, past a cluster of large mossy boulders on the right and a seasonal brook. Near the base of the descent, pass the edge of a wide gas pipeline clearing and right of way above the banks of Hubbard River. Bear left and follow the path to the confluence of Halfway Brook and Hubbard River. The river—a short at only 4.6 miles long but highly scenic tributary of Farmington River—originates in the nearby hills of Tolland and flows southeast through Granville State Forest to its mouth at Barkhamsted Reservoir in Hartland, Connecticut. Along the way it drops 450 feet in 2.5 miles.

Follow a narrow, unmarked path upstream along the banks of Halfway Brook, with more good views of mossy boulders and cascades. After a few hundred feet, rejoin Halfway Brook Trail and retrace your steps to the junction at the footbridge. Before crossing the bridge, you can make a short detour upstream to a small but photogenic cascade and pool, where marsh blue violets, which favor woodland springs, boggy areas, and wet meadows, grow in spring. One subtle feature that distinguishes them from other blue violets is their short lower petal.

After crossing the bridge, walk along a paved road for a few hundred feet to the marked junction with Camp Trail. (The road, which continues along the western banks of Hubbard River 0.6 mile to a trailhead on West Hartland Road, near the state forest entrance, offers an optional side trip extension to the walk). Turn left on Camp Trail and begin the moderately steep but short ascent along the north side of Halfway Brook. After passing a cascading seasonal brook on the right, Camp Trail bends south toward Halfway Brook and soon reaches an outlook at the crest of the wooded ravine. Turn right and reach the back of the campground picnic area then continue through the campground to West Hartland Road.

On the east side of the road, next to the parking area, follow Beaver Pond Loop Trail through an old red-pine plantation along the banks of Halfway Brook. After a quick 0.1-mile walk on the winding, needle-carpeted path, you'll reach the north end of the wetland at a stone wall near an old beaver dam. Continue through shady pines and hemlocks to an outlook behind the dam. Beaver Pond Loop Trail briefly parallels the northeastern corner of the fingerlike wetland

then bends left and passes an area of downed timber and a stone wall. At the junction with Sattler Trail, turn left to complete the 0.4-mile loop with a short walk back to the trailhead.

If you wish to further explore Hubbard River, the parking area at the bridge on West Hartland Road (0.4 mile south of the main entrance) offers direct access to trails on both sides of the river, including the aforementioned route on the western bank. Hubbard River Trail offers a pleasant walk along the eastern banks past cascades, small waterfalls, and pools then continues to the state forest's southeastern boundary.

DID YOU KNOW?

The Tunxis tribe's main settlement was in the fertile meadows along Farmington River, near present-day Farmington and Southington, Connecticut. The name Tunxis is derived from *Wuttunkshau*, a term for "where the river bends."

MORE INFORMATION

Open sunrise to sunset year-round. Biking and dogs are allowed; swimming is not allowed. Hunting is allowed in accordance with state laws. The campground, adjacent to Halfway Brook Trail, offers 22 sites. For more information, visit mass.gov/locations/granville-state-forest or call 413-357-6611.

WINTER ACTIVITIES

Skiing and snowshoeing are allowed. The trail network includes hiking trails and gated paved roads along both banks of Hubbard River. Halfway Brook Trail includes a moderate to steep descent to Hubbard River.

NEARBY

Mass Audubon's Richardson Brook Wildlife Sanctuary, which opened in 2015, offers two interconnected loop trails in the ravine of Richardson Brook, a tributary of Farmington River. The entrance is on MA 57 west of Tolland, near an overhead highway sign that reads, "Steep Curves" (massaudubon.org). The closest places to eat are in Southwick along US 202.

Facing page: Marsh blue violets are among the wildflowers that grow in the ravine of Halfway Brook, a tributary of Hubbard River.

20

WILLIAM CULLEN BRYANT HOMESTEAD

This walk begins at the pastoral former homestead of the acclaimed poet William Cullen Bryant then follows Rivulet and Pine trails through an enchanting forest of giant trees.

DIRECTIONS

From the south, on I-91 in Northampton, take Exit 19 and continue straight at the end of the ramp on Damon Road 1.1 miles to the junction with US 5/MA 10. (From the north, on I-91, take Exit 20 for US 5/MA 10 then take the first right on Bridge Road.) Continue straight on Bridge Road 2.3 miles. Turn right on MA 9 west and continue 17.3 miles to the junction with MA 112 at the Old Creamery Co-op in Cummington. Turn left and follow MA 112 up-hill 1.5 miles to a five-way intersection at the property boundary. Continue straight on Bryant Road 0.2 mile to the parking area at the red barn on the right. *GPS coordinates:* 42° 28.200' N, 72° 56.040' W.

TRAIL DESCRIPTION

When enjoying the bucolic views, towering trees, and cascading streams at the Bryant Homestead, it's easy to understand why the setting inspired the renowned poet and editor William Cullen Bryant during the nineteenth century. Bryant, who grew up on the property, purchased the land after becoming editor of the *New York Evening Post* and spent more than a dozen subsequent summers back at his boyhood home. The homestead, which includes the house and a photogenic red barn, is now on the National Register of Historic Places. Adjacent to the meadow is Rivulet Forest, where groves of giant old trees grow out of the ravine of Rivulet Brook, the subject of some of Bryant's best-known works. The homestead and Rivulet Forest are now part of a 195-acre property managed by The Trustees of Reservations.

LOCATION
Cummington, MA

RATING
Easy

DISTANCE
1.8 miles

ELEVATION GAIN
345 feet

ESTIMATED TIME
1.25 hours

MAPS
USGS Worthington; The Trustees of Reservations map: thetrustees.org/assets/documents/places-to-visit/trailmaps/Bryant-Homestead-Trail-Map.pdf

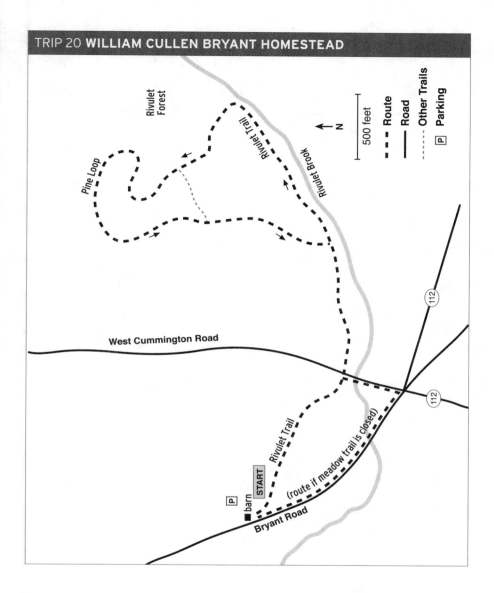

At the parking area, enjoy the pastoral view of the barn, the former Bryant home (not open to the public), and the hillside meadow. Barn swallows, distinguished from tree swallows by their rust-colored underparts and throats, dive over the field hunting the abundant insects during the summer. Breeding bobolinks and eastern bluebirds also benefit from the open grassland habitat.

From the information sign, follow the grass path across the hayfields, which are lined by a row of stately sugar maples that make for a classic New England scene, especially when fall foliage peaks in early to mid October. Visible across the field to the north are the hills of the upper Westfield River valley. At the end of the meadow path at West Cummington Road, look back across the field for a

From pastoral meadows lined with sugar maples to an old forest with giant trees, the trails at the William Cullen Bryant Homestead offer a variety of contrasts.

wide-angle perspective of the barn and house. (If the meadow trail is closed, walk along Bryant Road 0.2 mile past the sugar maples, a stone wall, and a small artificial pond to the five-way intersection then turn left and follow West Cummington Road to the Rivulet Trail trailhead on the right.)

Cross West Cummington Road and enter the woods on yellow-blazed Rivulet Trail, which begins at a trailhead adjacent to the bridge over Rivulet Brook. Descend along the western banks of the brook into an entirely different environment: a wooded ravine where huge old trees loom high above the cascading Rivulet. According to Anthony D'Amato, a University of Vermont professor who has conducted extensive research on old forests of Massachusetts, the prolific size of the trees is due to the ravine's rich soil. In spring and summer, watch and listen for ovenbirds, black-throated green warblers, and hermit thrushes. You may also glimpse a red fox or a flock of wild turkeys, especially near the forest-field edge.

Continue along the banks of Rivulet Brook through a grove of hemlocks to a sign emblazoned with the verses of "Yellow Violet," a poem Bryant composed in 1819. Here the loop begins, at a marked junction, 0.2 mile from West Cummington Road. Bear right and continue along the brook to marker 5 and a good view of the ravine, which, like many other waterways in western Massachusetts, was heavily eroded by floodwaters from Tropical Storm Irene in 2011. Numerous fallen trees, including a gigantic old hemlock, are evidence of the hurricane and other recent severe storms, including an ice storm in December 2008 and a blizzard in October 2011, which caused extensive forest damage when heavy snow accumulated on trees that were still in leaf. The mossy fallen logs, which also indicate these woods have not been disturbed by humans, are an important component of the forest ecosystem. The decaying wood offers habitat for ants and other insects, which in turn sustain migratory songbirds and woodpeckers. Black bears, which have highly varied diets, often tear apart fallen trees in search of insects.

At a sign with the verses of Bryant's "The Rivulet," near a large old gray birch and hemlock, continue left, away from Rivulet Brook, and cross gently rolling terrain to a footbridge over a seasonal brook. At the next junction (0.3 mile from the start of the loop), turn right on Pine Loop Trail, a recently completed extension of the original Rivulet Trail that leads through groves of giant white pines. Some of the trees are more than 150 feet high and rank among the tallest specimens in the Northeast. In June and July, look for wood sorrels, which grow in hilly, moist woods. With their white flowers and purple or pinkish veins, they are visually similar to spring beauties but bloom later in the season.

Follow Pine Loop Trail past more huge fallen trees (you may have to scramble over a few logs) then bear right and pass beneath more tall white pines. Near the property boundary, make a sharp left and continue along a ravine. Cross a creek in another pine grove then make a gentle ascent along a cascading brook. Listen for the long, warbling song of winter wrens, which are a characteristic species of forested ravines. As their name suggests, they are year-round residents in western Massachusetts.

At the end of Pine Loop Trail, turn right to rejoin Rivulet Trail. Near marker 16, pass through a small wet area, where you may see the tracks of white-tailed deer, eastern coyotes, or black bears. Continue the gradual climb through hemlock-hardwood forest to the end of the loop at the "Yellow Violet" sign. Turn right and retrace your steps along Rivulet Brook to West Cummington Road then follow either the meadow trail or Bryant Road back to the entrance at the red barn. The walk back to the trailhead gains about 350 feet in elevation, but the grades are mostly gentle.

DID YOU KNOW?

The scenery around Cummington inspired several of William Cullen Bryant's poems, including "Inscription for the Entrance to a Wood." In addition to Bryant's literary accomplishments, he was an early proponent of New York City's Central Park and Metropolitan Museum of Art.

MORE INFORMATION

Open sunrise to sunset year-round, no fee. Dogs are allowed; biking is not allowed. Limited bow hunting is allowed from mid-October to December. For more information, visit thetrustees.org or call 413-532-1631.

WINTER ACTIVITIES

Skiing and snowshoeing are allowed. The Rivulet and Pine Loop trails are narrow paths that follow easy to moderate grades along the ravine of Rivulet Brook, with a few large fallen logs.

NEARBY

The Old Creamery Co-Op, at the junction of MA 9 and MA 112 (445 Berkshire Trail) in Cummington, includes a deli, bakery, café, and grocery store. Open Monday to Saturday, 7:30 A.M. to 7:30 P.M., and Sunday, 8:30 A.M. to 7:30 P.M. (oldcreamery.coop, 413-634-5560). The Cummington Fairgrounds, at 97 Fairgrounds Road off MA 9, hosts several agricultural fairs annually (cummingtonfair.com).

21

DAUGHTERS OF THE AMERICAN REVOLUTION STATE FOREST

Beginning at a popular swimming beach at Highland Lake, this hike leads to scenic views from a fire tower atop Moore Hill then loops through quiet woodlands to the lake's eastern shore.

DIRECTIONS

From the south, on I-91 in Northampton, take Exit 19 and continue straight at the end of the ramp on Damon Road 1.1 miles to the junction with US 5/MA 10. (From the north, on I-91, take Exit 20 for US 5/MA 10 then take the first right on Bridge Road.) Continue straight on Bridge Road 2.3 miles. Turn right on MA 9 west and continue 9.7 miles to the junction with MA 112 in Goshen. Turn right and follow MA 112 north 0.7 mile then turn right on Moore Hill Road at a sign for the state forest and continue to the contact station at Highland Lake. *GPS coordinates:* 42° 27.390′ N, 72° 47.882′ W.

TRAIL DESCRIPTION

Located in the highlands of the eastern Berkshire foothills, Daughters of the American Revolution State Forest protects more than 1,500 acres of rolling hills, wetlands, and woods. The fire tower atop 1,697-foot Moore Hill, the property's highest point, offers sweeping views across the region.

At the base of the western slopes is boot-shaped Upper Highland Lake, the northernmost of two impoundments of the West Branch of Mill River.

From the main entrance at Upper Highland Lake, this hike combines several trails in a circuit that leads to the top of Moore Hill then returns to the north end of the lake via Long Trail. The route includes a 0.4-mile universally accessible segment on the southern shore of Highland Lake.

LOCATION
Goshen, MA

RATING
Moderate

DISTANCE
3.7 miles

ELEVATION GAIN
310 feet

ESTIMATED TIME
2.75 hours

MAPS
USGS Goshen;
Massachusetts Department of Conservation and Recreation map: mass.gov/eea/docs/dcr/parks/trails/dar-trail-map.pdf

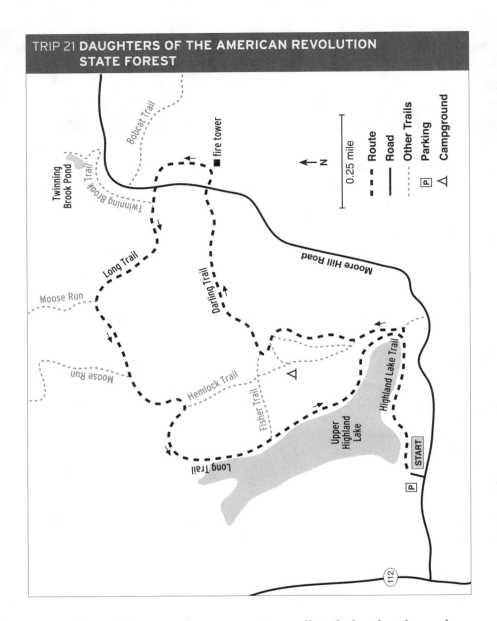

From the parking area at the contact station, walk to the beach at the southern end of Upper Highland Lake. Turn right and follow the grass path across the dam and past a row of picnic tables, where you may get a close-up view of the resident mallard ducks at the water's edge. Roughly half a dozen species of warm-water fish inhabit the lake, including largemouth and smallmouth bass. After passing the boat launch, enter the woods on the universally accessible Highland Lake Trail. Pass a small gazebo and continue beneath shady hemlock and birch trees on the southern shore.

At the east end of Highland Lake Trail, at 0.4 mile, turn left on the paved campground road and walk past another boat launch and the trailhead for Long Trail (your return route for this hike) to the campground office and recycling area. A short path on the right leads to an observation blind at the edge of an old beaver pond. Wetlands like this one are crucial ecosystems that often transition to meadows after the beavers move on. Listen for the chorus of spring peepers in early spring, and watch for colorful blue flag irises in June. Your best chance of seeing one of the many black bears present in these hills may be near the recycling dumpster, as evidenced by warning signs!

Bear right at a fork in the road and continue past a grassy clearing (watch for hawks circling overhead) then bear right again near campsite 50. At a red triangle marker, turn right and follow Darling Trail downhill into the woods, heading away from the campground. In spring and summer, listen for the calls of a variety of songbirds, including black-throated green and black-throated blue warblers, among the oaks, birches, maples, and hemlocks.

After crossing a bridge over a small creek, begin to ascend Moore Hill on Darling Trail, which is mostly unmarked but easy to follow. After passing a stone wall, bear left at an old stone foundation to follow a power line. Cross a boardwalk and continue through a pine grove to the junction with paved Moore Hill Road. Cross the road and follow the short, rocky path to the fire tower in a sunlit clearing at the crest of the 1,697-foot hill, roughly 250 feet above Highland Lake. Here you'll enjoy a fine perspective across the surrounding hills and ridges, including Chapel Ledge in Ashfield. On clear days, look for Mount Greylock to the west, Mount Monadnock to the northeast, and Mount Tom and the Holyoke Range to the east.

To continue the loop, follow an unmarked bridle path away from the tower, opposite the vehicle turnout. Pass a large forked birch tree and make a short descent to the base of the tower access road near its junction with Moore Hill Road. Cross the access road and continue through a rocky area then cross Moore Hill Road and continue straight on the upper end of blue-blazed Long Trail. Pass the junction with Twinning Brook Trail on the right; that trail leads downhill to a camping area at nearby Twinning Brook Pond.

Cross a footbridge and continue along the crest of a wooded ravine. Northern hardwoods, such as maple, birch, and beech, thrive in the relatively high elevation. On mild late-winter and early spring days, watch for mourning cloak butterflies, a welcome sign of the changing seasons. So named because their wings are dark, like garments worn by people in mourning, they are among a handful of hardy butterflies that overwinter in sheltered places, such as tree cavities.

After walking 0.5 mile from Moore Hill Road, reach the upper junction with Moose Run Trail at a stone wall and marker post near the Ashfield town line. You can extend the hike by turning right here on Moose Run Trail, which makes a 1.9-mile loop through the northern portion of the state forest before rejoining Long Trail at the lower junction. At the upper junction, Long Trail continues

Scenic Highland Lake is a popular destination for hikers, paddlers, anglers, and beach visitors.

straight ahead on a winding descent of Moore Hill's rocky northwestern slopes. In spring, watch for false hellebore, a characteristic species of open woods and stream banks. Farmers consider it a pest plant because its green leaves, although photogenic, are highly toxic. You may also see a common garter snake, New England's most abundant and visible snake, basking along the sunlit trail or slithering through fallen leaves.

Shortly after passing the lower junction with Moose Run Trail, reach the base of the descent at a grove of hemlock trees, near the inlet of Upper Highland

Lake. Cross a boardwalk through a swampy area then bear left and follow Long Trail south along the lake's eastern shores through groves of hemlock, pine, and mountain laurel, which add color to the barren forest during the winter months. Scan the water and shoreline for a variety of birds, including great blue herons, belted kingfishers, and black and mallard ducks.

Keep straight to follow Long Trail at the junction with Fisher Trail, which leads east to the campground. Shortly after crossing a knoll forested with tall pines, pass the small campground beach at the lake's southeastern corner. Complete the loop at the southern terminus of Long Trail, at the campground road. Turn right on Highland Lake Trail and retrace your steps along the southern end of the lake to the dam, beach, and parking area.

DID YOU KNOW?
The Daughters of the American Revolution (DAR), a patriotic women's organization that was established in 1890, donated 1,020 acres of land to establish the original state forest in 1929. Subsequent additions included Upper and Lower Highland lakes.

MORE INFORMATION
Open sunrise to sunset year-round. A seasonal parking fee ($8 MA residents, $15 out of state) is charged at the Highland Lake contact station, where maps and restrooms are available. The campground includes 51 campsites and a beach. The boat launch, picnic areas, and beach have universally accessible facilities. Biking (on designated trails) and dogs are allowed. Hunting is allowed in accordance with state laws. For more information, visit mass.gov/locations/daughters-of-the-american-revolution-dar-state-forest or call 413-268-7098.

WINTER ACTIVITIES
Skiing and snowshoeing are allowed. The trail network includes several hiking/bridle paths designated as suitable for skiing, most of which are in the southern and eastern portions of the state forest. These are marked on the Department of Conservation and Recreation map. Snowmobilers also use the trails.

NEARBY
Mass Audubon's Graves Farm Wildlife Sanctuary, located on Adams Road off MA 9 in Williamsburg, protects more than 600 acres of meadows, forests, and wetlands on an old farm. Two short, interconnected trails offer an easy, family-friendly loop that leads to a meadow, Nonnie Day Brook, and the surrounding forests (massaudubon.org, 413-584-3009). Spruce Corner Restaurant on MA 9 (190 Berkshire Trail West) in Goshen, is the closest place to eat, and there are many other restaurants in Northampton.

22

ARCADIA WILDLIFE SANCTUARY

This hike combines several trails as a circuit through a variety of wildlife-rich natural communities along Mill River, including an excellent example of a floodplain forest—a great outing for families and bird-watchers.

DIRECTIONS

From I-91 take Exit 18 in Northampton and follow US 5 south along the Connecticut River Oxbow for 1.3 miles. Turn right on East Street, and after 1.2 miles, turn right on Fort Hill Road at a sign for the sanctuary. Continue 0.7 mile to a three-way intersection. Bear right on Old Springfield Road, then turn left on Combs Road and continue to the sanctuary entrance at the road's end. *GPS coordinates: 42° 17.388' N, 72° 38.774' W.*

TRAIL DESCRIPTION

Situated at the confluence of Mill River and the Connecticut River Oxbow, Arcadia Wildlife Sanctuary encompasses more than 700 acres of floodplain and upland forests, beaver ponds, vernal pools, old orchards, and extensive grasslands. Thanks to these varied habitats, the sanctuary is an excellent destination for watching birds and other wildlife in all seasons. Portions of the trails along Mill River may be seasonally wet. Be prepared for biting insects during the spring and summer, especially during the early morning and evening.

Begin on the universally accessible Loop Trail, which starts between the nature center and schoolhouse buildings and follows the perimeter of the field adjacent to the parking area. Watch for a variety of wildlife, including eastern bluebirds, cedar waxwings, eastern cottontail rabbits, and woodchucks, the bane of many gardeners. During the summer, monarchs, fritillaries, and other butterflies feed on

LOCATION
Easthampton and Northampton, MA

RATING
Easy

DISTANCE
1.9 miles

ELEVATION GAIN
75 feet

ESTIMATED TIME
1.25 hours

MAPS
USGS Easthampton; Mass Audubon map: massaudubon.org/content/download/2666/28542/file/arcadia_trails.pdf

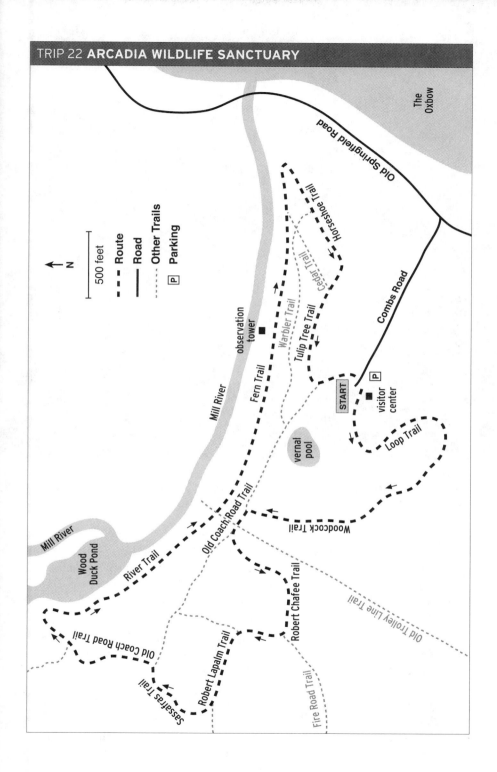

The Oxbow

Old Springfield Road

Horseshoe Trail

Cedar Trail

Combs Road

Warbler Trail

Tulip Tree Trail

observation tower

Fern Trail

Mill River

START

P

visitor center

Loop Trail

vernal pool

Woodcock Trail

Old Coach Road Trail

Mill River

Wood Duck Pond

River Trail

Robert Chafee Trail

Old Trolley Line Trail

Old Coach Road Trail

Robert Lapalm Trail

Sassafras Trail

Fire Road Trail

500 feet

← N

- - - Route
——— Road
········· Other Trails
P Parking

This uncommon floodplain forest on Mill River is an example of the many diverse habitats in Arcadia Wildlife Sanctuary, one of the Pioneer Valley's finest bird-watching destinations.

milkweed and other wildflowers in the meadow. Familiar backyard birds, including cardinals, woodpeckers, and black-capped chickadees, frequent feeders.

Continue to the junction with Woodcock Trail behind the nature center, where a universally accessible boardwalk and bridge offer close-up views of a large vernal pool. Watch for barred owls perched near the forest edge. Follow Woodcock Trail across the bridge and continue through a forest of hemlock, oak, and giant white pine trees. Though understory vegetation is relatively sparse beneath the tall evergreens, several species of wildflowers, including pink lady's slipper, eastern starflower, and mayflower, grow in the acidic soil.

At the end of Woodcock Trail, turn left on Old Coach Road, which was once part of a carriage road to Northampton, and continue downhill through a hemlock grove to a four-way junction with Old Trolley Line. Turn left at a sign for Chafee Trail and cross a short boardwalk through a wet area, then turn right and follow Chafee Trail up wooden steps and through more hemlock and pine groves. Watch for pileated and red-bellied woodpeckers hunting for insects in the tall trees. Turn right at the next junction and follow Fire Road Trail past more tall pines, then turn left on Robert Lapalm Trail, an old woods road with two boardwalks.

At the next junction, turn right on Sassafras Trail, so named for the many sassafras shrubs that line the path. Sassafras, which thrives in open woods and a variety of soils, is easily recognized by its three-pronged leaves, which are often described as mitten-shaped. Deer and black bears are among the species that browse the leaves, and rabbits feed on the shrub's bark in winter. One distinctive plant to watch for during the summer is Indian pipe, which blooms in the shady understory. This all-white member of the heath family has nodding flowers and receives nourishment from decaying plants.

Continue through growths of mountain laurel to the junction with Old Coach Road. Turn left on Old Coach Road and descend past a swampy wetland on Hitchcock Brook to the junction with River Trail near the sanctuary's northern boundary.

After all the intersections, begin a more straightforward segment along Mill River and its associated wetlands by following River Trail to Wood Duck Pond, which, befitting its name, is an excellent place to see waterfowl. Wood ducks have strongly benefited from the regrowth of mature forests and are thriving today after past population declines. Nesting boxes, which replicate the tree cavities the ducks raise their young in, have played a crucial role in their recovery. Continue through the floodplain forest on the south banks of Mill River. This uncommon natural community includes groves of shagbark hickory, black birch, green ash, and silver maple. The latter has gray, furrowed bark and pointed leaves that turn yellow in autumn. In summer, dense clusters of ferns and shrubs encroach on the narrow path.

At a three-way junction with Old Trolley Line, continue straight on Fern Trail, which offers easier walking on a wider, well-worn path. Stone abutments mark the site of a lost trolley bridge. At 0.1 mile from the junction, reach the observation tower at the edge of Arcadia Marsh. Climb the winding stairs to the top of the enclosed structure, where there's a fine view across the wetland to the sanctuary meadows. Scan the marsh for waterfowl, wading birds, river otters, muskrats, and other wildlife. Markers indicate water levels from the floods of 1936 and 1984. The great flood of March 1936, which occurred after heavy rain abruptly melted most of the snow in northern New England, caused significant damage throughout the Connecticut River watershed.

Return to Fern Trail and continue past a vernal pool, then make a short climb up the embankment to a junction where several trails (all of which lead back to the nature center) meet in a small clearing. This hike continues left on Horseshoe Trail, which bends to the right and follows an old farm road past an orchard and thickets at the edge of the sanctuary's farm fields. This is another good place to see a variety of bird species, such as gray catbirds, northern orioles, mocking-birds, rose-breasted grosbeaks, and migratory warblers. At the next junction, turn right and follow Tulip Tree Trail to the nature center.

To explore the grasslands, from the nature center follow Combs Road to the junction with Old Springfield Road, then turn left on Old Springfield Road and continue to the bridge at the confluence of Mill River and the Connecticut River Oxbow. Cross the bridge (which is closed during high water periods) and follow the dirt roads through the fields. Some of the uncommon species that have been seen here include short-eared owls, northern harriers (also known as marsh hawks), and red-headed woodpeckers. Bald eagles nest in the wetland adjacent to the field, which was also the site of a large great blue heron rookery (as of summer 2016, the heron colony had abandoned the site).

DID YOU KNOW?

The Connecticut River Oxbow, made famous by a Thomas Cole painting in 1836, was a broad, horseshoe-shaped bend in the river below Mount Tom and Mount Holyoke. During a flood in 1840, the river carved a new channel though the neck. Oxbow Lake, now separated from the river, is a popular boating and bird-watching destination.

MORE INFORMATION

Open dawn to dusk year-round. The visitor center is open Monday to Saturday, 9 A.M. to 3 P.M., and Sunday seasonally. The admission fee is $4 for adults and $3 for children and seniors. Admission is free for Mass Audubon members. Biking, dogs, and hunting are not allowed. For more information, visit massaudubon .org or call 413-584-3009 or 800-710-4550.

WINTER ACTIVITIES

Skiing and snowshoeing are allowed. The sanctuary is an excellent destination for viewing animal tracks, especially along Mill River and the field edges.

NEARBY

Look Park, on MA 9 in Florence (a village of Northampton), offers ponds and picnic areas on Mill River, a petting zoo, playgrounds, and seasonal activities, including a holiday light display. The park is open year-round; for hours and information, visit lookpark.org or call 413-584-5457. There are many places to eat in Easthampton and Northampton.

23

MOUNT TOM STATE RESERVATION

Mount Tom's distinctive high traprock summit ridge is arguably the most spectacular section of the New England Trail. This loop, rugged in places but not overly steep, leads from Lake Bray to outstanding views from Whiting Peak and Goat Peak.

DIRECTIONS

From the north, on I-91 in Northampton take Exit 18 and follow US 5 south for 4.0 miles. Turn right on Reservation Road and continue 0.3 mile to the entrance gate below the I-91 overpass, then continue 0.2 mile to the parking area at Lake Bray on the left. From the south, on I-91 take Exit 17 and follow US 5 north for 4.0 miles to the junction with Reservation Road on the left. If the entrance is closed, park at the gate and walk to Lake Bray. *GPS coordinates: 42° 16.124′ N, 72° 36.977′ W.*

TRAIL DESCRIPTION

Mount Tom, one of the Connecticut River valley's best-known and most prominent landmarks, is home to a wealth of natural features and hiking opportunities. The mountain's long summit ridge, formed by the ancient volcanoes that created the Metacomet Ridge, offers scenic views from dramatic basalt cliffs. The Mount Tom State Reservation, an oasis of more than 2,100 acres of protected land amid a developed area of the Pioneer Valley, offers habitats for a variety of flora and fauna, including several rare species.

This 4.8-mile circuit includes an easy to moderate ascent from Lake Bray to the New England Trail and Whiting Peak on the summit ridge and concludes with a steeper descent from Goat Peak to the trailhead. You can shorten the walk by hiking to only one of the peaks or by using Quarry Trail as a bypass. Signs may still reference the NET as the Metacomet-Monadnock Trail. Begin by following

LOCATION
Holyoke and
Easthampton, MA

RATING
Moderate to Strenuous

DISTANCE
4.8 miles

ELEVATION GAIN
1,150 feet

ESTIMATED TIME
3 hours

MAPS
AMC Massachusetts Trail Map 5; USGS Easthampton, USGS Mount Tom, and USGS Mount Holyoke; Massachusetts Department of Conservation and Recreation map: mass.gov/eea/docs/dcr/parks/trails/mtom.pdf

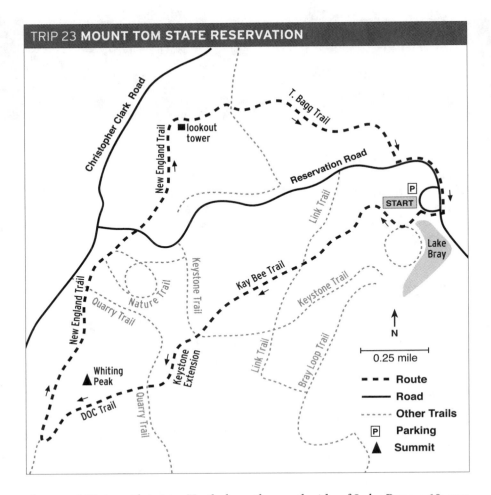

the gravel Universal Access Trail along the north side of Lake Bray, a 10-acre artificial lake formed by a dam on Bray Brook at the base of Mount Tom's west slopes. Continue straight at a junction where the accessible trail turns left toward the shore, and pass a picnic area. At the next junction, turn right on blue-blazed Kay Bee Trail (yellow-blazed Bray Loop Trail continues to the left along the road as part of a circuit around the lake).

Follow Kay Bee Trail uphill through a mixed forest of oak, maple, birch, pine, and hemlock. Cross Link Trail at a four-way junction and continue along a rocky woods road past a ledge to Keystone Junction. Go straight on red-blazed Keystone Extension Trail past an outcropping, then bear left and descend to a swampy area. Cross a boardwalk bridge and continue an easy walk over gently rolling terrain past beech trees and mountain laurels.

Thanks to its extensive unbroken forests in the midst of a heavily developed region and its location along the Connecticut Valley flyway, Mount Tom is an excellent birding destination. Several types of warblers (blackburnian, cerulean, and black-throated blue) are among the migratory songbirds that can be found here, and year-round residents include blue jays, golden-crowned kinglets, and white- and red-breasted nuthatches. Wildflowers include round-lobed hepatica, an early species that thrives in rocky woods, and pink lady's slipper, which blooms in late spring. Mount Tom offers habitat for more than half of the 80 species of native trees of Hampshire County. Unfortunately, many of the reservation's hemlocks have been killed by hemlock woolly adelgid, as evidenced by the defoliated trees visible along the trail.

After crossing a boardwalk at a swampy area and vernal pool, go straight at the next four-way junction on DOC Trail and begin a steeper 0.8-mile ascent to the summit ridge. Pass another rock ledge and continue through more hemlocks, hardwoods, and laurels. After crossing a section of exposed rock, continue the ascent through oak-dominated upland forest. A grove of damaged trees is the legacy of a powerful microburst (a downdraft in a rainstorm with winds that can exceed 100 miles per hour) in October 2014, which caused extensive destruction near the Route 141 entrance. (You can see striking views of the damage corridor from the auto road and the summit.)

After walking roughly 2 miles from Lake Bray, reach the crest of the ridge and the junction with the New England Trail (NET) between Deadtop Peak and Whiting Peak. The mountain's 1,201-foot summit, marked by communication towers and the remains of an old hotel, is 1.3 miles to the south. Turn right at the junction and follow the NET north along the ridge for 0.2 mile to 1,014-foot Whiting Peak. From atop the steep cliffs, the 180-degree panoramic views include Easthampton's neighborhoods, brick factories, and farm fields in the valley below and a glimpse of the Connecticut River Oxbow to the north.

Continue to follow the NET north on a steep descent to the junction with Quarry Trail near a maintenance area. At this point you have the option of shortening the hike by turning right onto Quarry Trail, which will lead you back to Keystone Extension Trail in another 0.2 mile. To continue to Goat Peak, follow the NET past Nature Trail to the upper end of Reservation Road. Turn right and walk along the road for roughly 75 yards, then bear left and follow the white-blazed NET up the north end of the ridge. At 0.3 mile from the road, bear right and make a moderately steep ascent to the clearing and observation tower at Goat Peak.

Though 822-foot Goat Peak is several hundred feet lower than the high points of the ridge to the south, its location at the north end of the mountain affords outstanding views. From the tower, there's a fine perspective of the western portion of the Holyoke Range, including the white summit house atop Mount Holyoke and the "Seven Sisters" peaks, across the Connecticut River to the east. On the western side of the river, the Connecticut River Oxbow and Easthampton are visible to the north and west.

At the end of summer and in early autumn, especially in mid-September, Mount Tom's lookouts are excellent places to view migrating raptors. On prime viewing days when the wind is blowing from the north, you may see hundreds or even thousands of southbound migrants, including broad-winged, sharp-shinned, and Cooper's hawks, American kestrels, ospreys, and bald eagles. In

late October (and sometimes early November), visitors are treated to outstanding fall foliage displays, when the densely forested slopes are alive with colorful oaks and other hardwoods.

Begin the descent to Lake Bray by following the NET north for another 0.3 mile. Immediately after passing the junction with blue-blazed Beau Bridge Trail (which connects to Hampden Field on Reservation Road), turn right off the NET onto red-blazed T. Bagg Trail and make a moderate to steep 0.8-mile descent through groves of hardwoods and mountain laurels. At the trail's end at Reservation Road, turn left and walk downhill on the road for 0.25 mile to the parking area at Lake Bray.

DID YOU KNOW?
The former Mount Tom Ski Area, which included fifteen runs, a popular ski school, and a racing league, operated on the eastern slopes of the mountain from 1962 to 1998. In April 2014, a forest fire burned about 30 acres of regenerating vegetation on the former ski slopes.

MORE INFORMATION
Open year-round; gates are open from 9 A.M. to 8 P.M. in summer and from 9 A.M. to 4 P.M. in winter. There is a seasonal parking fee ($5 MA residents, $10 out of state). Restrooms are available at Lake Bray. Leashed dogs are allowed; biking is not allowed. Hunting is allowed in accordance with state laws. For more information, contact mass.gov/locations/mount-tom-state-reservation, mount.tom@state.ma.us or call 413-534-1186.

WINTER ACTIVITIES
Approximately half of Mount Tom State Reservation's 20-mile trail network is designated as suitable for cross-country skiing, with generally easy to moderate grades. These trails are marked on the official Department of Conservation and Recreation trail map. Snowshoeing is allowed. The reservation gates close at 4 P.M. in winter.

NEARBY
Dinosaur Footprints, a property of The Trustees of Reservations, offers unique views of well-preserved dinosaur tracks and pathways on the banks of the Connecticut River at the base of Mount Tom. The roadside entrance is on US 5, 5.2 miles south of Exit 18 on I-91 in Northampton (thetrustees.org, 413-532-1631). The Tavern on the Hill restaurant is located opposite the Mount Tom State Reservation MA 141 entrance, and there are many other places to eat in Northampton, Easthampton, and Holyoke.

Facing page: Formed by the ancient volcanoes that created the Metacomet Range, the summit ridge of Mount Tom is arguably the most spectacular section of the New England Trail.

WHEN DINOSAURS ROAMED NEW ENGLAND

Imagine the Connecticut River Valley as a land of subtropical lakes, swamps, and mountains, roamed by dinosaurs and other prehistoric creatures. About 200 million years ago, during a geologic period known as the Mesozoic Era (or "Age of Reptiles" that lasted from 252 million to 66 million years ago), western Massachusetts was located just north of the equator. When the supercontinent of Pangea broke up, the Connecticut Valley formed along a geologic fault. The mild climate and abundant wetlands offered ideal habitat for a variety of reptiles, amphibians, birds, mammals, and fish. The most common dinosaurs were small to mid-sized species, while large carnivores were rare visitors.

Dinosaurs were present on Earth for approximately 150 to 175 million years before going extinct 66 million years ago. (Most scientists agree the Cretaceous–Paleogene extinction event, which eliminated 50 to 75 percent of the world's plant and animal species, was caused by an asteroid or meteor impact, a series of volcanic eruptions, climate change, or some combination thereof.) We know about these species' existence today because evidence was permanently recorded in the form of well-preserved tracks and fossil skeletons. When dinosaurs traveled along muddy lake shores and through swamps, they left behind footprints that filled in with sediments and eventually hardened into rock. Bones and skeletons were preserved after being buried in lake bottoms and other places sheltered from the effects of erosion and decomposition.

Visitors of all ages will thrill at the sight of dinosaur footprints deep in the rocks of the Connecticut River valley. Photo by Massachusetts Office of Travel and Tourism, Creative Commons on Flickr.

The Connecticut River valley is home to the world's largest concentration of dinosaur tracks. The first known discovery was made in 1802 by a young boy named Pliny Moody on his family's farm in South Hadley, Massachusetts. Scientific research began in earnest during the 1830s, after many tracks were uncovered in a quarry at Barton Cove on the Connecticut River in Turners Falls, Massachusetts. The noted geologist Edward Hitchcock eventually documented more than 20,000 tracks from 154 species at sites in the Connecticut Valley. At the time, the sources of the prints remained a profound mystery, even to Hitchcock. Somewhat presciently, he believed the tracks had been made by gigantic, ancient birds—a belief supported today by fossil records. We now know these birds descended from dinosaurs, having evolved from theropods (hollow-boned, three-toed dinosaurs) during the late Jurassic, and were the only dinosaur lineage to have survived the Cretaceous–Paleogene extinction event. Common tracks found in the Connecticut Valley include *Eubrontes,* a large carnivorous species that grew as large as 20 feet, and *Grallator,* a small theropod whose long strides indicate that it was likely a fast runner.

Dinosaur Footprints, a property owned by The Trustees of Reservations on US 5 in Holyoke (5.2 miles south of I-91 Exit 18), offers a unique and easily accessible opportunity to view dinosaur tracks in a natural setting. The site, on the west banks of the Connecticut River near Mount Tom, was originally discovered during highway construction in 1935, and nearly 800 tracks have been cataloged and mapped by researchers. Many fish, plant, and insect fossils are also preserved in the sandstone rock. Some of the prints are concentrated in parallel clusters called trackways, which scientists speculate may indicate the edge of a prehistoric lake or that the dinosaurs traveled in packs. The property is free to enter, open daily April 1 to November 30, sunrise to sunset. For more information, visit thetrustees.org/places-to-visit/pioneer-valley/dinosaur-footprints.html.

Dinosaur State Park and Arboretum, located at 400 West Street in Rocky Hill, Connecticut, encompasses a large collection of tracks that were unearthed during a construction project in 1966. Other attractions include nature trails and an arboretum. The exhibit center is open Tuesday to Sunday, 9 A.M. to 4:30 P.M. year-round (the grounds and trails close at 4 P.M.). For more information, visit dinosaurstatepark.org.

For those interested in learning more about dinosaurs and the Connecticut Valley's natural history, Beneski Museum of Natural History at Amherst College houses three floors of exhibits, including fossil skeletons and a large collection of tracks. It's open year-round Tuesday to Friday, 11 A.M. to 4 P.M.; Saturday to Sunday, 10 A.M. to 5 P.M. The museum is located at 11 Barrett Hill Road, just east of the junction of MA 9 and MA 116 in Amherst. For more information, visit amherst.edu/museums/naturalhistory.

24

SILVIO O. CONTE NATIONAL FISH AND WILDLIFE REFUGE: FORT RIVER DIVISION

This well-engineered, universally accessible nature trail, which includes several elevated boardwalks and observation areas, leads through diverse wildlife habitats in the floodplain of Fort River.

DIRECTIONS

From the south, on I-91 take Exit 19 in Northampton. Turn right at the end of the ramp and follow MA 9 east across Coolidge Bridge. (From the north, on I-91 take Exit 20. Turn left at the first traffic light at the end of the ramp, and follow Damon Road for 1.1 miles to the junction with MA 9 at Coolidge Bridge.) After crossing the bridge, bear right on Bay Road and continue 1.8 miles to the junction with MA 47. Go straight on MA 47/Bay Road for 0.6 mile, then turn left to continue on Bay Road for 0.2 mile. Turn left on Moody Bridge Road and continue 0.7 mile to the entrance road on the left. *GPS coordinates:* 42° 20.418′ N, 72° 33.910′ W.

TRAIL DESCRIPTION

Set amid the meadows and farmlands near the confluence of the Fort and Connecticut rivers in Hadley, the Fort River Division of the Silvio O. Conte National Fish and Wildlife Refuge is an ecologically significant area of grasslands, wetlands, and floodplain forests. It recently became the fifth major land acquisition project completed by the refuge, which was established in 1997 to protect land for native plants and wildlife throughout the four-state Connecticut River watershed. The universally accessible loop trail, a great walk for families, includes eight elevated boardwalks and seven observation decks with views of Fort River, the floodplain, and grasslands. The diverse habitats are ideal for watching birds and wildlife.

LOCATION
Hadley, MA

RATING
Easy

DISTANCE
1.2 miles

ELEVATION GAIN
25 feet

ESTIMATED TIME
45 minutes

MAPS
USGS Mount Holyoke

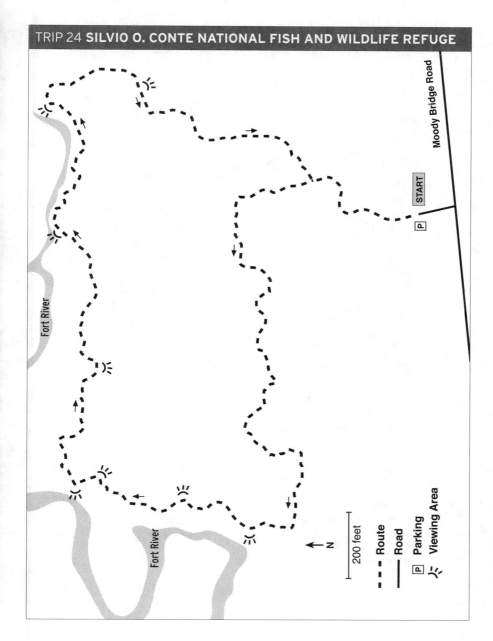

From the parking area, follow a short connecting trail past a pavilion to the start of the loop at a bench and an arrow marker at the field edge. A portion of the long ridge of the Holyoke Range is visible across the fields to the southeast. To make a counterclockwise circuit, follow the left branch of the loop to a board-walk bridge at a wet area and thicket. Areas where multiple habitats meet are especially valuable for wildlife because they offer benefits such as food, water,

The universally accessible trail at the Silvio O. Conte National Fish and Wildlife Refuge includes elevated boardwalks and observation decks with views of Fort River's diverse habitats.

and cover from predators. Watch for colorful eastern bluebirds, which thrive in fields, clearings, and forest edges. They are becoming increasingly common in Massachusetts during the winter months, especially in mild regions such as the Connecticut River valley, and if you're fortunate you may see a large flock. The wet meadows are also an ideal habitat for American woodcocks, which make evening courtship flights after the last snow melts in late winter or early spring. Eastern cottontail rabbits and other small mammals use the thickets to hide from predators, such as eastern coyotes, foxes, owls, and hawks.

Continue through the floodplain of Fort River, where the first elevated boardwalk offers dry passage through a seasonally wet area. In spring, you'll likely hear a loud chorus of spring peepers, which breed in the floodplain's seasonal pools. Later in the summer, patches of milkweed offer sustenance for a variety of insects, including monarch, fritillary, swallowtail, and skipper butterflies and hummingbird moths. An old farm road, a legacy of the property's past, is visible on the right. Young sapling trees and tall shrubs, such as staghorn sumac, offer additional diversity and cover for wildlife.

At 0.4 mile, reach an observation deck on the riverbank. Fed by numerous tributaries in the central Connecticut Valley, Fort River is the water supply for Amherst and Hadley and is the largest undammed tributary of the Connecticut River in Massachusetts, despite its proximity to developed areas. Watch for minks, muskrats, and wood ducks foraging along the riverbank.

Continue to two more viewing sites that overlook the river's floodplain. Water levels in the river and floodplain vary throughout the year (generally highest in spring and lowest during mid to late summer), and it's worth visiting in each season to observe the contrasts. In late winter and early spring, the shrill *conk-la-ree* call of red-winged blackbirds, among the earliest migrants to return, is one of the first signs of the changing seasons.

Follow a long elevated boardwalk past another view of the river, walk through a portion of the floodplain forest, and then continue past another seasonally wet area and a clearing with a partial view of the Holyoke Range to the right. One of the distinctive trees of the floodplain is shagbark hickory, named for its overhanging sections of bark. Another common wetland species is red maple, one of the Northeast's most adaptable trees. Some of the wildflowers that grow along the trail are jack-in-the-pulpit, which blooms in spring, and common mullein, a member of the snapdragon family that can grow as high as 7 feet. Rose-breasted grosbeaks, which often nest in tall shrubs near water, are among the migratory songbirds present in spring and summer.

Another elevated boardwalk will lead you through an area of gently rolling terrain near the southern banks of the river. The subtle depressions in the forest floor are ideal for vernal pools, which are fed by precipitation and floodwater and are a crucial breeding habitat for amphibians such as frogs and salamanders. After passing through a grove of tall white pines, reach another observation platform with open views across a large grassland to the central portion of the Holyoke Range, capped by Bare Mountain and Mount Norwottuck. The meadow offers a habitat for bobolinks, tree swallows, bluebirds, and butterflies, such as black swallowtails and fritillaries. Watch for eastern coyotes hunting along the field edge, especially early and late in the day.

Continue along another boardwalk past a seasonal wetland and pool, where you may see wood frogs, spring peepers, and basking painted turtles when water levels are high. Complete the circuit at the arrow marker, then follow the connecting trail back to the parking area.

DID YOU KNOW?

The boardwalks, observation platforms, and bridges were constructed entirely above ground to avoid disturbing the fragile floodplain habitat. Pads were used to support the boardwalk posts. The project took eighteen months to complete. While building the trail, workers also removed invasive species, such as water chestnut.

MORE INFORMATION

Open year-round, no fee. Portable toilets are available at the entrance. Hunting is not allowed near the trail but is allowed in other areas of the refuge in accordance with state laws. For more information, visit fws.gov/refuge/Silvio_O_Conte/about/ma.html or call 413-548-8002.

WINTER ACTIVITIES

Snowshoeing is allowed. The trail is not well suited for skiing because of the narrow path and boardwalks and heavy visitor use. Park at the stables building if the driveway is impassable. Watch for tracks and sign of animals in the various habitats, including the field edges.

NEARBY

Mount Warner, a property of The Trustees of Reservations, is another recently established conservation area in Hadley. Salamander Trail offers an easy to moderate 2-mile loop over the wooded summit and passes by two large vernal pools. The entrance is on Mount Warner Road off MA 47 in North Hadley. Contact thetrustees.org, or call 413-532-1631.

25

MOUNT HOLYOKE

Enjoy one of the finest views of the Connecticut River and Pioneer Valley from the popular summit of Mount Holyoke and visit a less-traveled overlook on the east side of Taylor's Notch.

LOCATION
South Hadley, MA

RATING
Moderate

DISTANCE
2.75 miles

ELEVATION GAIN
850 feet

ESTIMATED TIME
2 hours

MAPS
USGS Mount Holyoke; Massachusetts Department of Conservation and Recreation map: mass.gov/eea/docs/dcr/parks/trails/skinner.pdf

DIRECTIONS

From the south, on I-91 take Exit 19 in Northampton, then turn right at the end of the ramp and follow MA 9 east across Coolidge Bridge. (From the north, on I-91 take Exit 20, then turn left at the traffic light at the end of the ramp and follow Damon Road for 1.1 miles to the junction with MA 9 at Coolidge Bridge.) After crossing the bridge, bear right on Bay Road and continue 1.8 miles to the junction with MA 47. Continue straight on MA 47 south for 1.9 miles to the roadside parking area on the left (east) side of the road. *GPS coordinates: 42° 18.591′ N, 72° 35.055′ W.*

TRAIL DESCRIPTION

Mount Holyoke is the westernmost prominent summit of the Holyoke Range, which extends across the Pioneer Valley to Belchertown. The outstanding views gained national attention after acclaimed landscape painter Thomas Cole completed his famous *The Oxbow* (1836), which depicted a storm clearing the Connecticut River valley. Another significant historical event was the opening of the Summit House, America's first mountaintop hotel, in 1851. Mount Holyoke is the centerpiece of Joseph Allen Skinner State Park, which protects more than 400 acres at the western end of the range.

From the information sign at the parking area, follow an old cart road uphill into the woods along a brook. After 0.2 mile, begin the loop by bearing right on blue-blazed Halfway House Trail (yellow-blazed Taylor's Notch Trail on the left is the return route). Cross a footbridge at a grove of

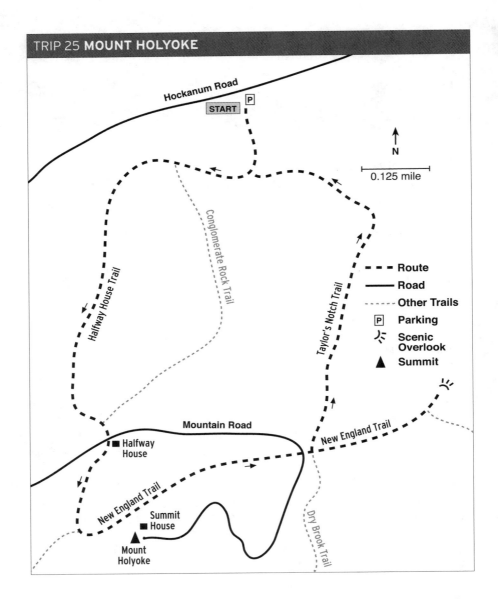

beech trees, then pass another brook and begin an easy, mostly level segment along the base of the north slopes, roughly parallel to MA 47. At marker 138 in a pine grove, stay straight (right) at the junction with red-blazed Conglomerate Rock Trail, then cross another brook. Bear left and begin the moderately steep ascent to the Summit House through mixed forest that includes hemlocks (now heavily infested with hemlock woolly adelgids), mountain laurels, and deciduous oaks, maples, birches, and beeches. Fall color lasts into late October and early November, thanks to the mountain's location in the mild Connecticut Valley lowlands.

The wooded slopes of the Holyoke Range offer habitat for a variety of flora and fauna, including many rare species. Because of its proximity to the Connecticut River flyway, the ridge is an excellent place to watch for migratory songbirds, which arrive in early spring and are most vocal through mid-July. Familiar year-round residents include blue jays, white-breasted nuthatches, and downy and hairy woodpeckers. Early spring wildflowers include round-lobed hepatica, red trillium, bloodroot, and trailing arbutus; among the species that bloom in the summer are nodding ladies' tresses, white snakeroot, and downy rattlesnake plantain.

After passing a grassy field and a snowmobile trail marker, reach the auto road and the Halfway House at 0.8 mile. The building was originally a carriage stop where guests of the Summit House would board a tram to the top of the mountain. Turn right and follow the paved road downhill past a garage and picnic shelter (portable toilets are available seasonally). Turn left at a sign on Halfway Trail and make a strenuous but short 0.2-mile ascent to the crest of the ridge. Shortly after the trail bends sharply to the left and levels, reach the junction with the white-blazed New England Trail (NET). Turn left and make a last quick climb to the Summit House at the top of the mountain.

The sweeping views from the summit and the viewing decks at the Summit House include the Connecticut River, the farm fields along the riverbanks, Northampton, Hadley, Amherst, Mount Toby, the University of Massachusetts campus, and the distant southern Green Mountains of Vermont. Across the river to the west are Mount Tom, the Berkshire foothills, and Mount Greylock on the northeastern horizon. To the south, the Connecticut River winds toward the greater Holyoke–Springfield area. Like Mount Tom, the Holyoke Range is an excellent place to view migrating raptors during the fall.

Follow the NET north through the summit picnic area, where there are more fine views. During the summer, blue harebell (also known as bluebell) wildflowers grow out of tiny cracks in the rocky outcroppings. At the edge of the clearing, enter the woods at a sign for the former Metacomet-Monadnock Trail (now the NET) and make a rocky 0.4-mile descent through a hemlock grove to the junction with the auto road and the upper end of yellow-blazed Taylor's Notch Trail at Taylor's Notch, a 650-foot-high gap between Mount Holyoke and the eastern portion of the range. Before continuing the loop, you have the option of following the NET on a 0.2-mile one-way ascent to another scenic vista on the east side of Taylor's Notch. This lookout is well worth the detour, as it offers another fine perspective of Mount Holyoke's upper slopes and the Connecticut River valley.

From the junction of the NET and Taylor's Notch Trail at the auto road, follow Taylor's Notch Trail downhill on a wide old carriage road past a rocky gully and groves of defoliated hemlocks. After approximately 0.5 mile, bear left (west) and pass through a rocky section at the base of the north slopes, where colonies of pink lady's slipper bloom in late spring. Complete the loop at the junction with Halfway House Trail at marker 139, then turn right to return to the parking area.

Thanks to its striking views of the Connecticut River valley, Mount Holyoke's summit has been a popular destination for hikers, tourists, and artists since the early nineteenth century.

DID YOU KNOW?

The long history of the Summit House dates back to 1821, when a cabin was first built atop Mount Holyoke. In 1851, the two-story hotel was built and regularly improved through 1900. Hotelier Joseph Allen Skinner donated the property to the state in 1939. The covered tramway to the summit operated until 1942, then was removed in 1965. After falling into disrepair, the building was restored as a historical site in 1981 following public opposition to a proposal to demolish it.

MORE INFORMATION

No parking fee at this trailhead; a parking fee ($5 MA residents, $10 out of state) is charged at the summit on weekends and holidays from Memorial Day to Veterans Day, and daily from mid-June to early September. The Summit House is open seasonally on weekends and holidays from 10 A.M. to 5 P.M. (contact the park for dates). Maps are available at the trailhead, the Skinner State Park main entrance on Mountain Road, and the Notch Visitor Center on MA 116. Biking (all trails except the New England Trail) and dogs are allowed. Hunting is allowed in accordance with state laws. The auto road entrance is located on Mountain Road, 0.4 miles from the junction with MA 47. For more information, visit mass.gov/locations/skinner-state-park or call 413-586-0350.

WINTER ACTIVITIES

Skiing and snowshoeing are allowed at Skinner State Park. Nearly all of the park trails are walking/bridle paths with moderate elevation gain and a few steep, rough sections. The New England Trail follows rocky terrain on the crest of the ridge.

NEARBY

The Mount Holyoke College Art Museum, at 50 College Street in South Hadley, offers exhibits, lectures, and other events. Open Tuesday to Friday, 11 A.M. to 5 P.M., and Saturday and Sunday, 1 to 5 P.M. For more information, visit artmuseum.mtholyoke.edu or call 413-538-2245. There are several restaurants in South Hadley on MA 116 and MA 47.

26

MOUNT NORWOTTUCK, THE HORSE CAVES, AND RATTLESNAKE KNOB

From an orchard and meadow on the north side of the Holyoke Range, this long circuit leads to two scenic overlooks at the summit of Mount Norwottuck, the Horse Caves, and another vista at Rattlesnake Knob.

DIRECTIONS

From the junction of MA 9 and MA 116 in Amherst, follow MA 116 south for 3.8 miles to the traffic circles at Atkins Farms. At the first rotary, follow Bay Road east for 0.2 mile. Park at the pullout on the north side of the road at a sign for the Sweet Alice Conservation Area. *GPS coordinates:* 42° 19.145′ N, 72° 31.438′ W.

TRAIL DESCRIPTION

The highest point of the Holyoke Range, Mount Norwottuck is well known for its scenic views, distinctive geology, and the Horse Caves, a giant ledge reputedly used as a hideout during Shays' Rebellion. Rattlesnake Knob, a low ridge in the gap between Mount Norwottuck and Long Mountain, offers a good view of the east end of the Holyoke Range. Most of the eastern portion of the range lies within Holyoke Range State Park, which combines with Skinner State Park to protect more than 3,000 acres.

This 5.5-mile circuit begins at Sweet Alice Conservation Area, a 41-acre property of the town of Amherst, then enters Holyoke Range State Park and follows the New England Trail (NET) over Mount Norwottuck. Another potential starting point is the Notch Visitor Center on MA 116, where there is direct access to the NET. The state park map (available online and at the Notch Visitor Center) is useful as a reference for the many numbered trail junctions.

From the roadside trailhead at Sweet Alice Conservation Area, follow the grass path through the orchard and

LOCATION
Amherst and Granby, MA

RATING
Moderate to Strenuous

DISTANCE
5.5 miles

ELEVATION GAIN
1,185 feet

ESTIMATED TIME
3.75 hours

MAPS
AMC Massachusetts Trail Map 5; USGS Mount Holyoke and USGS Belchertown; Massachusetts Department of Conservation and Recreation map: mass.gov/eea/docs/dcr/parks/trails/holyoke.pdf

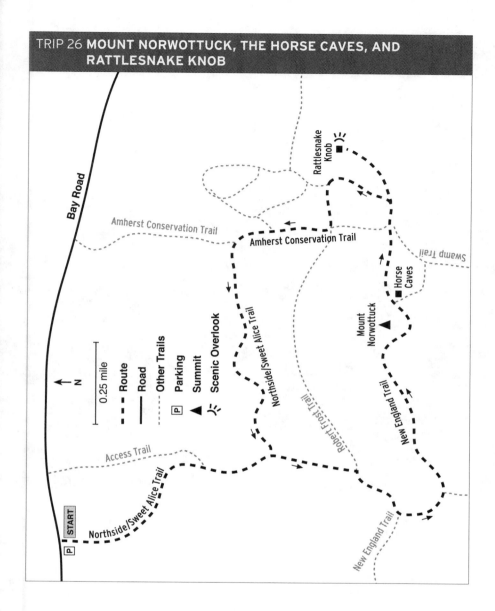

meadow, which provide habitat for wildlife. In spring and summer, watch for butterflies, such as spicebush swallowtails, pearl crescents, and tiny American coppers. American woodcocks make evening courtship flights in early to mid spring; yellow warblers and northern orioles are among the colorful songbirds that also benefit from the edge habitat. In June, magnolias bloom along the path.

Enter the woods at a trail sign and follow yellow-blazed Sweet Alice Trail across a footbridge to a posted junction at a power line. Bear left and follow Sweet Alice Trail through the clearing. (*Note:* If the path is impassable due to

At Mount Norwottuck, the highest point of the Holyoke Range, the New England Trail leads to two scenic overlooks, the dramatic Horse Caves, and Rattlesnake Knob.

overgrown vegetation, continue straight to the next junction then turn left to rejoin Sweet Alice Trail.) Prairie warblers, one of several songbirds that benefit from young, regenerating forests and thickets, nest in the brushy clearing. Look to the north for a view of Mount Toby in the distance.

Reenter the woods and follow Sweet Alice Trail across another footbridge and past a grove of beech trees to marker 277 and the Holyoke Range State Park boundary. At marker 276, turn right on blue-blazed Northside Trail and make an easy ascent through mixed woods of hemlock, birch, maple, beech, and oak. At the next junction, turn right on orange-blazed Robert Frost Trail and continue to the nearby junction with the NET, which enters from the Notch Visitor Center on MA 116.

Turn left on the NET and begin the most rugged portion of the hike, a 0.7-mile ascent of Mount Norwottuck's western slopes. Pass the junction with Southside Trail at marker 203 and continue to follow the NET through several rocky gaps and steep segments on the upper slopes. One benefit to the elevation gain is the lack of biting insects, which are more common in the moister lowlands. Familiar wildlife of this upland forest community includes migratory songbirds, mourning cloak butterflies, and six-spotted green tiger beetles. The beetles, which favor shaded openings in the forest, such as trail edges, are easily identified by their metallic green color. Gray squirrels and blue jays enjoy an abundant food supply of acorns in the oak woodlands.

After a last short, rocky scramble, reach Mount Norwottuck's 1,106-foot summit. The partial northerly views include Mount Toby, the University of Massachusetts Amherst campus, Mount Sugarloaf, and the southern Green Mountains of Vermont, including Mount Snow, on the northwestern horizon. Descend to the next overlook, which is more open and offers a fine perspective across the eastern portion of the Holyoke Range, including Rattlesnake Knob and 920-foot Long Mountain at the eastern end of the range. Also visible are the Pelham Hills and the Swift River valley; look carefully for the tower atop Quabbin Hill.

After enjoying the views, follow the NET on a winding, rocky descent past a series of outcroppings. Take your time and watch your footing on the loose traprock shards. At 0.2 mile from the summit, reach the Horse Caves, where you'll have to squeeze through a narrow crevice then carefully scramble around rocks to the base of the dramatic ledges. ("Caves" is a misnomer.) Legend has it that Daniel Shays and his followers used these ledges as a hideout after their raid on the Springfield Armory in 1787, during their revolt against taxation by the state government.

From the Horse Caves, continue to follow the NET on an easier descent along an old woods road to the eastern junction with orange-blazed Robert Frost Trail (RFT) at marker 206, in the saddle between Mount Norwottuck and Rattlesnake Knob. Turn right and follow the NET and RFT uphill to marker 207, where blue-blazed Ken Cuddeback Trail enters from the left. Follow the three trails, marked with white, orange, and blue blazes, to marker 208. Turn left here and walk about 300 feet to the vista from 787-foot Rattlesnake Knob, where there's a panoramic easterly view to Long Mountain. Watch for turkey vultures and other raptors soaring on thermal air currents created by the ridge.

Retrace your steps to marker 207 then turn right and follow Ken Cuddeback Trail on a steep descent via an old woods road. Shortly after the trail bends to the left, turn left at the next junction on a connecting trail (watch for a red marker at a footbridge) and follow it to the junction with yellow-blazed Amherst Conservation Trail. Turn right and make a quick 0.3-mile descent to marker 273. Turn left on the combined Sweet Alice and Northside trails, marked with yellow and blue blazes, which lead west through hemlock-hardwood woodlands on Mount Norwottuck's lower north slopes. Follow the blazed trail left at a wet area then complete the loop at marker 276, 1.6 miles from Rattlesnake Knob. Turn right and retrace your steps on yellow-blazed Sweet Alice Trail to the orchard and trailhead.

DID YOU KNOW?

After the aborted attack on the Springfield Armory, followers of Shays fled north and east to the towns of Amherst and Petersham and into neighboring states. Although the rebellion was unsuccessful, most scholars agree it had some influence on the development of the United States government and the Constitution, ratified one year later.

MORE INFORMATION

Open year-round, no fee. Maps, information, and restrooms are available at the Notch Visitor Center on MA 116 (1500 West Street), 1.0 mile south of the junction with Bay Road and West Street at Atkins Farms. Biking (on all trails except for the New England Trail) and dogs are allowed. Hunting is allowed in accordance with state laws. For more information about Holyoke Range State Park, visit mass.gov/locations/mount-holyoke-range-state-park or call 413-253-2883.

WINTER ACTIVITIES

Skiing and snowshoeing are allowed. The New England Trail on Mount Norwottuck has steep, rocky, and rough sections. The trails on the lower slopes, including Robert Frost Trail and Sweet Alice and Northside trails, are easier options.

NEARBY

From the Notch Visitor Center, the New England Trail southbound offers a moderately steep but quick 0.4-mile climb to the summit of Bare Mountain on the western side of the Notch, where there are fine views of Amherst and the Pioneer Valley. Atkins Farms Country Market, 1150 West Street at the junction with MA 116 and Bay Road, offers local produce, baked goods, and gift items (atkinsfarms.com, 413-253-9528).

27

MOUNT LINCOLN AND SCARBOROUGH BROOK CONSERVATION AREA

From a picnic area at an old mill pond, an easy climb on a new segment of the New England Trail leads to views from a fire tower atop Mount Lincoln in the Pelham Hills.

DIRECTIONS

From the junction of MA 9 and US 202 in Belchertown, follow MA 9 west 3.9 miles. Turn right on Gulf Road and continue 1.6 miles to the four-way intersection with North Gulf Road and South Gulf Road. Continue straight at the intersection then turn left to enter the Scarborough Brook Conservation Area parking lot. *GPS coordinates:* 42° 21.004′ N, 72° 26.061′ W.

TRAIL DESCRIPTION

At 1,240 feet, Mount Lincoln is the modest high point of the Pelham Hills, a chain of rolling hills east of the Connecticut River valley. Most of the mountain is protected as part of the University of Massachusetts's 1,200-acre Cadwell Memorial Forest, which is used for ecology and forestry research. At the base of the southern slopes is the Scarborough Brook Conservation Area, a 70-acre preserve managed by the town of Belchertown.

This hike follows the New England Trail (NET) from Scarborough Pond to Mount Lincoln's summit. The first segment is on a recently established portion of the trail, created after the original Metacomet-Monadnock Trail was rerouted by request of private landowners following the NET's federal designation. (The NET no longer passes through nearby Holland Glen and Buffam Brook conservation areas.)

From the information sign, follow the white-blazed NET, which enters Scarborough Brook Conservation Area from Gulf Road, into the meadow on the east side of Scarborough Pond, an old mill pond built in the

LOCATION
Belchertown and Pelham, MA

RATING
Easy to Moderate

DISTANCE
2.5 miles

ELEVATION GAIN
500 feet

ESTIMATED TIME
1.5 hours

MAPS
USGS Belchertown; New England Trail map: newenglandtrail.org; University of Massachusetts Amherst Department of Environmental Conservation map: eco.umass.edu/wp-content/uploads/2011/09/Cadwell-Map.pdf

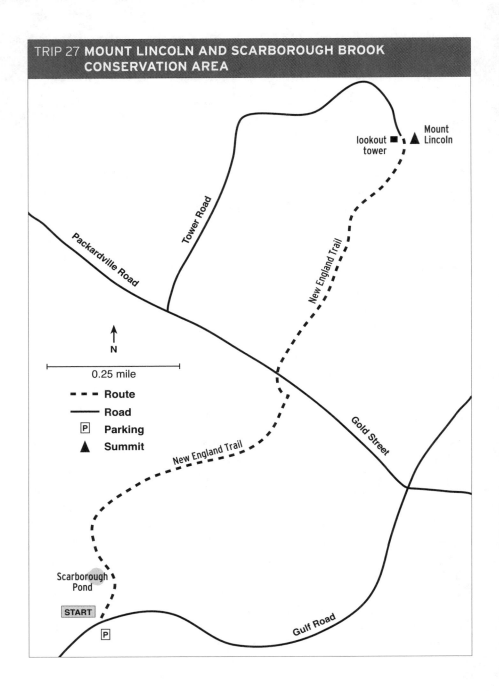

nineteenth century. For nearly 90 years, the property was part of the Pelham Game Club and used for fishing, target shooting, and other activities. The conservation area, established in 2007, encompasses the headwaters of Scarborough Brook. Protection of the watershed was crucial, as the brook drains into

Lawrence Swamp and an aquifer that serves as a public water supply for the towns of Belchertown and Amherst.

Follow the grass path across the field, past the pond dam and inlet. In spring, violets, bluets, wild strawberries, and other wildflowers bloom in the meadow, and you may see a few daffodils, holdovers from an old garden, around the pond edge. Take your time and watch for ducks, great blue herons, river otters, foxes, hawks, and owls.

At the north end of the field, enter the woods and pass several giant white pine trees. Begin an easy to moderate ascent along the ravine of Scarborough Brook through oak-hardwood forest. During the spring and summer, these densely wooded slopes are alive with the sounds of migratory songbirds, which venture north to the region to breed and take advantage of abundant food sources, such as insects and flowering plants. Some of the familiar species include black-throated green and black-throated blue warblers, ovenbirds, and scarlet tanagers. The songs and calls may seem cheerful, but they are part of a competitive territorial process as the birds search for mates and establish nests. Some of the squabbles can be rather animated and even result in injuries.

At roughly 0.3 mile from Scarborough Pond, pass the conservation area boundary and continue uphill through adjacent private land. Follow the NET left at a junction with an unmarked trail and continue through groves of oak and beech trees that offer colorful fall foliage viewing in mid to late October. After leveling off, the NET bends to the left and winds along the perimeter of several residences. (Please respect all private property.)

At 0.6 mile, about halfway to Mount Lincoln's summit, carefully cross Packardville Road (light traffic) at the Belchertown–Pelham town line. On the north side of the road, enter Cadwell Memorial Forest, established by the University of Massachusetts as a research forest in 1952. Here the NET continues along an old woods road on a portion of the original Metacomet-Monadnock Trail. The mixed forests include groves of red oaks, which serve as an important food source for white-tailed deer, gray and red squirrels, blue jays, and other wildlife. Many of the mountain's white oaks suffered heavily from gypsy moth infestations during the 1980s.

At 0.4 mile from the road crossing, bear right and follow the NET on a steeper but short 0.2-mile ascent through thickets of blueberry and huckleberry. At 1.2 miles from Scarborough Pond, reach Mount Lincoln's 1,240-foot summit, which is capped by an 80-foot fire tower and radio towers used by WFCR, the National Public Radio affiliate for western Massachusetts. Although the summit is wooded, the fire tower offers a fine 360-degree perspective across the hills of the central Pioneer Valley, including Mount Sugarloaf and Mount Toby to the northwest, the Holyoke Range to the southwest, the Swift River valley and a portion of Quabbin Reservoir to the east, and the distant cities of Holyoke and Springfield to the southeast. The paved tower access road is closed to public vehicles.

If you have time, you can extend your outing by continuing to follow the NET over the north slope of Mount Lincoln. From the summit, the trail

Mount Lincoln's summit fire tower offers views across Cadwell Memorial Forest and the Pelham Hills to the Connecticut River valley and Quabbin Reservoir.

branches off the access road and continues to a network of stone walls and a stream crossing. After crossing a power-line clearing and another stream on land owned by the town of Amherst for its municipal water supply, the NET reaches Amherst Road (where limited roadside parking is available) at 3.1 miles from the summit. To return to the trailhead, retrace your steps south along the NET to Scarborough Brook Conservation Area, where you can enjoy a break at the picnic site after your hike.

DID YOU KNOW?

Amherst Brick Company logged Mount Lincoln's forests for timber in the early twentieth century. Since the establishment of Cadwell Memorial Forest in 1952, researchers have conducted studies on a variety of topics, including gypsy moths, hemlock woolly adelgid, hardwood forest dynamics, and long-term vegetation monitoring.

MORE INFORMATION

Open year-round, no fee. At Cadwell Memorial Forest, biking is allowed on roads, and leashed dogs are allowed. For more information, visit eco.umass.edu. At Scarborough Brook Conservation Area, leashed dogs are allowed; biking and horses are not allowed. Hunting is allowed in accordance with state laws. For more information, visit belchertown.org or call the Belchertown Conservation Commission at 413-323-0405.

WINTER ACTIVITIES

Skiing and snowshoeing are allowed at Scarborough Brook Conservation Area and Cadwell Memorial Forest. Cadwell Memorial Forest has a 13.5-mile network of foot trails and cinder roads. The grade from Scarborough Pond to Mount Lincoln is moderately steep, with an easy 0.4-mile segment north of Packardville Road.

NEARBY

Holland Glen, a small waterfall on Hop Brook, is the centerpiece of a 120-acre property owned by the Belchertown Historical Society that abuts the 290-acre Holland Glen Conservation Area. A portion of the former Metacomet-Monadnock Trail offers an easy 0.25-mile walk to the cascade. The roadside parking area is on the north side of MA 9, 2.8 miles west of the junction with US 202 in Belchertown. There are many places to eat in Belchertown and Amherst.

28

QUABBIN RESERVOIR: QUABBIN PARK

Spectacular views from Quabbin Hill and Enfield Lookout, a segment along Quabbin Reservoir's shores, and wildlife-rich meadows are among the diverse attractions of this circuit in Quabbin Park.

LOCATION
Belchertown and Ware, MA

RATING
Moderate

DISTANCE
5.6 miles

ELEVATION GAIN
700 feet

ESTIMATED TIME
3 hours

MAPS
USGS Winsor Dam; Massachusetts Department of Conservation and Recreation brochure: mass.gov/eea/docs/dcr/ watersupply/watershed/ quabbinbrochure.pdf

DIRECTIONS

From the east, on the Massachusetts Turnpike (I-90), take Exit 8 in Palmer and follow MA 32 north 8.0 miles to Ware. Turn left at a sign for MA 9 West and follow Vernon Street 0.1 mile then turn left on MA 9 and continue 5.3 miles to the Quabbin Park middle entrance. Turn right and follow the auto road 0.3 mile to the parking area at the east end of Winsor Dam. From the west, from the junction of MA 9 and US 202 in Belchertown, follow MA 9 east 4.7 miles to the Quabbin Park middle entrance on the left. *GPS coordinates: 42° 17.150′ N, 72° 20.157′ W.*

TRAIL DESCRIPTION

The massive Quabbin Reservoir, created during the 1930s as the water supply for eastern Massachusetts, is southern New England's largest conservation area (see "The Lost Towns of the Quabbin Valley," page 201). The numerous attractions of Quabbin Park, located at the reservoir's south end, include an auto road with many scenic views, a visitor center, and a lookout tower at the summit of Quabbin Hill, the park's highest point. This 5.6-mile loop over Quabbin Hill combines several of Quabbin Park's foot trails, which are unnamed but well marked with yellow blazes. After a moderately steep ascent over Quabbin Hill, most of the return segment is easy walking along the reservoir shore and an old town road. You can also start at the Quabbin Park visitor center and walk across Winsor Dam to the trailhead, which adds 1.8 miles (0.9 mile each way).

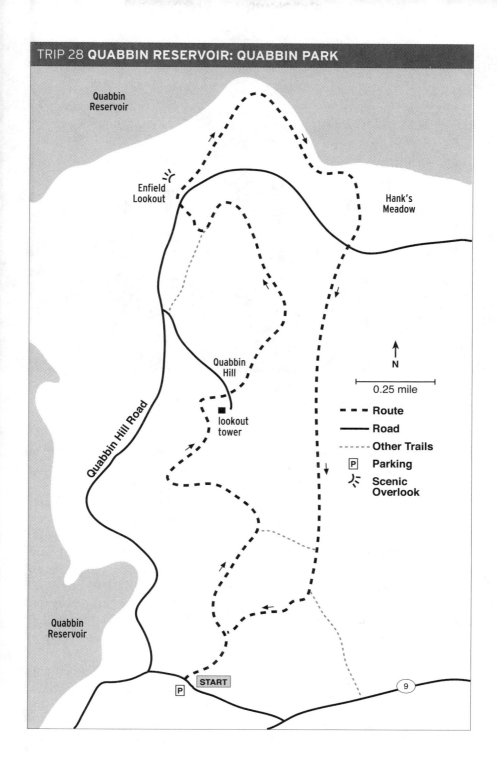

Quabbin
Reservoir

Enfield
Lookout

Hank's
Meadow

Quabbin
Hill

Quabbin Hill Road

lookout
tower

N

0.25 mile

- - - **Route**
—— **Road**
- - - - **Other Trails**
P **Parking**
))(**Scenic
Overlook**

Quabbin
Reservoir

P **START**

9

A white-tailed deer feeds near Quabbin Reservoir, one of two water supplies for Boston.

From gate WR25, follow the trail uphill past a power line, then continue roughly parallel to the clearing. At the next junction, begin the loop by bearing left at a yellow arrow marker (the woods road on the right is the return route). Pass the power line again and continue uphill on a narrow path through oak and paper birch groves, with glimpses of the top of Quabbin Hill through the trees. Walk through a pine grove, where you may have to step across a few fallen logs. Many of Quabbin Park's red pines, which were planted during the 1930s and are not native to central Massachusetts, have been infested with red pine scale, an introduced insect that kills trees by boring holes through the bark. Another intruder is Japanese barberry, an invasive plant species that often encroaches on native wildflowers and shrubs. More welcome are the violets and buttercups that bloom midspring in sunlit openings. Flocks of wild turkeys, which are common in Quabbin Park, frequent forest edges.

Continue the climb past the junction with an unmarked trail on the right. After passing a small pond, follow the blazed trail left, away from the power line. Shortly after the ascent resumes, turn right at a junction marked with three yellow blazes and continue through oak-hardwood forest on Quabbin Hill's upper slopes. When leaves are off, portions of the surrounding valley hills are visible through the trees.

At 1.4 miles (about 45 to 50 minutes), reach Quabbin Hill's 1,026-foot summit. The stone lookout tower, open seasonally, offers 360-degree views of the reservoir, Mount Monadnock, Wachusett Mountain, the Pioneer Valley, and the Berkshire Hills. From the grassy clearing at the base of the tower, there are westerly views to the Holyoke Range and Mount Tom in the Connecticut River valley. Watch for indigo buntings, porcupines, white-tailed deer, and other wildlife near the field edge.

From the tower, follow the paved path downhill to the summit parking lot. Continue straight across the lot to an overlook and picnic table. From the left side of the overlook, reenter the woods on a yellow-blazed trail. (The trail on the right side leads southeast to Webster Road.) After passing through dense blueberry thickets, make a winding descent of the north side of Quabbin Hill then continue past a glacial boulder and a large vernal pool in a depression on the right.

At roughly 1 mile from the summit, a small clearing offers an opportunity to watch for deer, wild turkeys, and other wildlife. After reentering the woods, turn right at the next junction and follow a woods road downhill to the paved auto road and gate WR18 at Enfield Lookout, one of the region's most scenic outlooks. Enjoy the spectacular views north across the Swift River valley to Mount Monadnock and watch for bald eagles above the hills. The valley below was once the site of Enfield, the largest of the four towns abandoned during the reservoir's creation during the 1930s.

From gate WR18, follow the path downhill and to the right, along the base of the lookout clearing, then continue down the valley slope 0.4 mile to the reservoir edge. At the base of the descent, turn right and follow the yellow-blazed path through the woods along the shoreline. Scan the water carefully for a variety of waterfowl, including long-tailed ducks and horned and pie-billed grebes, which are rare visitors to the region. If the water is frozen in winter, you may see eastern coyotes crossing the ice on hunting rounds.

Continue along the perimeter of a small cove then cross a stream and reach the corner of Hank's Meadow. Thanks to the convergence of diverse habitat— forest, field, and water—this is an excellent wildlife viewing area. White-tailed deer are frequently seen here, as hunting is prohibited in Quabbin Park. Since 1991, a limited annual hunt has been held in other sections of Quabbin Reservoir to maintain the population at a viable size and promote a healthy forest. Also watch for wild turkeys, eastern bluebirds, and a variety of butterflies and dragonflies in the meadows.

Follow the grass path along the perimeter of the field, heading away from the water, then bear right on the meadow access road. Cross the auto road and reenter the woods at gate 54 on Webster Road, an old woods road. On the left is the distinctive stone foundation of the former Powers mansion, one of Quabbin Reservoir's many historical sites. Continue to follow Webster Road south on an easy ascent over the east shoulder of Quabbin Hill.

At 0.6 mile from the auto road, pass the junction with the aforementioned yellow-blazed trail to Quabbin Hill's summit on the right then continue straight at junctions with Trail 34 on the left and a woods road on the right. When you reach the next intersection at a row of old sugar maples, turn right and follow a grassy woods road through a pine grove and a former timber harvest. Descend past a wetland and complete the loop at the power line. Turn left to return to gate WR25 and the parking area.

DID YOU KNOW?

Bald eagles were successfully reintroduced to Massachusetts at Quabbin Reservoir during the 1980s. Over the past 30 years, the eagles have steadily expanded their range across the state. Enfield Lookout is one of the region's most popular eagle-watching destinations.

MORE INFORMATION

Quabbin Park is open sunrise to sunset year-round (check posted gate closing times), no fee. The visitor center, located at the west end of Winsor Dam, offers maps, information, and historical exhibits. Dogs, hunting, and public access to the water are not allowed. Biking is allowed on the Quabbin Park auto road and in other designated areas. For more information, visit mass.gov/files/documents/2016/11/vp/quabbinbrochure.pdf or call 413-323-7221.

WINTER ACTIVITIES

Skiing is not allowed in Quabbin Park; snowshoeing is allowed. The park is an excellent place for animal tracking due to the abundant wildlife and diverse habitats. For a map of trails open to skiing on other Quabbin Reservoir watershed lands outside of Quabbin Park, visit mass.gov/eea/docs/dcr/watersupply/watershed/maps/quabski.pdf.

NEARBY

McLaughlin Fish Hatchery, located along the Swift River at 90 East Street off MA 9 in Belchertown, is open to the public daily from 9 A.M. to 3:45 P.M. For more information visit mass.gov/locations/mclaughlin-hatchery or call 413-323-7071. The adjacent Herman Covey Wildlife Management Area includes trails that lead to large open fields and wetlands. For more information visit mass.gov/orgs/division-of-fisheries-and-wildlife. There are many places to eat in Belchertown and Ware on MA 9, US 202, and MA 32.

29

LAUGHING BROOK WILDLIFE SANCTUARY

In the woods that once inspired the author Thornton W. Burgess, this pleasant hike leads you along the banks of East Brook and through hemlock-hardwood forests that rise above old stone walls.

DIRECTIONS

From I-91 in Springfield, take Exit 2 for MA 83 South. Turn left on Sumner Avenue (which becomes Allen Street and then Somers Road) and continue 8.1 miles to Hampden. After passing St. Mary's Church, turn left on Main Street and continue 2.0 miles to the sanctuary entrance on the left. *GPS coordinates:* 42° 03.857' N, 72° 24.305' W.

TRAIL DESCRIPTION

Laughing Brook Wildlife Sanctuary is well known as the setting and inspiration for many of the works of the noted author Thornton W. Burgess (1874–1965). Situated in the watershed of the Scantic River, this mostly wooded Mass Audubon property protects more than 350 acres of forests and wetlands along East Brook, the "Laughing Brook" that appears in many of Burgess's stories. A fire destroyed the nature center in 2004, and heavy flooding damaged the trails in 2005, but the sanctuary, now unstaffed, reopened in 2008. On Mass Audubon trails, blue blazes indicate that you're heading away from the entrance, and yellow blazes mark the way back to the trailhead.

At the entrance, scan the meadows and nesting boxes for eastern bluebirds and tree swallows. Both are territorial within their own species, and if you see a box being used by a bluebird, the adjacent box will likely be occupied by a swallow. You may notice descendants of the eastern cottontails that inspired Burgess's Peter Rabbit (not to be

LOCATION
Hampden, MA

RATING
Easy to Moderate

DISTANCE
4.2 miles

ELEVATION GAIN
350 feet

ESTIMATED TIME
2.25 hours

MAPS
USGS Hampden;
Mass Audubon map:
massaudubon.org/content/
download/8062/145292/file/
laughingbrook_trails.pdf

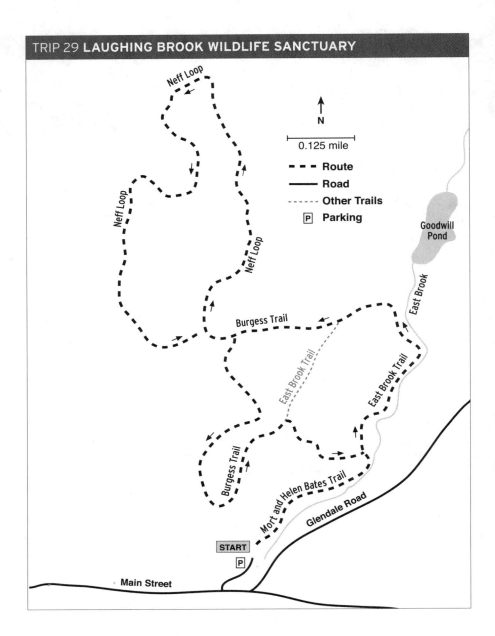

confused with the Peter Rabbit character of author Beatrix Potter) feeding on the edges of the field, especially early and late in the day.

From the information sign and gate, begin on Mort and Helen Bates Trail, named in honor of two of the sanctuary's benefactors. Continue to a gazebo and viewing area at a small artificial pond on East Brook. Watch for colorful yellow warblers, which frequent the shrubby vegetation at the pond edge, belted kingfishers, tree swallows hunting insects over the water, basking painted turtles, and other wildlife. Pass a small brushy field on the right then cross a footbridge over East Brook. In late spring, fragrant sweet bay magnolia blooms along the trail edge near the bridge.

Bear right and follow East Brook Trail into the woods, along the west banks of East Brook. Stay right at junctions with other trails and paths, keeping close to the brook and its pools and rocky bed. Continue through tall white pines and a hemlock grove to a stone wall then bear right at the junction with a discontinued trail and return to the brook. Ebony jewelwing damselflies, distinguished by their metallic green bodies and black wings, are common along the brook's banks in late spring and early summer. Look carefully and you may see a male guarding his female mate while she lays eggs.

At 0.6 mile from the trailhead, follow East Brook Trail left, away from the brook, and make a gentle ascent into a drier oak-pine forest. Bear left at a stone wall and continue through an old pine plantation. Turn right at a marked junction and follow Burgess Trail past granite outcroppings, mountain laurels, and a shady hemlock grove.

At the next junction, turn right and follow a short connecting path to the start of the Neff Trail loop at a tall, forked oak. (To save 1.8 miles and roughly 45 to 50 minutes of walking, you can bypass Neff Trail by continuing left on Burgess Trail.) To make a counterclockwise circuit on Neff Trail, follow the right branch of the loop on a gradual ascent through mixed woods that include some impressive large white and red oak trees. Common migratory songbirds include black-throated green warblers and veeries. The hemlock groves serve as crucial wintering areas for white-tailed deer and other animals, with the evergreen cover mitigating snowfall and retaining heat more efficiently than open hardwood forests. Fishers, members of the weasel family, have recently returned to these woods after being absent for many years. Often erroneously called fisher-cats, these active and energetic predators feed on a variety of prey, including porcupines.

While mature forests are predominant today, an extensive network of stone walls offers evidence that this land was mostly open and cultivated for agriculture in Colonial times. Follow the well-marked Neff Trail as it winds through hemlock-hardwood forests in the valley above Big Brook, another tributary of the Scantic River. Shortly after the trail passes a wet area next to a stone wall in a shady hemlock grove, the blazes change from blue to yellow, indicating you're past the halfway point of the loop. Continue along the crest of a wooded ravine, where there are glimpses of nearby valley hills through the trees. Pass more stone walls and descend through another hemlock grove. At the base of the descent, bear left and make a short climb through a sunlit open white pine grove. Tiny bluet wildflowers grow along the margins of the path in spring.

At the end of the Neff Trail loop, follow the connecting path back to the junction with Burgess Trail. Turn right and continue past a wetland where skunk cabbage, one of the first plants to emerge at the start of the growing season, flowers in abundance in spring. Cross a steep-sided glacial ridge, following Burgess Trail left at a junction with an unmarked path that leads down the slope. After crossing a creek, turn right at a three-way junction to rejoin East Brook Trail,

Once the inspiration for children's book author Thornton Burgess, Laughing Brook Wildlife Sanctuary offers diverse habitats for eastern bluebirds and other wildlife.

which will lead you on a short, winding descent through mixed forest. Bear right at the next junction and continue past a large stone wall to the end of the loop at marker 15 on the banks of East Brook. Turn right and retrace your steps along the brook to the pond and fields at the entrance.

DID YOU KNOW?

Thornton Burgess was a prolific writer and naturalist whose works include more than 170 books and 15,000 articles, including *Old Mother West Wind* (1910) and the syndicated *Bedtime Stories* newspaper column (1912–1960). He also broadcast a popular radio series for nearly 50 years. His former home on Main Street in Hampden is now used by Mass Audubon for staff housing.

MORE INFORMATION

Open dawn to dusk year-round, no fee. Biking, dogs, and hunting are not allowed. The sanctuary is unstaffed and managed by Mass Audubon's Arcadia Wildlife Sanctuary. For more information, visit massaudubon.org or call 413-584-3009.

WINTER ACTIVITIES

Skiing and snowshoeing are allowed. The trails mostly follow gently rolling terrain with some minor ups and downs, especially along Neff Trail.

NEARBY

The Zoo in Forest Park and Education Center (302 Sumner Avenue, Springfield) features exotic and native wildlife, educational programs, and special events. For seasonal hours (closed in winter) and information, visit forestparkzoo.com or call 413-733-2251. There are several places to eat in Hampden.

30

PEAKED MOUNTAIN

From Butternut Pasture, old fire roads form a loop past an orchard and over the summit ridge of Peaked Mountain, where overlooks offer some of the finest views in south-central Massachusetts.

DIRECTIONS

From the Massachusetts Turnpike (I-90) take Exit 8 in Palmer and follow MA 32 south 5.3 miles to Monson. Following signs for Peaked Mountain, turn right on High Street, then turn left on Ely Road and continue 1.0 mile to a stop sign. Keep straight for 2.0 miles on Lower Hampden Road. Turn left on Butler Road and continue 1.2 miles to the Peaked Mountain entrance on the left. *GPS coordinates:* 42° 02.940' N, 72° 21.120' W.

TRAIL DESCRIPTION

Located in the largely undeveloped uplands in Monson, near the Connecticut state line, Peaked Mountain is the centerpiece of a 333-acre property of The Trustees of Reservations that also includes nearby Miller Forest Tract and Lunden Pond. From the 1,227-foot summit and other points along the summit ridge, there are fine views across the surrounding countryside to Mount Monadnock, the Green Mountains, and the city of Springfield.

This walk combines red-blazed Summit Loop and orange-blazed Orchard Loop, both of which follow a series of named fire roads that were built after a large forest fire in 1984. You can shorten the hike and save some elevation gain by following Summit Loop alone for a 2-mile outing. From the trailhead at Butternut Pasture, an old hay field, begin by following the grass path to marker 1 at the forest edge. Indigo buntings nest at the meadow in spring and summer. Thistles, daisies, and other wildflowers offer nourishment for butterflies and other pollinating insects.

LOCATION
Monson, MA

RATING
Moderate

DISTANCE
2.6 miles

ELEVATION GAIN
700 feet

ESTIMATED TIME
2 hours

MAPS
USGS Monson;
The Trustees of
Reservations map:
thetrustees.org/
assets/documents/
places-to-visit/trailmaps/
Peaked-Mountain-Trail
-Map-1.pdf

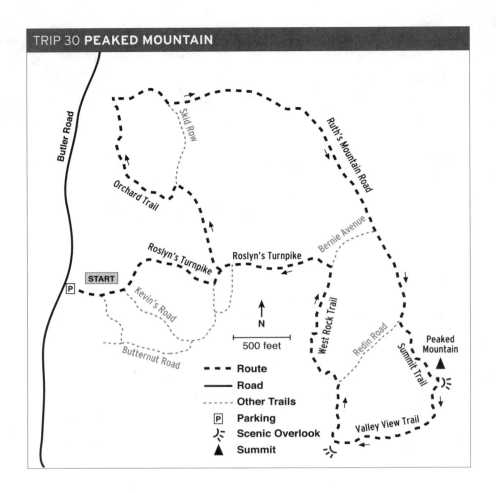

Enter the woods on red-blazed Summit Loop, which follows Roslyn's Turnpike uphill past junction 4, where Kevin's Road branches to the right. Cross a creek and continue the moderate ascent through hardwood forest of oak, birch, and maple. These woods have recovered from centuries of disturbances, including clearing for sheep pastures by early settlers, timber harvesting, and several forest fires. Many resident and migratory birds now benefit from the revitalization, including the red-bellied woodpecker, distinguished by its red head, striped back, and abrupt *chiv* call. Like the northern cardinal, it is a primarily southern species that has expanded its range into New England in recent decades.

Continue uphill to marker 5 at a bench and a small pond, which, like the roads, was created for fire control during the 1980s. Watch for resident bullfrogs in spring and summer. At 0.3 mile, turn left at marker 6 onto orange-blazed Orchard Loop and Skid Row—so named because the trail was used by a log skidder during a past timber harvest. After a gradual descent past a large twin white oak, turn left at the next junction and follow Orchard Loop down the lower western slopes. Continue through the woods, parallel to a pasture at the property boundary, to the edge of the orchard at marker 12. This sunlit opening is a good place to pause and watch for butterflies, dragonflies, songbirds, and raptors. Listen for the whistling calls of northern orioles during the spring and summer.

Reenter the woods and begin the ascent to the summit on Ruth's Mountain Road, also part of Orchard Loop. The initial portion of the climb is moderately steep, but as you gain elevation the grade lessens, and the walking becomes easier. A few glacial boulders, deposited at the end of the last ice age, are scattered amid the hardwood forest on both sides of the route. Follow the obvious main trail past junctions with several unmarked footpaths. The distinctive *pee-a-wee* call of the eastern wood peewee, one of the migratory songbirds that breeds in these woods, is a familiar sound during the spring and summer. Tiger beetles, easily identified by their bright metallic-green bodies, frequent the open path, where they hunt other insects. Pink lady's slipper blooms along the trail edge from late May to mid-June.

At a three-way intersection at marker 8, reach the end of Orchard Loop at the junction with Summit Loop and Bernie Avenue. Turn left on red-blazed Summit Loop to begin a clockwise circuit around Peaked Mountain's summit ridge. From this point, the rest of the hike is on Summit Loop. A few American chestnut saplings, identified by their toothed leaves, grow along the trail edge. American chestnut, once a crucial source of timber and food for wildlife, was eliminated by the chestnut blight fungus during the early twentieth century. An estimated 3 to 4 million trees were lost to the blight. However, chestnut stumps often produce saplings that live for roughly 20 years before dying.

At marker 9, follow Summit Loop left along the rocky upper end of Ruth's Mountain Road. Groves of stunted trees, their size inhibited by the thin soil at the top of the mountain and exposure to wind and storms, grow along the crest of the ridge, along with huckleberry and blueberry shrubs. At 1.5 miles, follow a short, rocky path to the summit, where an open ledge affords 180-degree views of Wachusett Mountain, the hills of the Swift River valley and Quabbin Reservoir, and, on clear days, Mount Monadnock and the southern Green Mountains of Vermont on the distant northern horizon. Look carefully for the damage corridor from a tornado that caused extensive destruction in June 2011 throughout Hampden County, including Monson. Listen for a variety of bird songs echoing across the valley, such as the distinctive *who-cooks-for-you* call of barred owls. Turkey vultures and other birds of prey often circle on updrafts along the ridge.

From the ledge, follow Summit Loop and Valley View Trail around and over exposed rocks to another overlook with views of a beaver pond and a portion of the nearby Norcross Wildlife Sanctuary. Descend past another ledge and a rocky section where mountain laurel blooms in June. The walking soon becomes easier as the path bends west along the ridge to Valley View, an open ledge with southwesterly perspectives of nearby Boulder Hill and the city of Springfield.

Peaked Mountain's ridge includes views to Mount Monadnock, Wachusett Mountain, and Springfield.

Continue to follow Summit Loop north along West Rock Trail past marker 10 and an old mound from a nineteenth-century charcoal operation, when trees cut from the mountain's forests were used to provide fuel for a local ironworks. At marker 7, turn left and follow the upper portion of Roslyn's Turnpike on a moderately steep descent to the end of the loop at marker 6. Turn left again and retrace your steps past the fire pond to Butternut Pasture and the trailhead, roughly 1 mile from the summit.

DID YOU KNOW?

After the 1984 forest fire, landowners on Peaked Mountain formed a co-op, built the fire roads that now serve as hiking trails, and created a research area to monitor regenerating forest vegetation. Peaked Mountain opened to the public in 1999.

MORE INFORMATION

Open sunrise to sunset year-round, no fee. Dogs are allowed; biking and hunting are not allowed. For more information, visit thetrustees.org or call 978-840-4446. The trail network at Miller Forest Tract, on Butler Road 0.7 mile north of the Peaked Mountain entrance, includes a circuit around Lunden Pond and two other easy loops.

WINTER ACTIVITIES

Skiing and snowshoeing are allowed. Most of the Peaked Mountain trails follow old fire roads with moderate grades and some steep sections. There are several rough and rocky segments around the summit. At Miller Forest Tract, easier options include Miller Forest Loop and Lunden Pond Loop.

NEARBY

Norcross Wildlife Sanctuary, at 30 Peck Road in Wales, offers 2 miles of easy trails through a variety of natural habitats and wildflower gardens and has a visitor center with natural history exhibits. The sanctuary is open from April to November (closed holidays), Tuesday to Saturday, 9 A.M. to 4 P.M. For information, visit norcrosswildlife.org or call 413-267-9654. There are several places to eat in Monson.

WORCESTER COUNTY

Located in the geographic heart of Massachusetts, Worcester County is an expansive region of rolling hills, mixed forests, and extensive wetlands. At 1,580 square miles, it is the commonwealth's biggest county, covering an area larger than the state of Rhode Island. Although it is home to roughly

800,000 residents and the development associated with Worcester and several other population centers, there are also many sizable sections of protected land. The 92-mile-long Midstate Trail corridor links many of the county's natural landmarks and conservation areas.

Most of Worcester County lies within two irregularly shaped ecoregions: the Worcester–Monadnock Plateau and the Lower Worcester Plateau. The former (425 square miles), which extends into adjacent southern New Hampshire and the eastern portion of Franklin County, is characterized by rocky, often steep hills that generally range between 500 and 1,400 feet in elevation. Transition forests, largely composed of northern hardwoods (oak and hickory in milder lowlands, spruce and fir on the highest hilltops) are predominant.

The larger Lower Worcester Plateau, which covers roughly 1,000 square miles, stretches from the foothills of the lower Connecticut River valley across most of south-central Massachusetts. Although this land is also quite hilly, the elevations are lower than in the Worcester–Monadnock Plateau, averaging between 300 and 500 feet, and the slopes are gentler. The mixed forests include oak and

Facing page: An oriole perches on a blossoming apple tree branch in the Ware River watershed.

hickory, central hardwoods, and white pine. The easternmost portion of Worcester County sits along the transition to the Southern New England Coastal Plain, a geographically similar region of low hills and wetlands.

Northwestern Worcester County is lightly populated, with several large conservation corridors in the watersheds of the Millers and Tully rivers. The remote glacial valley of Falls Brook, home to the picturesque cascades of Royalston Falls (Trip 33), also marks the northern terminus of the federally designated New England Trail. The nearby ridge of Jacobs Hill (Trip 34) rises high above Long Pond and the Tully Lake Flood Control Area, where the many recreational opportunities include a scenic hiking trail around Tully Lake and Doane's Falls (Trip 35). In Athol, Bearsden Conservation Area (Trip 32) encompasses five rugged hills and unbroken forests in a remote, heavily wooded section of the Millers River valley. It is part of a network of conservation areas that protects a considerable portion of the upper watershed.

On the east side of Quabbin Reservoir, the former town common of Dana (Trip 37), now listed on the National Register of Historic Places, serves as a memorial to the Swift River valley communities that were abandoned during the reservoir's creation in the 1930s. The diverse habitats of Rutland Brook Wildlife Sanctuary (Trip 36) are part of a large area of conservation land along the East Branch of Swift River, the reservoir's largest source.

The state water supply network also includes an expanse of undeveloped land in the Ware River valley, where several contiguous properties, including Barre Falls Dam and Ware River Reservation (Trip 39), protect more than 20,000 acres. The extensive wetlands and forests are home to a wide variety of wildlife, including one of the state's largest moose populations. At the Mandell Hill Conservation Area in Hardwick (Trip 38), old fields on a former hilltop farm offer panoramic views of the valley and a glimpse of the property's past, when agriculture was the predominant land use. (While much of central Massachusetts has reverted to forest since Colonial times, farming remains an important component of several communities.) In nearby West Brookfield, the rock ledges and caves at Rock House Reservation (Trip 40) were once used as shelter by the Nipmuck.

The region's highest point and most prominent landmark is 2,006-foot Wachusett Mountain (Trip 41), a monadnock in Princeton that has long been one of Massachusetts's most popular hiking destinations. At Wachusett Meadow Wildlife Sanctuary (Trip 42), an old farm at the base of Wachusett Mountain now offers diverse habitats for a variety of wildlife, including monarch butterflies and grassland birds. Nearby Leominster State Forest (Trip 43) is home to the sheer cliff of Crow Hill, one of the region's most impressive natural features; the forest also includes several scenic ponds and rolling hills with colorful mountain laurels.

At the boundary of Worcester and Middlesex counties, Willard Brook State Forest (Trip 45) protects a large expanse of forest and wetlands in the Nashua

River watershed north of Fitchburg. At the southern end of the Wapack Range, at the New Hampshire state line, 1,832-foot Mount Watatic (Trip 44) offers sweeping views from Boston to the Berkshires. Mount Watatic and Wachusett Mountain are both outstanding hawk-watching destinations, thanks to locations along an active migratory corridor.

Amid the development of Worcester, New England's second-largest city, Mass Audubon's Broad Meadow Brook Wildlife Sanctuary (Trip 47) serves as a crucial 450-acre oasis of protected natural habitats. Moore State Park (Trip 46), just outside the greater Worcester area in the town of Paxton, is a former mill village and country estate that now features diverse habitats, historical sites, and colorful gardens. A unique combination of nature and history is also evident at Blackstone River and Canal Heritage State Park in Uxbridge (Trip 48), where trails lead to old canals, locks, and scenic views of the Blackstone River, one of America's most significant industrial waterways. The river, which stretches 45 miles from Worcester to Providence, is the centerpiece of a designated National Heritage Corridor. Another of the Blackstone Valley's distinctive landmarks is Purgatory Chasm (Trip 49), a dramatic rocky gorge that is popular not only with hikers and tourists but also with scientists, who continue to investigate its origins.

At the southern end of the Midstate Trail corridor, Douglas State Forest (Trip 50), the largest conservation area in southern Worcester County, protects nearly 6,000 acres of forests and wetlands along the Massachusetts–Rhode Island state line. The various natural and historical features include a rare Atlantic white cedar swamp, beaver wetlands, former railroad lines and mill sites, and a portion of scenic Wallum Lake.

The ledges of Soapstone Hill offer spectacular views of Quabbin Reservoir. Other attractions of this less-traveled loop include a rocky gorge and a wildlife-rich beaver pond on Fever Brook.

LOCATION
Petersham and
New Salem, MA

RATING
Moderate

DIRECTIONS

From MA 2 take Exit 16 in Orange and follow US 202 south 2.0 miles to the junction with MA 122 in New Salem. Turn left and follow MA 122 south 3.6 miles to the entrance at the New Salem–Petersham town line. Turn right on the access road and continue 1.7 miles to the parking area on the right near the campground gate. (The access road is unmaintained in winter, and may be impassable for vehicles. However, visitors can park at the entrance and walk or ski to the trailhead.) *GPS coordinates:* 42° 29.249′ N, 72° 15.362′ W.

DISTANCE
3.3 miles

ELEVATION GAIN
450 feet

ESTIMATED TIME
2 hours

MAPS
USGS Quabbin Reservoir

TRAIL DESCRIPTION

While enjoying the spectacular views of Quabbin Reservoir from Soapstone Hill, one of the low, rocky eminences that characterize the Swift River watershed, you may feel like you've ventured to the lakes regions of New Hampshire or Maine. At the base of the hill, the West Branch of Fever Brook serves as the source for a chain of beaver wetlands at the reservoir's northern tip. This hike begins in the southwestern corner of the 984-acre Federated Women's Club State Forest and enters adjacent Quabbin Reservoir land near the campground (see "More Information" for rules). Although the route is generally easy to follow, it is sparsely marked with blue blazes and flagging, and a portion below the gorge is narrow and partially overgrown. Apart from a steep climb to the Soapstone Hill lookout, the walking is mostly easy.

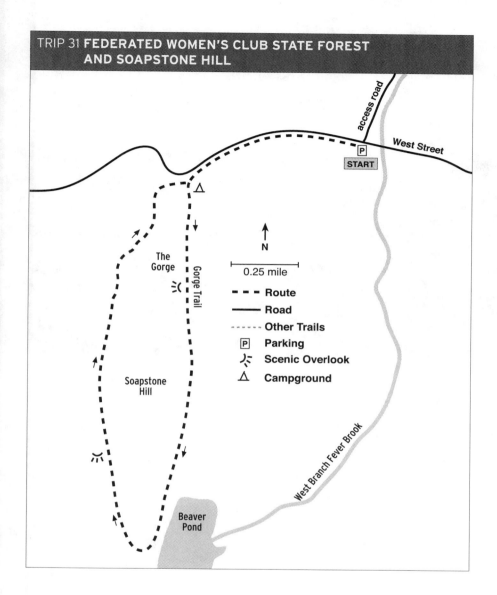

Opposite the parking area is a view of Fever Brook, which flows out of a nearby beaver pond en route to its confluence with Quabbin Reservoir, downstream from the trailhead. From the orange gate, follow the dirt campground road past a small pond and continue uphill through a power-line clearing, where New England and white wood aster, goldenrod, Queen Anne's lace, fringed gentian, and other colorful wildflowers bloom in summer. Moose, black bears, white-tailed deer, coyotes, and other wildlife often use the clearing as a travel corridor and foraging area, and butterflies feed on the abundant flowers.

Soapstone Hill, which rises high above beaver wetlands in the valley of Fever Brook, offers spectacular views across the north end of Quabbin Reservoir.

Bear left at a Y junction and enter the campground. (The woods road on the right leads downhill to beaver ponds and the shores of Quabbin Reservoir, on the west side of Soapstone Hill.) At 0.5 mile from the trailhead, begin the loop by turning left onto Gorge Trail, opposite campsite 1; the junction is unmarked as of this writing. Pass campsites 2 and 3 and continue to an overlook on the right with a view of the Gorge, a rocky ravine on the east side of Soapstone Hill. Here the trail becomes narrow and partially overgrown in places but is still easy to follow. Descend into the valley of Fever Brook through mountain laurel thickets and white pine saplings. Watch for the tracks and signs of moose, which are common here.

At the base of the descent, the trail widens into a more prominent woods road. Continue through a small grassy clearing and along the west side of a large beaver pond on the West Branch of Fever Brook, reached at 1.3 miles. This wetland offers habitat for a variety of wildlife, including wood and black ducks, common and hooded mergansers, great blue herons, beavers, river otters, snapping turtles, dragonflies, and moose. Near the south end of the wetland, look carefully for a junction on the right, marked with a blue blaze on a tree at a stone wall. Although the loop continues to the right, a short detour straight on the road leads to an outlook where Fever Brook empties into Quabbin Reservoir, at the junction with the former Monson Turnpike, one of many roads that were abandoned when the reservoir was built during the 1930s.

Follow the narrow path past a former timber harvest site and begin the ascent of Soapstone Hill's steep southern slope, which was shaped by glaciers. Pass the edge of an abandoned quarry where rocks were once extracted for use by factories in the former industrial village of North Dana, which is now beneath the waters of Quabbin Reservoir. (Although the trail is safe, use caution near dropoffs.) Bullfrogs and raccoons now frequent the algae-filled pool at the base of the steep walls. Continue the moderately steep ascent to the rocky ledges at the top of the ridge, which rises about 350 feet above the beaver pond. Yellow false foxglove blooms around the ledges in late summer.

At 1.8 miles, make a short scramble to a lookout with picturesque southeasterly views of the north end of Quabbin Reservoir and the forested hills of the Swift River valley. When leaves are off the trees, you can also see a portion of the beaver pond in the valley below. Listen for the distinctive laughing calls of common loons, which often echo across the reservoir coves, and watch for bald eagles soaring above the valley. You may also hear barred owls and whip-poor-wills, especially in the evenings. Scan the southern horizon carefully for a glimpse of the observation tower atop Quabbin Hill at the reservoir's south end.

From the ledges, continue north along the ridge past an outlook on the right with a glimpse of Mount Monadnock on the northern horizon. Red columbine, a characteristic wildflower of rugged, rocky habitats, grows along the ridge in mid to late May. In 2017, these oak-hardwood forests suffered heavily from an infestation of gypsy moths, which defoliated nearly all of the trees on Soapstone Hill and in the surrounding area. Gypsy moth outbreaks, which are linked to droughts, occur at irregular intervals in southern New England.

At the end of the ridge, bear right and descend past another former timber harvest site to an overgrown clearing at the state forest boundary. Follow the path left to the junction with an unmarked footpath on the right; take the footpath to the campground field and picnic area, in roughly five minutes. If you miss the turn, continue to the nearby junction with a woods road at gate 36B then turn right to reach the campground. Watch for wild turkeys and tiny spring peepers in the field.

Rejoin the campground road and complete the loop at campsite 1 then backtrack downhill past the power line to the parking area. Before leaving, you can explore Fever Brook and the beaver pond near the trailhead, where you may see a wood duck, river otter, or one of the numerous moose that inhabit the northern portion of Quabbin Reservoir.

DID YOU KNOW?

The West and East branches of Fever Brook are two of Quabbin Reservoir's largest source waters. Both have extensive chains of beaver wetlands that offer habitat for a variety of wildlife.

MORE INFORMATION

Open year-round, no fee. The access road is unmaintained in winter. Restrooms are available seasonally at the campground. Biking, dogs, and hunting are not allowed on Quabbin Reservoir land, which includes most of this hike. Hunting is allowed at Federated Women's Club State Forest in accordance with state laws. A map is posted at the campground, but it does not include all of the trails. The state forest is unstaffed; for information and camping access, contact Erving State Forest (978-544-3939) or visit mass.gov/locations/federated-womens-club-state-forest.

WINTER ACTIVITIES

Skiing is not allowed on Quabbin Reservoir land, which accounts for most of this hike, but is allowed at Federated Women's Club State Forest, which includes the trailhead, campground, and access road. The road, which is not maintained in winter, is a good option for skiers when conditions permit, since it is wide and level from the MA 122 entrance to the campground gate. Snowshoeing is allowed on all trails.

NEARBY

The Bear's Den, managed by The Trustees of Reservations, is a picturesque waterfall and gorge on the Middle Branch of Swift River. A 0.25-mile trail offers an easy walk to the falls and the site of an old gristmill. The entrance is at 18 Neilson Road off US 202 in New Salem. For more information, visit thetrustees.org.

32

BEARSDEN CONSERVATION AREA

Scenic vistas (at Sheep Rock and Round Top Hill), Duck Pond, and a ridge trail highlight this moderately rugged circuit in the hills of the Millers River valley.

DIRECTIONS

From the west, on MA 2, take Exit 17 in Athol and follow MA 32 north 0.9 mile to the junction with MA 2A. From the east, on MA 2, take Exit 18 and follow MA 2A west 1.2 miles to the junction with MA 32. Follow MA 2A/MA 32 west 0.4 mile then turn right on Bearsden Road at a sign for Bearsden Conservation Area and continue uphill past Adams Farm. Turn right at another conservation area sign and continue to follow Bearsden Road past a pond and gate to the parking area at the road's end, 1.6 miles from the junction with MA 2A/MA 32. *GPS coordinates: 42° 36.258′ N, 72° 11.552′ W.*

TRAIL DESCRIPTION

Bearsden Conservation Area, one of the region's hidden gems, protects more than 1,000 acres of rolling hills, wetlands, and forests in the Millers River valley. The numerous attractions include five rocky hills, scenic vistas, beaver ponds, cascading brooks, Newton Reservoir, and frontage on Millers River. These forests have been classified by the Massachusetts Bureau of Natural Heritage as one of the state's best examples of interior forests. Many stone walls offer evidence that the hills were formerly cleared and used as sheep pastures.

This 3.6-mile loop combines several foot trails and woods roads in the western portion of the forest. From the yellow gate at the parking area, head north on Bearsden Road, which was the main road from Athol to South Royalston until the bridge over Millers River was washed out by floodwaters from the 1938 hurricane (see "A Terrible

LOCATION
Athol, MA

RATING
Moderate to Strenuous

DISTANCE
3.6 miles

ELEVATION GAIN
580 feet

ESTIMATED TIME
2.5 hours

MAPS
USGS Athol; North Quabbin Community Coalition map: northquabbinwoods.org/pdfs/bearsden_map.pdf

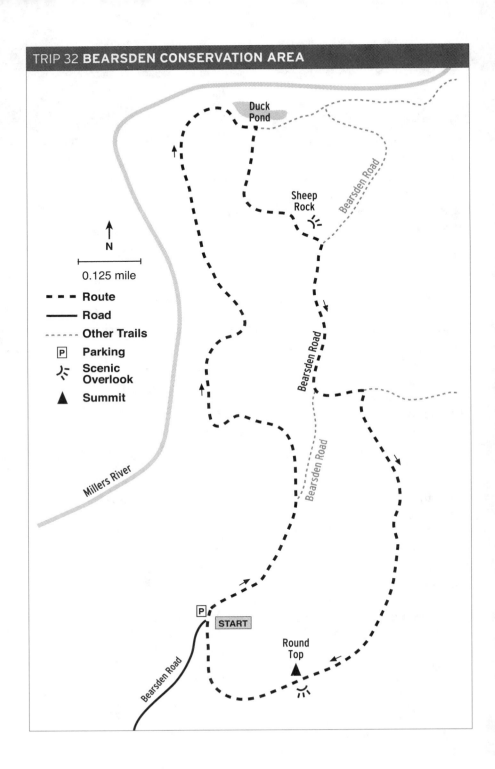

TRIP 32 **BEARSDEN CONSERVATION AREA**

Duck Pond

Bearsden Road

Sheep Rock

N

0.125 mile

- - - Route
—— Road
- - - - Other Trails
P Parking
Scenic Overlook
▲ Summit

Bearsden Road

Bearsden Road

Millers River

P
START

Bearsden Road

Round Top
▲

Trio," page 189). At 0.3 mile, turn left at a sign for Fire Road–Thompson's Corner and begin a long descent into the valley. Follow the road, built for fire control during a lengthy drought in the 1960s, past several large glacial boulders and a tall white oak. In midspring, look for the tiny pink and white blossoms of trailing arbutus, Massachusetts's state flower, on the embankments. At Thompson's Corner, the road turns right and continues north over gently rolling terrain to a footbridge. You may hear or glimpse freight trains rumbling along the railroad tracks that parallel the river in the valley below.

Shortly after passing Scott's Corner, where the trail bends to the right along an oxbow in Millers River, reach Duck Pond, the literal low point of the hike, in the base of the valley at 1.5 miles. The pond, nestled in the floodplain next to Millers River and the railroad embankment, is a pleasant spot to watch for waterfowl, dragonflies, frogs, turtles, and other wildlife as you enjoy a break before beginning the climb to Sheep Rock. Overnight camping is available at the Duck Pond camping shelter by reservation (see "More Information"). On a future visit, or if you have time to extend this outing, you can follow the red-blazed trail along the river to Old Stage Road and the Buckman Brook shelter in the eastern portion of the property.

At a marked junction, turn right on Sheep Rock Trail and make a steep 0.4-mile ascent of the valley slope to Sheep Rock, so named because it was once the site of an upland sheep pasture. A wooden observation tower offers panoramic views across the forested slopes of the Millers River valley from 285 feet above the riverbed. This small clearing is periodically visited by eastern coyotes, red foxes, and fishers, which den in the nearby rocky ledges.

From Sheep Rock, follow a woods road east 0.3 mile to a T junction, where you'll rejoin Bearsden Road. Turn right and pass through Deep Cut Gorge, where the road was blasted through rock ledge. The gorge offers a shady break from summer heat and the walls are often lined with interesting ice formations in winter. Continue past a grove of large red oaks and a gate at the junction with the trail to Bemis Hill on the left. At a small picnic area, turn left off Bearsden Road and follow an old logging road uphill toward Round Top Hill.

At the next marked junction, turn right, following a sign for Sunday Walls, Warren Vista, and Round Top. At 0.2 mile past the junction, a 50-yard detour leads to Sunday Walls, stone walls that reputedly were built in the eighteenth century as part of a competition between two brothers from one of the town's first settler families; the story has it that the winner completed 19 feet. Continue the easy ascent along the ridge past more stone walls, holdovers from Colonial times when the hill was cleared for pastures. The next point of interest is Warren Vista, a lookout on a plateau below Round Top's summit, with partial westerly views.

After passing another stone wall, make a last climb to the 1,278-foot summit of Round Top, the highest of the conservation area's five hills. A few red spruce trees, which thrive in high-elevation conditions many other trees can't tolerate, grow along the crest of the ridge. The mixed-aged forests at the summit are the

legacy of a forest fire in 1957 and a recent timber harvest. A wooden observation deck offers easterly views across the wooded countryside to Wachusett Mountain and the wind turbines at Mount Wachusett Community College, in Gardner. Visitors may also glimpse Mount Monadnock to the north when leaves are off the trees. The hilltop is a good place to observe migrating hawks and monarch butterflies in late summer and early autumn.

From the summit, follow Round Top Trail on a steep but quick 0.25-mile descent through groves of tall pines on the southwestern slopes. Bear right at the base of the hill and complete the loop at the parking area, 0.4 mile from the summit.

DID YOU KNOW?

Bearsden Conservation Area is part of a largely undeveloped section of the Millers River valley in Athol and Royalston known as the Gulf. This remote expanse of protected land, which also encompasses the 2,500-acre Millers River Wildlife Management Area, includes a 7-mile-long catch-and-release fishing area that extends from South Royalston to the Starrett tool company dam in Athol.

MORE INFORMATION

Open dawn to dusk year-round, no fee. Biking and dogs are allowed. Hunting is allowed in accordance with state laws. Overnight camping is available by reservation at the Paige Cabin, near the conservation area's main entrance, and at the Duck Pond and Buckman Brook shelters. For more information, visit athol-ma .gov/parks-trails/pages/bearsden-conservation-area.

WINTER ACTIVITIES

Skiing and snowshoeing are allowed. The trails range from wide woods roads to narrow paths. Some, such as Sheep Rock Trail and the lower portion of Round Top Trail, have steep sections. In the eastern part of the property, reached from the entrance on South Royalston Road off MA 2A, options include an easy loop around Newton Reservoir and a gradual descent to Millers River on Old Stage Road.

NEARBY

Alan E. Rich Environmental Park, on MA 2A in Athol, offers a boat launch and trails through a meadow on the banks of Millers River. The park is the starting point for the popular River Rat canoe race held annually in April. Millers River Environmental Center, at 100 Main Street, is adjacent to the park and is the headquarters for several organizations, including the Athol Bird and Nature Club, which offers public programs and field trips (atholbirdclub.org). There are several places to eat on MA 2A in Athol and Orange.

Facing page: A hiker pauses on Sheep Rock in Bearsden Conservation Area.

33

ROYALSTON FALLS RESERVATION

From the dramatic gorge and waterfall at Royalston Falls to a series of pools, rocky cascades, and a natural bridge, the relentless carving power of water is evident throughout the valley of Falls Brook.

LOCATION
Royalston, MA

RATING
Moderate

DISTANCE
1.6 miles

ELEVATION GAIN
350 feet

ESTIMATED TIME
1.25 hours

MAPS
USGS Royalston; The Trustees of Reservations map: thetrustees.org/assets/documents/places-to-visit/trailmaps/Tully-Trail-Map.pdf

DIRECTIONS

From the west, on MA 2, take Exit 17 in Athol and follow MA 32 north 0.9 mile to the junction with MA 2A. Turn left onto MA 32/MA 2A and continue 1.4 miles. Turn right on MA 32, cross the bridge over Millers River, and continue 9.2 miles on MA 32 to the reservation entrance on the right, next to the Newton Cemetery.

From the east, on MA 2, take Exit 19 in Phillipston and follow US 202 north 2.4 miles. Turn left and follow MA 68 north 8.6 miles to Royalston town common. Turn left at Newton Library and continue 3.8 miles on MA 68 to the junction with MA 32. Turn right on MA 32 and continue 1.7 miles to the reservation entrance on the right. *GPS coordinates: 42° 42.969′ N, 72° 15.383′ W.*

TRAIL DESCRIPTION

Royalston Falls, the northernmost of three scenic waterfalls in the hills of Royalston, is one of Massachusetts's most picturesque cascades. The 217-acre Royalston Falls Reservation, managed by The Trustees of Reservations, protects the falls and the adjacent wooded valley of Falls Brook in the Tully River watershed. This hike, the most straightforward of several approaches to the falls, follows portions of the long-distance New England Trail (NET) and Tully Trail, which overlap from the reservation entrance to Falls Brook. (An alternative route from a more remote trailhead on Falls Road is described in the last paragraph.) Winter is a great time to view unique conditions at the falls, but be prepared for potentially icy

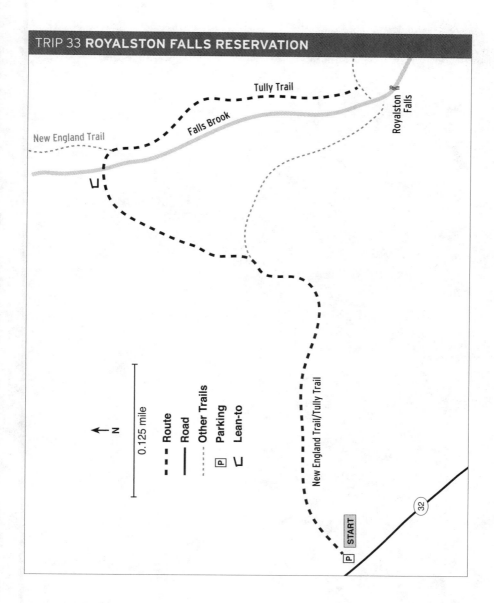

conditions. Portions of the trail near the entrance may be wet in spring or after heavy rain.

From the gate and information sign, follow the combined white-blazed NET and yellow-blazed Tully Trail along an old woods road past Newton Cemetery and a stone wall. Eastern starflower, one of the most abundant wildflowers of the Northeast, grows in clusters along the path in spring. Follow the trails past a seasonally wet area and begin the moderately steep descent into the Falls Brook valley. Cross a cascading seasonal brook twice and pass an unmarked trail on the left. Tall oaks, birches, and maples grow out of the rich soil on the valley

slopes. The reservation's forests and wetlands offer habitats for about 50 species of breeding birds. Common year-round residents include downy and hairy woodpeckers, which are similar in appearance; the latter can be distinguished by its larger size and proportionally longer bill.

At 0.5 mile, reach a footbridge and camping shelter on the banks of Falls Brook, which cascades through groves of eastern hemlock trees. The shelter, built by the Pioneer Valley Hiking Club in 2003, is available on a first-come, first-served basis. At a marked junction on the east side of the bridge, the NET and Tully Trail split. The route to Royalston Falls continues to the right on Tully Trail, but a short detour left (north) on the NET leads to a small natural bridge where the brook has eroded a gap in the sandstone rock. North of the bridge, the federally designated NET ends at the New Hampshire state line, and the Meta-comet-Monadnock Trail continues roughly 20 miles to the summit of Mount Monadnock.

To continue to Royalston Falls, follow yellow-blazed Tully Trail downstream along the east banks of Falls Brook. Although the walking is generally easy, numerous rocks and tree roots creep into the narrow path, so be sure to watch your footing. Upstream from the falls are a variety of interesting features that have been scoured by the brook, including a rocky chasm, several small cascades, and a pool at the confluence with another brook.

A colorful mushroom often visible in the ravine is the hemlock varnish shelf, which grows on the bark of conifer trees and has demonstrated medicinal benefits. Bluebead lily, indentified by elongated leaves and yellow flowers that bloom in May, produce dark blue berries (not poisonous, but rather foul tasting) during the summer. Unfortunately, many of the hemlock trees are now infested with hemlock woolly adelgid, which is spreading throughout the uplands of central Massachusetts after several mild winters.

At 0.3 mile from the footbridge and NET junction, reach the lip of Royalston Falls and the junction with a white-blazed trail that leads to Falls Road (see last paragraph). A cable fence offers several safe perspectives of the 45-foot cascade and the dramatic rocky gorge. Falls Brook usually runs high in spring and after seasonal rains but often shrinks to a trickle during dry periods. In winter, tall icicles form along the gorge walls.

The falls are quite photogenic in all seasons. Overcast days are ideal for photographing waterfalls and forest streams because the diffused light reduces contrast and shadows in shady ravines. Use a sturdy tripod and a long exposure to create a blurred, flowing effect for the moving water. A polarizing filter will reduce glare and lengthen exposure times.

You can explore the base of the gorge by carefully descending the embankment below the falls. (Use caution on the steep slope and around the water when

Facing page: Falls Brook plunges 45 feet through a dramatic, high gorge.

the flow is high.) To complete this hike, retrace your steps on Tully Trail to the footbridge then backtrack uphill on the NET and Tully Trail to the trailhead, following the white and yellow blazes.

Falls Road, which was the main hiking route to Royalston Falls before the MA 32 trailhead was established, offers an optional approach from the east. From the Royalston town common, follow MA 68 for 1.4 miles then turn right on Falls Road and continue 2.3 miles to the end of the maintained road. Here the road becomes rough; parking is recommended at a pullout about 100 feet from the last residence. (*Note:* There are several other pullouts farther along; use caution and do not block the road.) Follow Falls Road downhill at a moderately steep grade to a stream crossing at a washed-out bridge. Make a short climb past several former timber harvest sites to the junction with the white-blazed connecting trail, which offers a quick 0.3-mile walk over rolling terrain to the junction with Tully Trail at the falls. The round-trip takes about 1.25 hours with an overall elevation gain of 585 feet.

DID YOU KNOW?

In the nineteenth century, the land around Royalston Falls was mostly cleared for agriculture, and the falls were the site of a town playground, a picnic area, and a casino with a dance band. Visitors used a ladder to reach the base of the falls. The property was donated to The Trustees of Reservations by the Foote family during the 1950s.

MORE INFORMATION

Open sunrise to sunset year-round, no fee. No restrooms. Biking and dogs are allowed. Hunting is allowed in accordance with state laws. For more information, visit thetrustees.org or call 978-249-4957. For information on the New England Trail, visit newenglandtrail.org.

WINTER ACTIVITIES

Skiing and snowshoeing are allowed. The portion of the route from the main entrance to Falls Brook is moderately steep, with some wet and rocky areas. The segment of Tully Trail from Falls Brook to Royalston Falls is narrow, rocky, and potentially icy in winter; hikers should bring traction devices for hiking boots and use caution around the brook and falls.

NEARBY

For waterfall enthusiasts, Doane's Falls (Trip 35) and Spirit Falls (Trip 34), also located in Royalston, are excellent options for day trips. Seasonal camping is available at Tully Lake Campground, near Doane's Falls Reservation. Food is available at Royalston General Store on MA 68 in South Royalston; there are restaurants in Athol and Baldwinville (a village of Templeton).

34

JACOBS HILL RESERVATION

Panoramic valley views, a ridge trail through hemlock-hardwood forests, Little Pond, and Spirit Falls reward visitors to this scenic, lesser-known destination near the Royalston town common.

LOCATION
Royalston, MA

RATING
Easy to Moderate

DISTANCE
2.7 miles

ELEVATION GAIN
480 feet

ESTIMATED TIME
2 hours

MAPS
AMC Massachusetts Trail Map 4; USGS Royalston; The Trustees of Reservations map: thetrustees.org/assets/documents/places-to-visit/trailmaps/Tully-Trail-Map.pdf

U.S. Army Corps of Engineers map: www.nae.usace.army.mil/Portals/74/docs/Recreation/TUL/TULParkMap2013.pdf

DIRECTIONS

From the west, on MA 2 in Athol, take Exit 17 and follow MA 32 north 0.9 mile to the junction with MA 2A. Turn left onto MA 32/MA 2A and continue 1.4 miles then turn right to stay on MA 32. After crossing the bridge over Millers River, turn right on Chestnut Hill Road and continue 6.4 miles to the junction with MA 68 at Royalston town common. At Newton Library, turn left and follow MA 68 north 0.6 mile to the reservation entrance on the left.

From the east, on MA 2, take Exit 19 in Phillipston and follow US 202 north 2.4 miles. Turn left on MA 68 and continue 8.6 miles past Birch Hill Dam to Royalston. Turn left at Newton Library to stay on MA 68 and continue 0.6 mile to the reservation entrance on the left. *GPS coordinates: 42° 40.572' N, 72° 11.916' W.*

TRAIL DESCRIPTION

Jacobs Hill Reservation, another highlight of Tully Trail, protects 175 acres along the crest of a ridge above Long Pond and the East Branch of Tully River, where overlooks at Jacobs Hill and the Ledges offer panoramic easterly views across the valley. Between the overlooks is Spirit Falls, where the seasonal outflow from Little Pond drops 150 feet in a long series of cascades. This hike, which includes a portion of Tully Trail, combines the reservation's 1.5-mile loop trail with an optional side trip to the Ledges, separated from the main tract by private land.

From the information sign, follow the white-blazed trail across a wide power-line clearing at the swampy edge of

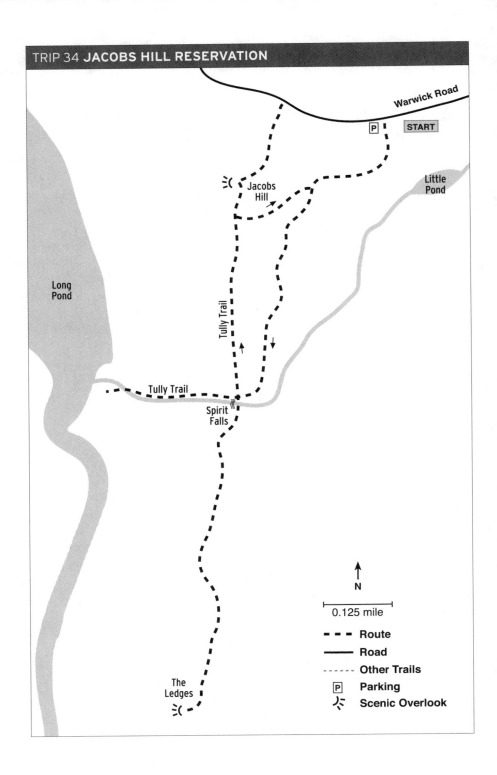

Warwick Road

P

START

Little Pond

Jacobs Hill

Long Pond

Tully Trail

Tully Trail

Spirit Falls

The Ledges

N

0.125 mile

- - - Route
——— Road
------- Other Trails
P Parking
Scenic Overlook

Little Pond. Watch for moose, great blue herons, and black bears, which often feed on fruit shrubs in the clearing and at the edge of the wetland during the summer. Enter the woods and head uphill through hemlock-hardwood forest to a Y junction at 0.25 mile, where the loop begins. Bear left toward Spirit Falls. (The right fork of the trail, your return route, leads up the slope toward Jacobs Hill, at the crest of the ridge.) Continue over rolling terrain through the woods above Little Pond, which can be glimpsed through the trees on the left. A variety of mushrooms grow along the forest floor during the warm months, including *russula emetica*, which is distinguished by its bright red cap. The beech and maple groves are characteristic of the northern hardwood forests that thrive in cool upland settings, such as Jacobs Hill.

At 1.0 mile (about 25 to 30 minutes), reach an open point at the outlet of Little Pond, a boggy wetland bordered by tamarack and spruce trees. The outflow is the source of Spirit Falls, a long series of cascades created by Spirit Falls Brook tumbling 200 feet down the steep slope of the Tully River valley to Long Pond. The brook's flow is highly seasonal, and the best time to see the falls running at a high volume is in the spring or after heavy rain. Follow the trail along the crest of the falls to a four-way junction with the long-distance, yellow-blazed Tully Trail and the white-blazed side trail to the Ledges. For the best views of Spirit Falls, continue straight and follow Tully Trail (south) on a steep descent along the rocky cascades; backtrack uphill to return to the junction. To continue the loop and bypass the side trip to the Ledges, turn right and follow Tully Trail north uphill, toward Jacobs Hill.

To make the 0.6-mile (one-way) trip to the lookout at the Ledges, step across the brook (easy most times of the year but may be wet during high water periods) and follow the white-blazed trail uphill through mixed forest of hemlock, pine, and hardwood, to the edge of the ridge. After passing the reservation boundary, continue roughly 0.25 mile through privately owned land; you'll pass a former timber harvest site, the headwaters of a seasonal brook in a rocky area, and a birch grove that offers golden foliage in autumn. Shortly after reentering the reservation, bear right to reach the rocky lookout at the trail's end, where the panoramic views include the north end of Tully Lake to the south, Tully Mountain across the valley to the west, and the distant profile of Mount Grace in Warwick on the northwestern horizon. A stone bench offers a great spot for a rest break or a picnic.

After enjoying the sights, retrace your steps to the junction at Spirit Falls. Resume the circuit on yellow-blazed Tully Trail, which will lead you on a steady but fairly easy northerly ascent along the ridge, through groves of shady hemlocks. At an area of exposed rock, there are partial glimpses of the valley through the trees on the left.

At 0.4 mile from Spirit Falls, reach a junction where a white-blazed trail departs downhill, to the right. Continue straight on Tully Trail for a few hundred feet to the Jacobs Hill overlook, which offers another fine 180-degree

The long ridge of Jacobs Hill, a highlight of Tully Trail, includes two overlooks with sweeping views across Long Pond and the Tully River valley.

perspective of the valley, including the north end of Long Pond and the winding Tully River above the inlet. Sunsets can be spectacular from this point. In late September and early October, enjoy a bird's-eye view of the bright red foliage of the swamp maples in the wetlands bordering the pond's inlet. Watch for common ravens, which are larger than crows and have a deeper *cronk* call, soaring along the valley ridge. They are known for their intelligence and often work together when gathering food.

From the lookout, backtrack to the junction with the white-blazed trail, which will lead you downhill to the start of the loop. (You can also continue north on Tully Trail for a few hundred feet to a posted junction then turn right and follow another white-blazed connecting trail to the start of the loop.) Retrace your steps past the swamp and power line to the trailhead.

DID YOU KNOW?

The views from Jacobs Hill inspired Massachusetts Secretary of Environmental Affairs Robert Durand to authorize the Tully Initiative, which protected nearly 10,000 acres of the Tully River valley, in 2000. The valley is part of the North Quabbin Bioreserve, which encompasses 120,000 acres in eleven north-central Massachusetts towns.

MORE INFORMATION

Open sunrise to sunset year-round. No restrooms. Dogs are allowed; biking is not allowed. Hunting is allowed in accordance with state laws. For more information, visit thetrustees.org or call 978-249-4957.

WINTER ACTIVITIES

Skiing and snowshoeing are allowed. The loop trail and the side trail to the Ledges mostly follow rolling terrain, with a few rocky areas. The portion of Tully Trail from Spirit Falls to Long Pond is very steep and rocky. Nearby Long Pond Mountain Bike Trail is an excellent skiing route in winter.

NEARBY

Seasonal camping and boat rentals are available at Tully Lake Campground at 25 Doane Hill Road (tullylakecampground.org, 978-249-4957 March to October, 413-684-0148 November to February). The Long Pond boat launch, adjacent to the campground, offers access to Long Pond, where there are excellent views of the Jacobs Hill ridge, and to Tully Lake. Food is available at Royalston General Store on MA 68 in South Royalston; there are restaurants in Athol and Baldwinville (a village of Templeton).

35

TULLY LAKE AND DOANE'S FALLS

The loop trail around Tully Lake and Doane's Falls leads to many scenic outlooks from the shores and a dramatic quarter-mile series of waterfalls and cascades.

DIRECTIONS

From the west, on MA 2, take Exit 17 in Athol and follow MA 32 north 0.9 mile to the junction with MA 2A. From the east, on MA 2, take Exit 18 and follow MA 2A west 1.2 miles to the junction with MA 32. Follow MA 32/MA 2A west 1.4 miles then turn right to continue on MA 32. Cross the bridge over Millers River and continue 3.3 miles on MA 32 to Tully Dam and the Tully Lake Recreation Area entrance at the Athol–Royalston town line. *GPS coordinates:* 42° 38.729′ N, 72° 13.349′ W.

TRAIL DESCRIPTION

Destructive storms in the early twentieth century, including the great flood of 1936 and the 1938 hurricane (see "A Terrible Trio," page 189), motivated the construction of Tully Dam in 1949 at the confluence of the East Branch of Tully River and Lawrence Brook, two of Millers River's largest tributaries. Tully Lake, which opened in 1966, is the centerpiece of a popular recreation area. At its northeast corner is Doane's Falls, where Lawrence Brook drops more than 250 feet in a quarter-mile series of cascades. The U.S. Army Corps of Engineers manages Tully Lake; The Trustees of Reservations manages Doane's Falls Reservation and Tully Lake Campground.

Blue-blazed Tully Lake Loop Trail offers a scenic 4.5-mile loop around the lake and Doane's Falls. It coincides with yellow-blazed Tully Trail from Tully Lake Campground to the recreation area entrance on MA 32. The route described here starts from the recreation area, where

LOCATION
Royalston and Athol, MA

RATING
Easy to Moderate

DISTANCE
4.5 miles

ELEVATION GAIN
225 feet

ESTIMATED TIME
2.5 hours

MAPS
AMC Massachusetts Trail Map 4; USGS Royalston; The Trustees of Reservations map: thetrustees.org/assets/documents/places-to-visit/trailmaps/Tully-Trail-Map.pdf

U.S. Army Corps of Engineers map: www.nae.usace.army.mil/Portals/74/docs/Recreation/TUL/TULParkMap2013.pdf

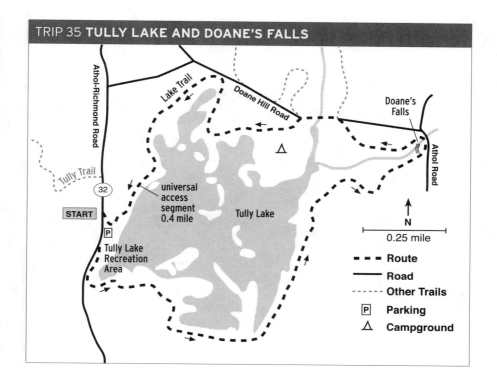

maps, restrooms, and picnic areas are available. Other trailheads are located at Tully Lake Campground, Doane's Falls, and Tully Dam. There are two universally accessible sections: a 0.4-mile segment along the west shores of the lake and a 0.2-mile segment at lower Doane's Falls. To visit Doane's Falls without completing the full loop, park at the Doane's Falls Reservation entrance on Doane Hill Road.

From the recreation area, walk up the access road to MA 32 then turn left and follow MA 32 (light traffic) 0.3 mile to Tully Dam, where there is a scenic overview of Tully Lake and a westerly view to Tully Mountain. From the sign at the start of the disc golf course, walk down the grassy slope and follow Tully Lake Loop Trail past the course fairways and land that was logged to create wildlife habitat. Common yellowthroats, chestnut-sided warblers, and other songbirds frequent the regenerating vegetation in spring and summer. Continue over gently rolling terrain through groves of white pines and hemlocks, past a swampy area. Carefully cross a rocky stream at the lake's southeastern corner and follow the narrow path as it swings northeast along the eastern shores, past several brook crossings.

Tully Lake is one of approximately 50 sites in the state that has hosted nesting pairs of bald eagles, a species that has made a strong comeback in Massachusetts after being reintroduced at the nearby Quabbin Reservoir in the 1980s. Watch

The loop trail around Tully Lake provides near-constant views of the scenic shore.

for eagles soaring high above the tall pines or searching for food on ice in winter. In early spring and late fall, common mergansers, ring-necked ducks, and other migratory waterfowl use the lake as a resting point during migrations. Double-crested cormorants, which are common along the coast and have expanded their range inland, have also been seen here. In spring, painted trillium, pink lady's slipper, eastern starflower, and other wildflowers bloom in the acidic soil beneath the pines and hemlocks.

At the lake's northeastern corner, follow the trail away from the water to the boundary of Doane's Falls Reservation. You'll hear the cascades of Lawrence Brook through the trees, but the views of the falls are from the opposite bank. Make a moderately steep ascent of the east side of the hemlock-lined ravine to Athol Road. Turn left and follow the road to the nearby bridge over Lawrence Brook at the upper falls at 2.3 miles, where there is parking for two or three cars.

Cross the bridge and continue to an outlook at a cable fence, where there's a photogenic perspective of the upper falls and the stone arch bridge. Unlike waterfalls on seasonal streams, Doane's Falls usually has a steady flow year-round. Make a steep 0.25-mile descent along the west bank of the ravine, past a view of the middle falls on the left. (Use caution around dropoffs.) At the base of the cascades is the block-shaped, 20-foot lower falls. A few hundred feet farther downstream, Lawrence Brook empties into the northeast corner of Tully Lake. In summer, cardinal flower, a familiar sight along river and stream edges, grows along the banks of the brook. The bright red blossoms offer nourishment for ruby-throated hummingbirds and bees.

From the lower falls, bear right and continue along a universally accessible path to the Doane's Falls Reservation lower parking area. Turn left and follow Doane Hill Road to the bridge over the East Branch of Tully River, where the loop trail merges with Tully Trail, which enters from the east side of Long Pond. At 2.8 miles, enter Tully Lake Campground, where information, camping supplies, and boat rentals are available seasonally. At the day-use parking area, reenter the woods on Tully Trail and begin a pleasant segment along the north shore, with several fine views of the lake and its small islands. In mid to late summer, blue bottle gentians bloom along the trail edge. Cross a footbridge over the outlet of a marshy wetland and continue over a low knoll. Walk quietly and you may see common mergansers and wood ducks, which favor forested wetlands and swamps.

At the lake's northern tip, at the edge of Doane Hill Road, turn left to continue the loop, heading south along the western shore. White-tailed deer, as well as wood thrushes and other songbirds, are common here. Continue over gently rolling terrain past several stream crossings to a junction at the north end of the universally accessible trail, at 4.1 miles. A short path on the right leads to a beaver pond, where you may see dragonflies, including widow and slaty skimmers, in summer. At the next junction, a 300-foot-long side trail on the left leads to a small peninsula and picnic area with fine views of the lake.

This location is ideal for photographing sunrises, foggy scenes, and fall foliage, especially when the red maples on the lake edge are at peak color. Complete the circuit with a pleasant and easy 0.4-mile walk along the universally accessible trail past several interpretive signs to the recreation area entrance.

DID YOU KNOW?

Several mills, including a sawmill, a gristmill, a fulling mill, and a scouring mill, were built to harness the power of Doane's Falls in the eighteenth and early nineteenth centuries. The fulling and scouring mills were used to process wool. The falls are named for Amos Doane, who built the last mill near the upper pool in the early 1800s.

MORE INFORMATION

Open year-round, no fee. Dogs are allowed. Hunting is allowed in accordance with state laws. Tully Lake Recreation Area includes a boat launch, picnic area, disc golf course, playground, and restrooms. For more information, visit www .nae.usace.army.mil or call 978-249-9150. Swimming and biking are prohibited at Doane's Falls Reservation; for more information, visit thetrustees.org or call 978-248-9455. Tully Lake Campground, managed by The Trustees of Reservations, offers waterfront campsites and canoe and kayak rentals (tullylakecampground .org, 978-249-4957).

WINTER ACTIVITIES

Skiing and snowshoeing are allowed on marked trails. Tully Lake Loop Trail is narrow with a few rough areas and requires three short road walks. The segment at Doane's Falls Reservation is steep and rough in places. A good option for skiing is the 7.5-mile Mountain Bike Trail, which follows a narrow single-track path on the west and north sides of Long Pond and Tully River, and a wide, mostly level woods road on the east side.

NEARBY

Otter River State Forest, Lake Dennison Recreation Area, and Birch Hill Dam protect a large section of contiguous wetlands and forests in the upper watershed of Millers River. Attractions include many miles of woods roads and trails, boat launches, campgrounds, and swimming beaches. The Otter River State Forest and Lake Dennison entrances are on US 202 north of Baldwinville (a village of Templeton), and Birch Hill Dam is on MA 68 in South Royalston. For more information, visit mass.gov (Otter River State Forest, Lake Dennison Recreation Area) or www.nae.usace.army.mil/Missions/Recreation/Birch-Hill-Dam. Food is available in Athol and at the Royalston General Store on MA 68 in South Royalston.

A TERRIBLE TRIO: THE STORMS OF THE EARLY TWENTIETH CENTURY

During an infamous eleven-year period in the early twentieth century, western Massachusetts was ravaged by three devastating storms that caused substantial property damage and had lasting effects on the landscape. With its annual precipitation of 45 inches, plentiful rivers and streams, narrow mountain valleys, and proximity to the coast, the region has long been prone to flooding and to weathering the effects of coastal and tropical storms.

In early November 1927, the remnants of a tropical storm tracked up the Connecticut River valley then stalled between two other weather systems in northern Vermont. The storm dropped 5 to 10 inches of rain in places that were already saturated from unusually heavy precipitation that autumn, leading to extensive flooding throughout the watersheds of the Connecticut, Merrimack, Hudson, and Androscoggin rivers. In the town of Becket in the Berkshire Hills, Wheeler Reservoir Dam failed, releasing a wave of water that destroyed more than 50 buildings in the town center. Three of the giant Keystone Arches railroad bridges on Westfield River were washed out, although crews were able to reopen the rail line in eleven days. The Connecticut River crested at 15 feet above Holyoke Dam, and severe flooding extended downstream to Hartford. In Vermont, where the storm is regarded as the worst natural disaster in the state's history, 85 people were killed, 9,000 were left homeless, many towns were uninhabitable for weeks, and nearly 1,300 bridges were destroyed.

The great floods of March 1936 caused even more widespread damage throughout New England and the eastern United States. During the winter of 1935 to 1936, prolonged cold temperatures and heavy snowfall created a deep snowpack in the mountains and many ice jams on rivers. The pattern changed suddenly in March, when a series of unusual late-winter rainstorms abruptly melted the snow, causing massive flooding that destroyed many homes, businesses, mills, roads, railways, and bridges. In the narrows below Mount Tom, an ice jam caused the Connecticut River to carve a new channel and shear off a 1,000-foot section of the granite Holyoke Dam. A 6-mile ice buildup damaged the giant hydroelectric dam at Vernon, Vermont, prompting evacuations in fears of a potentially catastrophic flood—which fortunately didn't happen. Many residents of the towns of Sunderland and Hadley were evacuated to the nearby colleges in Amherst, which were pressed into service as emergency shelters.

The flooding finally began to recede in late March, leaving behind corridors of destruction along many waterways. In New England, about 200 people were killed, transportation and communication infrastructures were crippled, and 50,000 residents of the lower Connecticut Valley were left homeless. The long duration of the rains allowed meteorologists to issue advance warnings that prevented additional fatalities.

A mere year and a half later, the region felt the force of the most destructive weather event in New England's history: the hurricane of September 1938. Only two other hurricanes, in 1635 and 1815, have caused significant destruction in interior New England since European settlement. Unlike most other hurricanes, which track along the coast, this storm, also known as the Long Island Express due to its rapid movement, took an unprecedented northwesterly turn across the interior uplands. Winds blew down an estimated 275 million trees, causing long-lasting effects on forests that linger today. Spurred by fears of potential fire hazards, people stored fallen trees in lakes and ponds. In addition to the wind damage, which mostly occurred on the east side of the storm, a round of catastrophic flooding once again impacted many communities. In Ware, Massachusetts, the floodwaters crested 6 feet higher than during the 1936 storm.

In the aftermath, the government authorized the U.S. Army Corps of Engineers to construct a network of flood-control dams in the Connecticut River basin, including Knightville Dam and Littleville Lake on Westfield River, Birch Hill Dam and Tully Lake in the Millers River watershed, and Barre Falls Dam on Ware River. Although severe storms, including Hurricane Diane (1955), the heavy rains of April 1987, and Tropical Storm Irene (2011), have continued to affect central Massachusetts, these impoundments have saved river communities millions of dollars by mitigating flood damage. In addition to their value for public safety, the dams are also the centerpieces of conservation areas that offer a variety of recreational opportunities and provide habitats for wildlife.

36

RUTLAND BROOK WILDLIFE SANC[TUARY]

From the shores of Connor Pond, this hike follows the cascades of Rutland Brook through an enchanting forest of giant hemlocks and pines. An optional extension leads to the dramatic Porcupine Ledge atop Sherman Hill.

DIRECTIONS

From MA 2 take Exit 17 in Athol and follow MA 32 south 6.3 miles to the junction with MA 122 in Petersham. Turn left and follow MA 32/MA 122 south 3.0 miles to Connor Pond at the Petersham–Barre town line. Turn left on Pat Connor Road, then bear left and follow the dirt road along the shore 0.2 mile to the sanctuary parking area and information sign. *GPS coordinates: 42° 27.791′ N, 72° 09.677′ W.*

TRAIL DESCRIPTION

Rutland Brook Wildlife Sanctuary is one of several properties, including the Swift River Reservation, Brooks Woodland Preserve, and Harvard Forest, that form a large conservation corridor along the East Branch of Swift River, Quabbin Reservoir's largest water source. The protected land helps ensure high-quality drinking water for more than 2.5 million residents of eastern Massachusetts. This mostly easy outing (apart from a short climb up Sherman Hill, which can be bypassed), combines several of the sanctuary's well-marked trails. As on other Mass Audubon trails, blue blazes indicate that you're heading away from the trailhead, and yellow blazes mark the return route.

Begin by following John Woolsey Trail along the northeast shores of Connor Pond, an impoundment of the East Branch of Swift River. In early spring and late autumn, flocks of migratory waterfowl, such as common and hooded mergansers and ring-necked ducks, use the pond as a resting place during travels to and from their northern

LOCATION
Petersham, MA

RATING
Easy to Moderate

DISTANCE
2.6 miles

ELEVATION GAIN
500 feet

ESTIMATED TIME
1.75 hours

MAPS
USGS Petersham;
Mass Audubon map:
massaudubon.org/content/
download/7925/144302/file/
rutland_trails.pdf

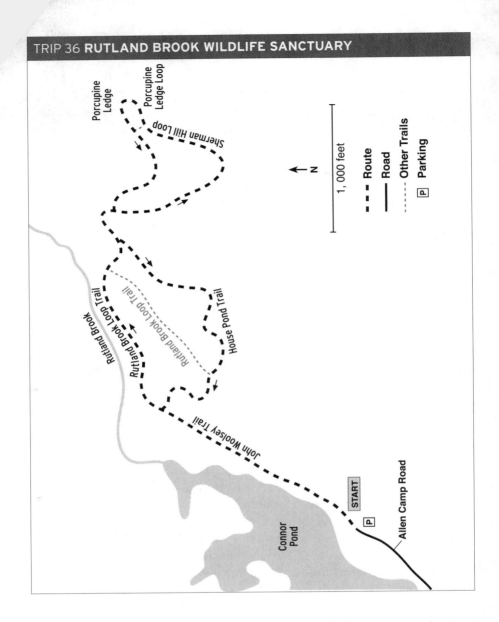

breeding grounds. Familiar year-round residents include river otters, beavers, and mink. Watch for belted kingfishers diving into the water on hunting rounds.

The pond, stocked annually by the Division of Fisheries and Wildlife, is a popular destination for anglers; mink sometimes visit, looking for a free meal. From Connor Pond dam, the East Branch of Swift River flows south through the adjacent Swift River Reservation before emptying into Quabbin Reservoir at Pottapaug Pond.

Follow John Woolsey Trail along the edge of a meadow that offers habitat for bluebirds, tree swallows, red and gray foxes, and white-tailed deer. From the edge of the field, continue past wetlands at the pond's north end. In spring, you may see a few nonnative wildflowers, including white trillium, mayapple, and yellow flag iris, which blooms along the pond edge in late May and early June. Some of these are holdovers from gardens planted by Mary Allen, whose family owned a summer camp on the land in the mid-twentieth century.

At a marked junction 0.4 mile from the trailhead, reach the start of Rutland Brook Loop Trail. Continue straight for a few hundred feet to a footbridge at the sanctuary boundary, where Rutland Brook empties into Swift River at the north end of Connor Pond. The property on the opposite side of the bridge is part of the Brooks Woodland Preserve, which offers additional trails (see "More Information"). Turn right and follow Rutland Brook Loop Trail on an easy ascent along the east banks of the rocky, cascading brook. This portion of the trail is especially scenic in spring, when the brook is often roaring with a high volume. Giant hemlocks and white pines grow out of the well-watered soil.

At the crest of the cascades is a beaver wetland, another good place to watch for waterfowl, river otters, and wading birds. The beaver dam and a lodge are visible from the pond's edge. At the junction with Ridge Trail, bear left and make a short climb to the nearby junction with House Pond Trail. Here you can make the side trip to Sherman Hill and the Porcupine Ledges or turn right to bypass the climb and continue the loop on House Pond Trail.

To reach Sherman Hill, follow Ridge Trail up to the start of Sherman Hill Loop. The right branch of the loop offers a slightly longer but easier ascent to the top. After passing a large shagbark hickory tree, the trail turns sharply left (north) and reaches the 1,210-foot summit: the highest point in Petersham, although trees obscure the views. A quick 0.1-mile detour on Porcupine Ledge Trail will bring you to the base of the striking 40-foot Porcupine Ledge, so named because it is the site of a porcupine den. Eastern coyotes and fishers also make dens in similar rocky openings and caves. Notoriously slow movers, American porcupines use their coating of about 30,000 quills to deter potential predators. The quills are large, stiff hairs with tiny barbs that are difficult to remove, as many dog owners can attest. In late spring, hardy red columbines, a wildflower that thrives in rocky habitats with marginal growing conditions, sprout from thin cracks in the ledge.

After exploring, return to Sherman Hill Loop and turn right to make a quick, steep descent back to the junctions with Ridge Trail and House Pond Trail. Turn left on House Pond Trail and descend to a grove of "wolf trees," or giant forked white pines that foresters left uncut. The adjacent hemlock forests serve as important wintering areas for white-tailed deer, moose, and other wildlife. The dense evergreen cover provides shelter from heavy snow and insulation from cold temperatures. Watch for "runs," or well-defined trails in snow made by deer

Rutland Brook cascades through hemlocks and pines to its confluence with Swift River at Connor Pond.

herds, and the large, heart-shaped tracks of moose. Unfortunately, hemlock woolly adelgid, an insect pest, arrived in the Swift River valley in recent years and is spreading through the sanctuary.

Continue to follow House Pond Trail along the north side of House Pond, which was once part of the Allen family camp. At 0.3 mile from the Ridge Trail junction, turn left to rejoin Rutland Brook Loop Trail and continue a few hundred feet to the end of the loop, at the junction with John Woolsey Trail. Turn left and retrace your steps along the shore of Connor Pond to the parking area.

DID YOU KNOW?

The dam at Connor Pond was damaged by the Worcester tornado of 1953, one of Massachusetts's worst natural disasters. The storm formed near Quabbin Reservoir in Petersham and killed nearly 100 people in the city of Worcester and surrounding areas.

MORE INFORMATION

Open dawn to dusk year-round, no fee. The sanctuary is unstaffed and has no restrooms. Biking, dogs, and hunting are not allowed. For more information, visit massaudubon.org or call 978-464-2712.

WINTER ACTIVITIES

Snowshoeing is allowed on all trails. Watch for animal tracks along the shores of Connor Pond and in the forest. Skiing is not allowed at the sanctuary but is allowed at neighboring Brooks Woodland Preserve, North Common Meadow, and Swift River Reservation (see "Nearby," below).

NEARBY

Brooks Woodland Preserve, North Common Meadow, and Swift River Reservation, all managed by The Trustees of Reservations, protect more than 1,200 acres in the Swift River watershed. The 25-acre North Common Meadow includes a small pond and a former town pasture now maintained for grassland birds and butterflies. Trailheads for Brooks Woodland Preserve are on Quaker Drive and East Street; for North Common Meadow, on MA 32 and East Street; and for Swift River Reservation, on MA 122 and Nichewaug Road. Visit thetrustees.org for maps and information. The Fisher Museum at Harvard Forest, at 324 North Main Street (MA 32) offers a series of well-crafted dioramas on forest and landscape history and two interpretive trails. Visit harvardforest.fas.harvard.edu for information.

37

QUABBIN RESERVOIR: DANA COMMON

At the former town common of Dana, stone foundations and old roads serve as artifacts of the Swift River valley communities that were abandoned to create the Quabbin Reservoir.

DIRECTIONS

From MA 2 take Exit 17 in Athol and follow MA 32 south 6.3 miles to the junction with MA 122 and MA 32A in Petersham. Turn right onto MA 122/MA 32A and continue 0.5 mile to a four-way intersection. Turn left and follow MA 32A south 3.0 miles to the Quabbin Reservoir gate 40 parking area on the right (west) side of the road. *GPS coordinates: 42° 26.465′ N, 72° 12.535′ W.*

TRAIL DESCRIPTION

When Quabbin Reservoir was created during the 1930s as the water supply for the greater Boston area, four towns and several villages in the Swift River valley were abandoned and then flooded (see "The Lost Towns of the Quabbin Valley," page 201), dislocating 3,500 residents. The town common of Dana was located above the water line, so it was not flooded but was abandoned due to its proximity to the watershed. Although the 30 buildings that once ringed this classic New England village green are long gone, the mowed common, stone foundations, and old roads remain as evidence of the former community. The common and surrounding 68 acres were added to the National Register of Historic Places in 2013, the 75th anniversary of the disincorporation of the lost towns.

The former Dana–Petersham Road offers an easy, nearly level 1.8-mile (one-way) walk to the common, where several other old town roads converge. From the gate 40 parking area, follow the road past a small stream where marsh marigold and skunk cabbage, two of the first plants to emerge in spring, bloom in April. Pass the information

LOCATION
Petersham, MA

RATING
Easy

DISTANCE
3.6 miles

ELEVATION GAIN
75 feet

ESTIMATED TIME
2 hours

MAPS
USGS Petersham; Massachusetts Department of Conservation and Recreation map: mass.gov/eea/docs/dcr/watersupply/watershed/maps/eastquabbike.pdf

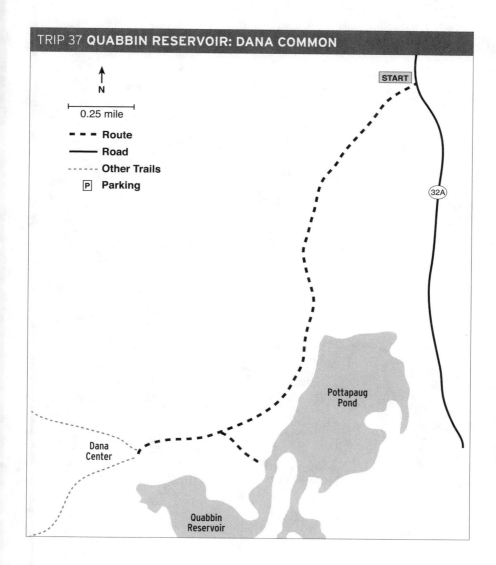

sign, where a portable toilet may be available, and walk by an old pine plantation and a small field. At 0.5 mile, reach a large meadow at the site of the former Eastview Farm, one of several farms once located along the road to Dana. Today the old fields are maintained as meadows to benefit wildlife and preserve the historic landscape. A small wood structure here is used as a checking station during the annual Quabbin Reservoir deer hunt, which is held for two days in early December. The foundations of the farm buildings are visible on the left side of the road.

Watch for a variety of wildlife in these clearings, including white-tailed deer, eastern coyotes, red and gray foxes, and eastern bluebirds. One of the most visible butterflies is the tiger swallowtail, easily identified by its bright-yellow and

black color. In midsummer, milkweed serves as the host plant for breeding monarchs, which are recovering from a significant population crash in 2013. A songbird that benefits from the mixed habitats is the eastern (or rufous-sided) towhee, whose distinctive *drink-your-tea* call is a familiar sound during spring and summer. Deerflies also thrive in mixed habitats and can be especially troublesome here in summer.

At 0.8 mile, more fields on both sides of the road mark the former site of Dana's "poor farm," which was a community farm, similar to those in many other rural New England towns, where people in need performed chores in exchange for room and board. Apple trees on the right, holdovers from an old orchard, offer food for deer, porcupines, and other wildlife. Through the trees on the left you can see a portion of Pottapaug Pond, the northeastern arm of Quabbin Reservoir.

At 1.5 miles, marker 40-2 signals the junction with the former Barre–Dana Road at a tall, spreading white oak tree. An optional 0.2-mile detour to the left leads to an old bridge site at a narrow channel of Pottapaug Pond. Watch for bald eagles, which nest at the pond, perched in the pines or soaring overhead on hunting rounds. River otters are often visible, especially when the pond is partially or wholly frozen in winter. During the summer, colorful dragonflies, such as eastern pondhawks and widow and slaty skimmers, frequent the vegetation at the pond edge.

From the junction, continue on Dana–Petersham Road past another large meadow, a portion of an old road on the right, and the former site of a blacksmith shop, marked with an interpretive sign. At 1.8 miles, reach the former Dana town common and a small stone monument dedicated to the former valley residents. On the northeast side of the common, an old walkway leads to the foundation of the former village school, which was next to the town hall and cemetery. On the opposite side are the sites of the Congregational church and the Vaughn residence, distinguished by its foundation of small, rounded stones and an old sugar maple that grows out of the cellar hole. The adjacent road leads to two other former houses in a clearing and a wooded knoll above Pottapaug Pond. On the west end of the common are the remains of several elaborate homes, a general store, and the former Eagle Hotel, which is easily identified by its large foundation.

Before retracing your steps to the trailhead, you can extend your walk by exploring the other old town roads that meet at Dana Common. From the west end of the common, the former Greenwich Road continues over rolling terrain along the north side of Pottapaug Hill then reaches scenic views from the reservoir shore at 2.0 miles from the common. Pottapaug Pond Road, a shorter

Facing page: The former town common of Dana serves as a memorial to the Swift River communities that were abandoned during the creation of Quabbin Reservoir in the 1930s.

extension, branches left off Greenwich Road roughly 400 feet west of the common and leads south 1.0 mile to the north shore of Pottapaug Pond. Skinner Hill Road, which begins near the hotel foundation, leads over Skinner Hill to a sharp bend known as Dead Man's Curve and the reservoir shore at Graves Landing, 1.8 miles from the common. Biking is allowed on these roads.

DID YOU KNOW?

Although most of the buildings of the lost Swift River towns were razed, some were moved by their owners to other locations. The former village church in Prescott is now part of the Mount Holyoke College campus in South Hadley. Guy Marvel, the valley's last holdout resident, left Storrsville (a small village near Dana Common) in 1941 after unsuccessfully suing the state over compensation for his land.

MORE INFORMATION

Open sunrise to sunset year-round. Biking is allowed on designated roads. Dogs are not allowed. Portable toilets may be available near the information sign near Gate 40 and at Dana Common. Hunting is not allowed, with the exception of two days in early December, when the area is closed to the public. The Quabbin Reservoir visitor center is located in Quabbin Park off MA 9 (485 Ware Road) in Belchertown. For more information, visit mass.gov/locations/quabbin-reservoir or call 413-323-7221. For information on the deer hunt, visit mass.gov/service-details/quabbin-reservation-deer-hunt.

WINTER ACTIVITIES

Skiing is not allowed; snowshoeing is allowed. The road to Dana Common is usually plowed for administrative use and is a good option for those who wish to avoid hiking in snow. A map of trails open to skiing on other Quabbin Reservoir watershed lands is available at mass.gov/eea/docs/dcr/watersupply/watershed/maps/quabski.pdf.

NEARBY

The Petersham Art Center, on MA 32 (8 North Main Street), offers monthly exhibits, as well as classes and workshops and sells gifts made by local artists. Call 978-724-3415 or visit facebook.com/petershamartcenter for hours and other information. Food is available at the Petersham Country Store and Quabbin Woods Restaurant on MA 32 in Petersham.

THE LOST TOWNS OF THE QUABBIN VALLEY

The year 2018 marked the 80th anniversary of the disincorporation of the four Swift River valley towns—Dana, Enfield, Greenwich, and Prescott—that were abandoned and then flooded during the creation of Quabbin Reservoir. Although the buildings of the Dana town common and the other communities are long gone, many stone foundations, old roads, railroad beds, mill ruins, and other historical sites remain as important artifacts of the residents whose lives were changed.

While the reservoir has great value as a resource for eastern Massachusetts, its story is also controversial. More than 3,500 residents were forced to abandon their homes, neighborhoods, and businesses in return for low compensation during the heart of the Great Depression, causing regional tensions that still linger.

After struggling to find adequate water sources for the greater Boston area for nearly 300 years, the state began plans for a giant artificial reservoir in the Swift River valley in the early twentieth century. The site was chosen because of its low human population, bowl-shaped topography, and relatively clean rivers and streams.

After the project was formally proposed during the 1920s, officials and residents of the doomed towns were powerless against the political interests of eastern Massachusetts. People gradually exited the vicinity in the 1930s, and the reservoir was filled in 1945.

Dana was established in 1801 from portions of the towns of Petersham and Hardwick. The common, which served as the town's institutional center, was located at the convergence of five major roads. North Dana, on the Middle Branch of Swift River, was a thriving industrial village with hat and soapstone factories and a box company. The Athol and Enfield Railroad, also known as the "Rabbit Run," transported these goods to outside markets and brought many tourists to the valley to escape the increasing congestion of nearby Boston, Worcester, and Springfield.

Originally known as *Quabbin*, from a Nipmuck term for "well-watered place," Greenwich, the oldest of the four lost towns, was established in 1754. Its waterways—the East and Middle branches of Swift River and numerous lakes and ponds—supported a thriving ice-harvesting industry in the winter and were popular camping destinations in the summer. Many farms were located on a fertile plain flanked by rocky hills; two of those hills, Mount Lizzie and Mount Pomeroy, are now islands in the reservoir.

Enfield, the largest of the communities, was located at the confluence of the East and Middle branches of Swift River at the south end of the valley, nestled in the lowlands between Prescott Peninsula and Quabbin Hill, a site visible today from the popular Enfield Lookout in Quabbin Park (Trip 28). From the 1770s onward, Enfield was an active center of industry, with many textile, wood, and woolen mills. In April 1938, an emotional and well-attended farewell gathering was held in the town hall, which was the last building standing in the valley when it was torn down in 1940.

In the northwest corner of the valley, Prescott sat atop a long ridge high above the Middle and West branches of Swift River. It was largely an agricultural community, with many orchards and dairy farms. With a population of only 300 residents in the early twentieth century, Prescott was the smallest of the towns, and it was abandoned shortly after the reservoir was authorized in 1928. Prescott Peninsula, which is above the flood line but closed to the public, was the site of a radio astronomy observatory used by area colleges from 1969 to 2011.

On the west side of the Swift River valley, the state also took over portions of the towns of New Salem and Pelham, including several neighborhoods and villages. In central Worcester County, residents had to vacate the villages of Coldbrook Springs, White Valley, and Barre Falls when the Ware River watershed was added as a supplement to the water supply network. Less known than the lost Swift River valley towns, they are also an important component of the local history.

In addition to Dana Common, there are many other historical sites to discover along Quabbin Reservoir's numerous roads and trails. At gate 30 at the junction of MA 122 and US 202 in New Salem, the former road to Millington (a village that is now underwater) offers an easy walk with views of the Keystone Bridge, restored farm fields, old sugar maples, a former tavern site, and a cove where the road ends in the water. At gate 35 off MA 122 in New Salem, segments of an abandoned railroad bed and the former Route 21 lead to scenic views, an old ice harvesting pond, the foundation of the former New Salem railroad station, and an observation tower used during World War II bombing practice. The Quabbin Park visitor center, in Belchertown, offers exhibits and trail information.

38

MANDELL HILL CONSERVATION AR

Situated on the grounds of a former hilltop farm, Mandell Hill Conservation Area offers scenic country views, outstanding wildlife habitat, and a pleasant loop trail through fields and forests.

DIRECTIONS

From the Massachusetts Turnpike (I-90) take Exit 8 in Palmer and follow MA 32 north 8.4 miles to the junction with MA 9 in Ware. Turn right onto MA 32/MA 9 and continue 1.7 miles through downtown Ware. Turn left on MA 32 and continue 3.4 miles to the junction with MA 32A in Gilbertville then bear left on MA 32A and continue 2.6 miles to Hardwick town common. Turn right on Barre Road and continue 1.0 mile to the entrance on the right, opposite the junction with Ridge Road. *GPS coordinates:* 42° 20.561′ N, 72° 10.632′ W.

TRAIL DESCRIPTION

Mandell Hill Conservation Area, managed by the East Quabbin Land Trust, encompasses an old farm atop Ruggles Ridge in the town of Hardwick. The fields are maintained for grassland birds, butterflies, and other wildlife. The 1.3-mile loop trail, an excellent walk for families, is marked with blue diamond blazes, and portions of the route are also delineated with wire fences that enclose livestock. Please keep gates closed and use caution around fences, livestock, and farm machinery.

From the white gate at the parking area, follow an old farm road south into the main fields, where there are fine open views. On the left are the large, well-preserved stone foundations of the former Mandell Farm buildings. At Opa's Garden, planted native wildflowers at the base of a large white birch tree offer nourishment for black swallowtails and other butterflies. The fields, formerly used to

LOCATION
Hardwick, MA

RATING
Easy

DISTANCE
1.3 miles

ELEVATION GAIN
100 feet

ESTIMATED TIME
1 hour

MAPS
USGS Ware; East Quabbin Land Trust map: eqlt.org/wp-content/uploads/2015/03/Mandell-Hill-Map-2016.pdf

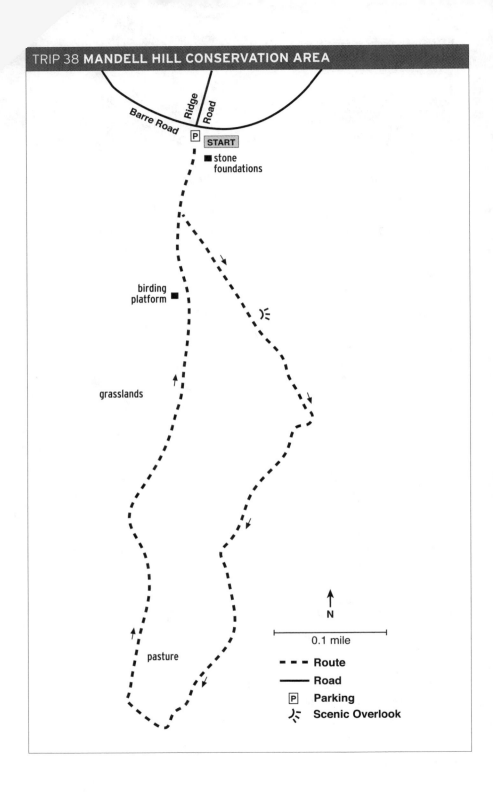

Barre Road

Ridge Road

P START

■ stone foundations

birding platform ■

grasslands

N

0.1 mile

- - - **Route**

——— **Road**

P **Parking**

)≔ **Scenic Overlook**

pasture

grow corn and hay and as pastures, are now leased to a local farmer who provides grass-fed beef for local and regional markets.

The loop trail begins at a junction at a stone wall. To make a clockwise circuit, bear left and follow the grass path along the right-hand side of the cow pasture. The sweeping views include the farmland abutting the conservation area, the Ware River valley and Wachusett Mountain to the east, and the hills of the Swift River valley to the west. Look carefully for a glimpse of the twin church steeples of Hardwick's historic town common.

In addition to providing fine views, the restored grassland, a habitat that has become increasingly rare in the Northeast due to forest regrowth, development, and a decline in farming, is crucial for a variety of wildlife. Watch for bobolinks and meadowlarks in spring and summer, especially in the fields to the right. Tree swallows and eastern bluebirds use the nesting boxes, and if you walk quietly and slowly, you may get a good look at bluebirds feeding along the trail or perched on the boxes. Near the pasture edge is a nesting box on a tall pole for American kestrels, small falcons that favor open areas. Sedge wrens, which are rare in New England and often well hidden in dense, low vegetation, have also been seen here. All of these species benefit from the ongoing habitat management.

At the edge of the field and stone wall, pass a gate at a low knoll shaded by a giant European beech tree. A chair-shaped boulder on the left makes for a fine spot to sit and enjoy the scenery. From there, enter the hardwood forest on the upper east slopes of Mandell Hill, an entirely different environment from the open fields. Here the trail narrows into a footpath and leads down past more stone walls, further evidence of former agricultural activity. In late summer, white wood aster, a characteristic species of dry eastern hardwood forests, grows along the trail edge.

After a 0.5-mile segment in the woods, turn right and make a quick climb to President's Field, an old pasture so named because George Washington's army reputedly camped there during Shays' Rebellion. Grazing cattle are rotated in from the main fields to help maintain the open habitat.

Flocks of wild turkeys frequent the forest-field edge, and chestnut-sided warblers, indigo buntings, and other songbirds forage on insects and seeds in late spring and summer. Milkweed serves as the host plant for monarch butterflies, which are recovering from a significant population decline.

Bear left and follow the blue-blazed trail through the woods around the south and west sides of the field. At the north end of the pasture, bear left again (you may have to step across a wire fence) and continue along an old farm road for a few hundred feet to the south end of the main fields. Pass a gate and a large rock pile and follow the marked grass path past stone walls and brushy thickets. Watch carefully for poison ivy, which grows along the trail as both a low and a tall shrub. The habitat benefits a variety of wildlife, including white-tailed deer, red and gray foxes, eastern coyotes, wild turkeys, butterflies, and dragonflies. In

The restored grasslands and farm fields at Mandell Hill include a viewing platform with sweeping, 360-degree views to Wachusett Mountain.

summer, goldenrod and other wildflowers are crucial nectar sources for bees and other pollinating insects.

Cross a wood stile over a stone wall and continue to a wooden viewing platform named in memory of Chris Ellison, a naturalist from Hardwick who recorded many interesting bird sightings at Mandell Hill and other places around the region. The 12-foot structure is an excellent location for bird-watching and enjoying scenic 360-degree views across the fields and countryside. You may even catch a colorful sunset or a rainbow after a passing storm. From the platform, complete the walk by following the grass path to the start of the loop and the trailhead.

DID YOU KNOW?
Mandell Hill and the surrounding open farmland offers a glimpse of the past, when Colonial settlers cleared three-quarters of central New England's

landscape for agriculture. Today the proportion has been reversed, and forests have reclaimed roughly 75 percent of the land.

MORE INFORMATION

Open year-round. Biking and leashed dogs are allowed; however, dog walking is discouraged to protect nesting birds. Hunting is allowed in accordance with state laws. The East Quabbin Land Trust office is on 120 Ridge Road near the Mandell Hill entrance; visitors are welcome to check out the scenic view. For more information, visit eqlt.org or call 413-477-8229.

WINTER ACTIVITIES

Skiing and snowshoeing are allowed. The trail is mostly level in the fields; it is narrower with a short section of rolling terrain in the woods. Use caution around wire fences and stone walls. Watch for animal tracks, especially around the forest-field edges.

NEARBY

The East Quabbin Land Trust manages several other properties with walking trails that can be combined easily with a visit to Mandell Hill, including Coxhall Kitchen Garden and Deer Park Preserve, on Barre Road, 0.3 mile west of Mandell Hill Conservation Area, and Patrill Hollow Preserve, on MA 32A, 0.5 mile south of the Hardwick town common. Food is available in Barre, Ware, and Gilbertville (a village of Hardwick).

This circuit, which combines a less-traveled segment of the Midstate Trail and old woods roads, leads through prime wildlife habitat in the Ware River watershed, including meadows, wooded hills, and Blood Swamp.

DIRECTIONS

From the junction of MA 62 and MA 68 in Hubbardston, follow MA 62 west 4.4 miles. Turn left at a four-way intersection on Coldbrook Road, enter Barre Falls Dam Recreation Area, and continue 1.1 miles to the parking area adjacent to Barre Falls Dam and the picnic shelter. *GPS coordinates:* 42° 25.673' N, 72° 01.507' W.

TRAIL DESCRIPTION

The Ware River valley is home to one of the largest sections of protected land in Massachusetts, where Barre Falls Dam Recreation Area, Ware River Wildlife Management Area, and Rutland State Park encompass more than 22,000 acres. The diverse habitats—swamps, beaver ponds, large meadows, forests, and rolling hills—support a wide variety of wildlife, including a thriving moose population. This circuit begins at Barre Falls Dam, follows a segment of the Midstate Trail over Harding Hill and along the perimeter of Blood Swamp, then loops back to the trailhead on old woods roads. This is an excellent route for bird-watching and wildlife viewing, with the opportunity to see a broad range of species in the different habitats.

At Barre Falls Dam Recreation Area, scan the open fields and the disc golf course for red foxes, bobolinks, eastern bluebirds, wild turkeys, and other wildlife. On spring evenings, American woodcocks make courtship displays over the fields. In late summer, this is one of the region's best places to see migrating hawks and monarch butterflies, which navigate thermal currents along the

LOCATION
Hubbardston, Barre, and Rutland, MA

RATING
Easy to Moderate

DISTANCE
5.8 miles

ELEVATION GAIN
405 feet

ESTIMATED TIME
2.75 hours

MAPS
USGS Barre; U.S. Army Corps of Engineers map: www.nae.usace.army.mil/ Portals/74/docs/Recreation/ BFDMap.pdf

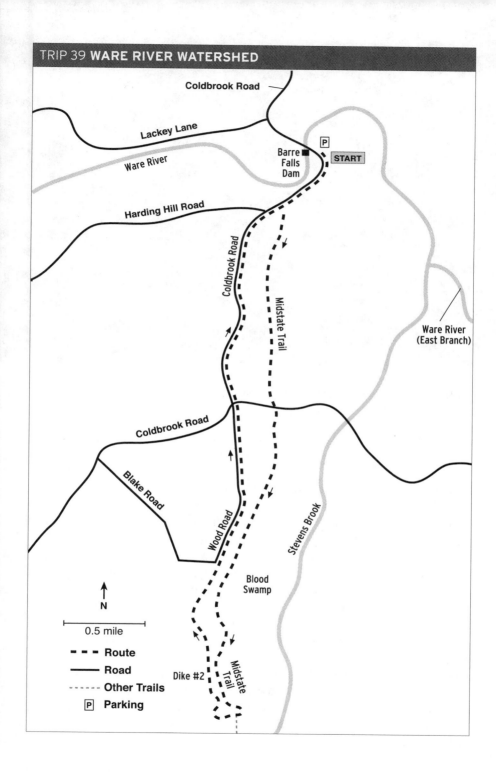

The Midstate Trail follows the edge of Blood Swamp, a wildlife-rich wetland that offers habitat for waterfowl and moose.

valley ridge. Barre Falls Dam was built in 1958 to mitigate flooding in the Ware and Chicopee River watersheds, and it has saved downstream communities millions of dollars of damage from storms, such as the flooding rains of 1987.

From the parking area, follow the Midstate Trail, marked with yellow triangle blazes, south along Coldbrook Road past a small cemetery. Shortly after the road becomes dirt, turn left at 0.2 mile and continue to follow the Midstate Trail on an easy ascent over the east side of Harding Hill, one of the rolling hills of the Ware River valley. Old stone walls mark former farm fields that have been reclaimed by mature forests of oak, maple, birch and other hardwoods. After crossing over the height-of-land (no views), descend the south slopes to the junction with Ruben Walker Road at a small pond at 0.9 mile.

Cross the road and follow the Midstate Trail through an old orchard adjacent to the pond, where apple trees with purple blossoms make for a colorful scene in May. Places where different habitats meet, known as "edges," are especially beneficial for wildlife because they offer food and water, cover from predators, and travel corridors. Watch for northern orioles in the apple trees, yellow warblers at the wetland edge, and turtles, dragonflies, and butterflies in the clearing.

Reenter the woods at a stone wall and continue through a shady old pine plantation to the edge of Blood Swamp, part of a series of wetlands on Stevens Brook, a tributary of nearby Ware River. Continue along the perimeter of the swamp past more stone walls. If the trail is flooded during high water periods, detour to the higher ground on the right. Walk quietly and you may see wood, black, and mallard ducks navigating around tall dead trees and shrubby coves, as well as river otters or raccoons foraging along the muddy wetland edge. The Ware River watershed is home to one of the state's highest concentrations of moose, thanks to the combination of wetlands, mixed-aged forests, and timber harvests, which creates a food source of regenerating vegetation favored by herbivores. The chances of seeing moose around the swamp are highest in summer, when they feed on aquatic plants and cool off in the water.

Follow the Midstate Trail as it bends away from the swamp to drier ground beneath tall pines and oaks along the perimeter of the wetland. After passing a woods road on the right, follow boardwalk bridges across a small brook and through a wet area. At 1.25 miles from Ruben Walker Road, the trail continues through the woods along the base of dike number 2, one of three flood-control impoundments at the south end of the swamp. Bear left at a marker post and follow the narrow footpath to the tip of the wetland. Then turn right and make a short climb to the junction with an administrative road at the west end of dike number 3 at the Rutland–Oakham town boundary. The junction marks the end of this hike's segment on the Midstate Trail. The remainder of the loop (3.1 miles) follows woods roads, portions of which are open seasonally to vehicles, snowmobiles, and other recreational uses. You have the option of backtracking on the Midstate Trail to the starting point.

To continue the loop, turn right (heading away from dike number 3) and follow the road west and north 0.4 mile to the next junction. Bear right and continue to follow the paved road across the top of dike number 2, where there are partially open views. After passing a brushy field on the right, cross the smaller dike number 1 and continue to a yellow gate and parking area at the end of the paved road. Bear right on Wood Road (labeled as Old Wood Road on some maps) and continue north 0.6 mile to the junction with Coldbrook Road.

Turn right and follow Coldbrook Road past the junction with the upper end of Ruben Walker Road on the right and a large meadow on the left, a good place to watch for white-tailed deer, porcupines, foxes, eastern coyotes, blue-winged and prairie warblers, and other wildlife. Continue uphill to a brushy meadow at gate CB16 on the right, where black-eyed Susans, New England asters, daisies, Queen Anne's lace, bottle gentians, and other colorful wildflowers bloom in the summer. The field is also a good place to see eastern bluebirds, indigo buntings, and a variety of butterflies and dragonflies.

From the crest of the climb, complete the loop by following Coldbrook Road downhill to the Midstate Trail junction and the Barre Falls Dam Recreation Area, 1.2 miles from the junction with Wood Road.

DID YOU KNOW?

Like the four towns lost to Quabbin Reservoir, the villages of Barre Falls, Cold-brook Springs, and White Valley were also abandoned when the Ware River watershed was added to the state water supply network, supplementing the Quabbin and Wachusett reservoirs during the 1930s. Coldbrook Springs, named for mineral springs that were believed to have healing powers, was once home to several mills and two popular resort hotels.

MORE INFORMATION

Open year-round, no fee. Biking and dogs are allowed. Hunting is allowed in accordance with state laws. Barre Falls Dam Recreation Area includes a sheltered picnic site, restrooms, a boat launch, and a disc golf course. For more information, visit www.nae.usace.army.mil or call 978-928-4712. For information about the Ware River watershed, visit mass.gov/locations/ware-river-watershed. The Midstate Trail Committee of the Appalachian Mountain Club's Worcester Chapter has a website and offers a guidebook for the Midstate Trail (midstatetrail.org).

WINTER ACTIVITIES

Skiing and snowshoeing are allowed. The trails include a network of wide woods roads that are good for beginner and intermediate skiers. These trails are also used by snowmobilers. The Midstate Trail is mostly a narrow footpath with a moderately steep segment over Harding Hill. In addition to Barre Falls Dam, there are several other access points, including Whitehall Pond in Rutland State Park off MA 122.

NEARBY

Rutland State Park, at the southern end of the conservation corridor along Ware River, includes a swimming beach and a fishing area at Whitehall Pond. The park also offers access to several woods roads and trails, including a portion of Ware River Rail Trail, a 12-mile recreational trail that leads from Coldbrook to Bald-winville. The entrance is at 49 Whitehall Road in Rutland off MA 122 near the Rutland–Oakham town line. For more information, visit mass.gov/locations/rutland-state-park.

THE RETURN OF THE MOOSE

If you spend enough time exploring central Massachusetts, there's a good chance you'll encounter a moose somewhere along the trails. This hasn't always been the case, as the moose population only rebounded in southern New England during the last quarter-century, following a 200-year absence. Their return is a testament to successful conservation efforts and the region's abundant protected land, but a recent population dip and the changing environment may reverse the cycle.

In pre-Colonial times, moose were present throughout the inland forests of Massachusetts. But like many other familiar woodland species, they were nearly extinct in southern New England by the early eighteenth century due to widespread forest clearing and unregulated hunting. In the early and mid twentieth century, there were only a few sightings of stragglers that had wandered south from New Hampshire and Vermont. In the 1990s, however, an increasing number of females with calves indicated the return of a breeding population, and by the turn of the century, the number of moose residing in Massachusetts was roughly 1,000. A smaller population gained a foothold in Connecticut in the late 1990s, and individual moose periodically have been reported in Rhode Island.

The resurgence is the result of a combination of short- and long-term factors. Central Massachusetts offers an abundance of ideal habitat, especially in protected areas, such as Quabbin Reservoir and the Ware and Millers River watersheds. The regrowth of forests over the past 150 years and hunting restrictions have greatly benefited moose and other species, such as black bears, white-tailed deer, fishers, beavers, wild turkeys, and wood ducks, all of which also have made strong recoveries in recent decades. The return of beavers was especially important, as their wetlands are crucial for moose, which feed on aquatic plants and use the water to cool off during the summer.

During the 1960s and 1970s, a widespread outbreak of spruce budworm disease in northern New England prompted many timber harvests to salvage dying trees. This created an abundance of mixed-age forests with hardwood saplings, which are an important food source for moose. The population grew rapidly with a high survival rate, and many moose dispersed to southern New England.

In recent years, though, certain North American moose populations have declined significantly, including northern New England. New Hampshire and Vermont moose numbers are estimated to have decreased by about 50 percent since 2000, which in turn has reduced the dispersal to southern New England. Although research is ongoing, some of the primary causes include the spread of diseases and parasites likely linked to the warming climate.

Many moose in northern New England have suffered significantly from winter tick infestations, which cause blood loss, malnourishment, and poor reproductive health. According to studies by researchers in Maine and New Hampshire, 75 to 80 percent of moose calves have died after being parasitized by ticks. Many biologists believe these outbreaks are linked to warmer and shorter winters with reduced snow cover, which allow ticks to thrive and feed on moose at the most vulnerable time of the year. Infested individuals, often known as "ghost moose," rub off much of their fur in an attempt to get rid of the ticks, leading to their sickly, pale appearance and vulnerability to cold temperatures.

Moose are also suffering from increasing incidences of brainworm, a parasite that causes fatal neurological damage, and liver flukes, which can weaken infested individuals and make them susceptible to predation and starvation. Both are spread by white-tailed deer, which have expanded their range north over the past century and now overlap with moose in many areas. In addition to promoting the spread of deer, warm temperatures cause heat stress for moose, which are boreal creatures adapted to cold environments.

In spite of these issues, the Massachusetts moose population appears to be holding steady for now at around 900 to 1,000 individuals. There have been fewer deaths from tick infestations than in northern New England, likely due to lower population densities. State officials have discussed enacting a moose hunting season, but that has received little legislative support as of this writing, especially with the downturn in moose populations elsewhere. While the future is uncertain, we can hope moose will continue to thrive in the wilds of Massachusetts for years to come.

Once scarce in Massachusetts, moose have seen a steady rise in population due to successful conservation efforts. Photo by Jerry Monkman.

40

ROCK HOUSE RESERVATION

Shaped by glaciers and once used by the Nipmuck as a shelter, the distinctive Rock House serves as the centerpiece to this popular reservation, where other attractions include giant ledges and boulders, the scenic Carter Pond, and a butterfly garden.

DIRECTIONS

From the Massachusetts Turnpike (I-90) take Exit 8 in Palmer and follow MA 32 north 8.4 miles to the junction with MA 9 in Ware. Turn right onto MA 32/MA 9 and continue 1.7 miles through downtown Ware. At the second junction of MA 32 and MA 9, continue straight 1.1 miles on MA 9 to the entrance on the left (north) side of the road. *GPS coordinates:* 42° 16.050′ N, 72° 11.874′ W.

TRAIL DESCRIPTION

Thousands of years ago, the Nipmuck, American Indians who inhabited much of central Massachusetts, used the giant outcropping now known as the Rock House as a hunting camp and shelter from cold winter winds. Today the well-marked trails and old cart and fire roads of the 196-acre Rock House Reservation lead visitors past ledges and other outcroppings, through forests cleared for agriculture in Colonial times, and along the shores of Carter Pond. This walk, which combines several of the marked trails, is excellent for families.

From the information sign, follow Inner Loop Trail on a quick climb to a junction on the south shores of Carter Pond. The former property owner, F. Adams Carter, built the spring-fed pond in 1930. Watch for painted turtles and frogs basking on exposed rocks and fallen trees, and dragonflies and damselflies in the vegetation on the shores. A large, angular boulder makes for a fine photo opportunity, especially when fall foliage peaks in early to mid-October.

LOCATION
West Brookfield, MA

RATING
Easy

DISTANCE
2 miles

ELEVATION GAIN
370 feet

ESTIMATED TIME
1.5 hours

MAPS
USGS Ware; The Trustees of Reservations map: thetrustees.org/ assets/documents/ places-to-visit/trailmaps/ RockHouseLoopTrailsMap.pdf

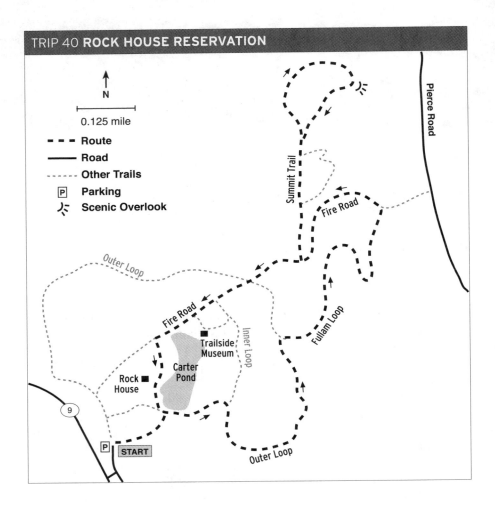

To begin the circuit, turn right at the junction and follow Inner Loop Trail past Carter Pond's earthen dam and into the woods. At a rock outcropping on the right, turn right on yellow-blazed Outer Loop Trail and continue past another giant boulder on the right. Cross a short boardwalk in a swampy area and make an easy winding ascent through mixed woods. In spring, listen for the chorus of wood frogs and spring peepers at vernal pools. At the next junction, at a wooden bench, turn right on Fullam Loop, marked with light blue blazes, and continue through an old pine plantation. Watch for a giant twin white pine on the right. Dense colonies of ferns grow beneath the pines in late spring. Listen for the territorial chattering call of red squirrels, which favor mixed conifer forests. In early spring, the musical trilling of pine warblers, one of the first migratory songbirds to arrive in the region, is a welcome sign of the changing seasons.

Cross a brushy power-line clearing where wild geranium, buttercup, bluet, and other wildflowers bloom in late spring. The evergreen juniper shrubs are a characteristic species of old pastures, clearings, and rocky hills. Reenter the woods and pass a giant red oak and the swampy headwaters of a seasonal brook. Follow Fullam Loop as it bends south back toward the power line then curves north and merges with Fire Road at the reservation boundary near Pierce Road. Turn left and keep following Fullam Loop on an easy walk along the needle-covered road to the junction with Summit Trail at two boulders on the north side of the power line at 1.1 miles.

Here you can turn right on Summit Trail to make a side trip detour up the hill or continue straight to bypass the climb, which shortens the hike by 0.6 mile. Summit Trail will lead you on a moderately steep ascent to the 1,020-foot hilltop, the reservation's highest point. At the crest of the climb, begin a short loop that leads past a privately owned field at the reservation boundary and a lookout with partial easterly views, especially when leaves are off the trees. Listen for the warbling calls of bobolinks from the field and watch for deer, foxes, wild turkeys, and other wildlife near the forest edge. Common ravens, easily distinguished from crows by their larger size and deep guttural call, may be seen (or heard) circling overhead. Like moose and black bears, they are one of many species that has returned to central Massachusetts in recent decades. Retrace your steps downhill to the junction with Fire Road and Fullam Loop and turn right to resume the loop.

Cross the power-line clearing, where the butterfly garden on the left includes butterfly bush, summersweet, globe thistle, bellflower, and other colorful perennials. Some of the common butterflies are tiger and black swallowtails, silver-bordered fritillaries, monarchs, duskywings, and a variety of tiny skippers. Also watch for hummingbird moths, logically named because they hover like hummingbirds while feeding on flowers. Many dragonflies also frequent the clearing, including twelve-spotted and spangled skimmers and eastern pondhawks. The latter is a familiar midsummer sight; the females are bright green, and the males light blue.

From the power line, where Fullam Loop ends, continue to follow Fire Road, which now briefly joins yellow-blazed Outer Loop. At the next junction, where Outer Loop branches to the right, rejoin Inner Loop Trail adjacent to Balance Rock, a glacial boulder neatly perched at the edge of a giant outcropping. A few hundred feet ahead is a side trail to the Trailside Museum, an unstaffed cabin that sits atop the ledge on the north side of Carter Pond. Inside are several natural history displays that were updated by volunteers and a University of Massachusetts geology student in 2017. There are fine views across the pond from the front of the cabin, but use caution near dropoffs.

Return to the road and bear left at the next junction to follow Inner Loop Trail to the Rock House at the pond's southwest corner. The boulders and ledges, which offered shelter from cold northerly winds, made an ideal winter camp site for the Nipmuck. Rock tripe lichens—which are common in northern regions, such as New England and the Rockies, and were used as emergency food by

Scenic Carter Pond, built during the 1930s, is nestled between a series of giant ledges and boulders at the aptly named Rock House Reservation.

early explorers—grow along the ledges. In late spring, enjoy the colorful magenta blooms of the planted rhododendrons next to the Rock House. Complete the loop at the south end of Carter Pond and retrace your steps downhill to the parking area.

DID YOU KNOW?

The Rock House is situated near two historical American Indian travel routes. The Nipmuck (or Nipmuc) tribe inhabited central Massachusetts and adjacent portions of Connecticut and Rhode Island, which was known as *Nippenet*, or "Freshwater Pond Place."

MORE INFORMATION

Open year-round, no fee. Dogs are allowed. Biking is allowed on Fire Road only. Hunting is permitted on a portion of the property on the west side of Outer Loop Trail. A portable toilet is available seasonally. Visit thetrustees.org or call 978-840-4446 for more information.

WINTER ACTIVITIES

Skiing and snowshoeing are allowed. The trails generally follow gently rolling terrain, with steep grades on Summit Trail. Fire Road, which connects the main entrance to Pierce Road, is a good skiing route. Use caution around the ledges and rocky areas.

NEARBY

Brookfield Orchards, at 12 Lincoln Road off MA 148 in North Brookfield, offers a country store and seasonal apple picking (brookfieldorchardsonline.com, 508-867-6858). Tip Top Country Store, at 8 Central Street off MA 9 in Brookfield, sells natural foods and has a gift shop featuring products by local artisans (tiptoponline.us, 508-867-0460).

41

WACHUSETT MOUNTAIN STATE RESERVATION

Views from Boston to the Berkshires, old-growth forests, East Wachusett Brook, and Echo Lake are among the many attractions of this moderately difficult loop on the southwest slopes of Wachusett Mountain, one of Massachusetts's best-known natural landmarks.

LOCATION
Princeton and
Westminster, MA

RATING
Moderate

DISTANCE
3.4 miles

ELEVATION GAIN
755 feet

ESTIMATED TIME
2.5 hours

MAPS
AMC Massachusetts Trail
Map 3; USGS Wachusett
Mountain; Massachusetts
Department of Conservation
and Recreation map:
mass.gov/files/documents/
2016/12/xg/wachusett.pdf

DIRECTIONS

From MA 2 take Exit 24 in Westminster and follow MA 140 south 2.1 miles. Turn right on Mile Hill Road and continue 0.5 mile. Bear left on Mountain Road and continue 1.2 miles to the reservation's main entrance, visitor center, and auto road on the right. Continue on Mile Hill Road for another 1.9 miles then turn right on Westminster Road and continue 0.7 mile to the roadside parking area at the Administration Road gate. *GPS coordinates:* 42° 28.453′ N, 71° 53.658′ W.

TRAIL DESCRIPTION

At 2,006 feet, Wachusett Mountain, a monadnock and prominent landmark of central New England, is the highest summit east of the Berkshires in Massachusetts. Thanks to its 360-degree views from Boston to the Berkshires, extensive trail network, and proximity to the greater Worcester and Boston areas, it has long been one of the region's most popular hiking and tourist destinations. Wachusett Mountain State Reservation was established as one of Massachusetts's first state parks in 1900. The upper slopes are home to several groves of rare old-growth forest that were discovered by researchers during the 1990s.

This hike, which begins at the Westminster Road trailhead near the reservation's southern boundary, combines several trails on the south and west slopes as a 3.4-mile

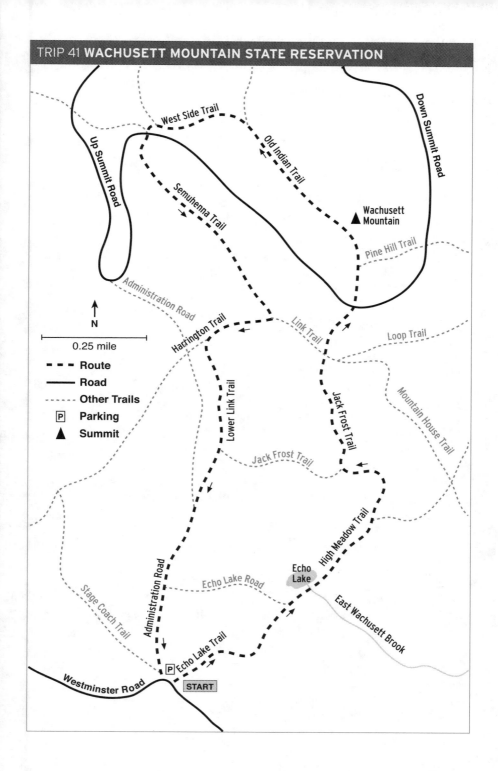

circuit. From Machias Pool, a small artificial pond next to the gate and roadside parking area, follow Echo Lake Trail uphill through an old pine plantation, where eastern starflower, mayflower, and other wildflowers bloom in midspring. Pass a stone wall and descend to a footbridge over East Wachusett Brook then continue to the junction with Echo Lake Road at 0.4 mile. Turn right and follow the road along the south side of Echo Lake, a pond with a splendid view of Wachusett Mountain's upper slopes. A grove of old hemlock trees is visible just below the summit.

From a picnic table and the remains of an old chimney at the east end of Echo Lake, begin the 0.9-mile ascent to the summit on blue-blazed High Meadow Trail. A short climb will bring you to the trail's namesake, an old orchard with fine easterly views. Pass the junction with Bicentennial Trail (which leads to the main entrance) and continue the moderately steep ascent past a series of rocky ledges. In midspring, this portion of the trail comes alive with the blooms of bloodroot, dutchman's breeches, trout lilies, and violets.

At the next junction, turn right on Jack Frost Trail, named for Dr. Harold Frost, who surveyed and created the route. Continue through an enchanting forest of old hemlocks on a mostly level ridge. Sadly, these trees are now threatened by hemlock woolly adelgid, although cool temperatures on the upper slopes may impede the spread of these insect pests. After 0.3 mile, turn left on Mountain House Trail, a wide, rocky old road so named because it once was the main route to the former summit hotels, which were built between 1874 and 1908. After passing the junction with Link Trail on the left, make the final ascent to the summit on the steep, rugged path. Cross the auto road and continue to follow Mountain House Trail another 0.1 mile to the parking area on the south side of the summit.

From the observation deck and other lookouts around the open, windswept summit, enjoy the long views in all directions. The most prominent landmark is Mount Monadnock, which rises above the surrounding hills of southern New Hampshire to the north, including the ridge of the Wapack Range. On the eastern horizon, the tall buildings of downtown Boston, 45 miles to the east, are visible on most days. To the west are the numerous hills and low mountains of central and western Massachusetts, capped by the rounded profile of Mount Greylock on the horizon.

In late summer and early autumn, the summit is one of the Northeast's finest places to see migrating raptors. The greatest overall numbers generally occur in mid-September, during the peak of the broad-winged hawk flights, when it's possible to see hundreds or even thousands of birds passing over the mountain. More than 10,000 have been recorded on especially active days. Other species regularly observed include sharp-shinned and Cooper's hawks, bald eagles, and

Facing page: From a platform on Wachusett Mountain's summit, where the viewshed extends from Boston to the Berkshires, hikers enjoy a striking perspective of the rising moon.

osprey; golden eagles have been sighted but are much rarer. The best viewing conditions are usually on partly cloudy days when the wind is blowing from the north. Experienced hawk-watchers are present most days counting the various species, and park rangers may offer interpretive programs on weekends.

From a posted trail sign near the observation platform, resume the loop on the combined Midstate Trail (marked with yellow triangle blazes) and Old Indian Trail. After passing the top of the ski area on the right, begin a steep descent of the rocky northwest slopes through unique groves of stunted old-growth trees. In spite of their diminutive size, some of the birches and maples are more than 300 years old. These woods have fortuitously survived the mountain's long history of development, which included clearing of the lower slopes for sheep pastures and timber, the establishment of the summit hotels, and the construction of the ski area. Use caution and watch your footing in this rugged segment.

At 0.4 mile from the summit, turn left on West Side Trail and continue 0.2 mile to a picnic area adjacent to the auto road. Make another left on Semuhenna Trail, cross the road, and continue 0.5 mile along a mostly level contour (a welcome break from the rugged terrain) across the southwest slopes. At the east end of Semuhenna Trail, turn right on the combined Harrington Trail and Midstate Trail and descend to a footbridge over the headwaters of East Wachusett Brook. In May, this section of the trail is adorned with the white blossoms of hobblebush, a shrub that thrives in wooded ravines.

Turn left on Lower Link Trail, which will lead you south along the banks of East Wachusett Brook and through dense mountain laurel thickets. Shortly after passing the lower end of Jack Frost Trail, cross the brook again and turn left on Administration Road (closed to vehicles). Trout lilies and other wildflowers bloom along the trail edge in spring. Complete the circuit with an easy descent past the junction with Echo Lake Road to the Westminster Road trailhead.

DID YOU KNOW?

In *A Walk to Wachusett* (1843), the writer and naturalist Henry David Thoreau chronicled an overnight visit to Wachusett Mountain. He described a large fire on Mount Monadnock that lit up the northwest horizon. Mount Monadnock's famous barren summit is the result of several large nineteenth-century fires, most of which were started by farmers to clear pastures and eradicate wolves.

MORE INFORMATION

Open year-round. No fee at the Westminster Road trailhead; a fee ($5 MA residents, $10 out of state) is charged for parking at the Wachusett Mountain State Reservation main entrance (345 Mountain Road in Princeton) or driving the auto road. Biking (on roads only) and dogs are allowed. Hunting is allowed in accordance with state laws. The visitor center at the main entrance offers maps, exhibits, restrooms, and vending machines. Seasonal restrooms are also available at the summit. The auto road is open from Memorial Day weekend to the last weekend in October. For more information, visit mass.gov/locations/wachusett-mountain-state-reservation or call 978-464-2987.

WINTER ACTIVITIES

Snowshoeing and cross-country skiing are allowed. Many of the hiking trails have steep, rough, and rocky sections, especially on the upper slopes. There are several wide unpaved roads, including West Road, Balance Rock Road, and Administration Road, that are easier alternatives. The adjacent Wachusett Mountain Ski Area offers 100 acres of downhill skiing and snowboarding trails (wachusett.com).

NEARBY

Wachusett Brewing Company, on MA 2A (175 State Road) in East Westminster, offers a retail store and free tours of the brewery, open Monday, Wednesday, and Thurday noon to 5 P.M., Friday and Saturday noon to 8 P.M., and Sunday noon to 6 P.M. For more information, visit wachusettbrew.com or call 978-874-9965.

42

WACHUSETT MEADOW WILDLIFE SANCTUARY

From the summit of Brown Hill to meadows, forests, and wetlands, this hike leads through diverse habitats on the grounds of an old farm with scenic views and outstanding opportunities to see birds and wildlife.

LOCATION
Princeton, MA

RATING
Easy to Moderate

DISTANCE
4 miles

ELEVATION GAIN
350 feet

ESTIMATED TIME
2.5 hours

MAPS
AMC Massachusetts Trail Map 3; USGS Wachusett Mountain; Mass Audubon map: massaudubon.org/content/download/8108/145671/file/wachusett_trails.pdf

DIRECTIONS

From I-190 take Exit 5 in Sterling and follow MA 140 north 2.4 miles to the junction with MA 62. Turn left on MA 62 west and continue 4.2 miles to the junction with MA 31 in Princeton. From the town common continue on MA 62 west 0.6 mile then turn right and follow Goodnow Road 1.0 mile to the sanctuary entrance at the road's end. *GPS coordinates: 42° 27.337′ N, 71° 54.306′ W.*

TRAIL DESCRIPTION

Situated on the grounds of an old farm at the base of Wachusett Mountain, Wachusett Meadow Wildlife Sanctuary is known for its diverse habitats and abundant wildlife. More than 2,000 plant and animal species, including 120 breeding birds and 73 butterflies, have been recorded on the grounds. While most of the farm fields have reverted to forest since 1956, when Mass Audubon acquired the property, several former pastures are maintained as meadows for wildlife. The trails are well marked, but a map, available at the headquarters, is recommended due to the numerous junctions.

At the parking area, enjoy views across South Meadow to Wachusett Meadow, a wet meadow on South Wachusett Brook. You may see the sanctuary's sheep herd at work grazing the fields, helping maintain the open habitat. Eastern cottontail rabbits, gray and red squirrels, and familiar backyard birds, such as cardinals, blue jays, juncos, and

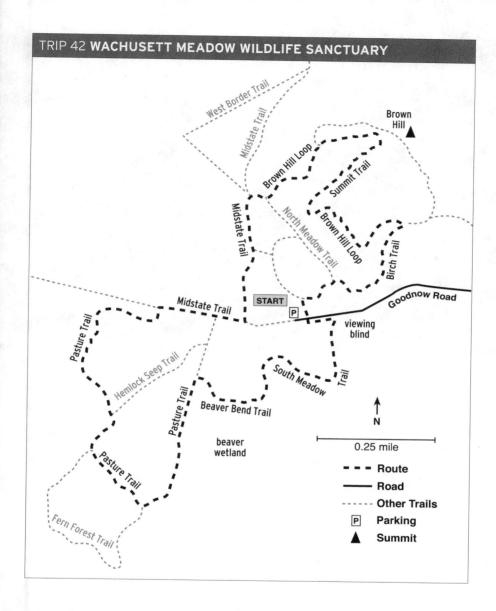

black-capped chickadees, frequent the entrance and bird feeders adjacent to the headquarters.

After signing in, begin on the north side of the building, where a butterfly garden attracts tiger and black swallowtails, among others, in summer. Follow the right fork of North Meadow Trail uphill past an old farm pond and its resident bullfrogs. In late spring and summer, the fields are alive with the blooms of milkweed, joe-pye weed, thistle, and goldenrod and other wildflowers, which

The wildflower meadows at Wachusett Meadow Wildlife Sanctuary are crucial habitat for monarch butterflies, which are recovering from a recent population crash.

are crucial food sources for butterflies and other pollinating insects. Milkweed is the only host plant for monarch butterflies, which are gradually recovering from a population crash in 2013 (see "Monarch Butterflies and Pollinating Insects," page 231). Other common butterflies include red-spotted admirals, great spangled and silver-bordered fritillaries, and silver-spotted skippers. The meadows also offer habitat for bobolinks, meadowlarks, eastern bluebirds, and other grassland birds.

At the meadow's northeast corner, turn right at a marked junction and follow Birch Trail through an old sheep pasture now forested with red oak and birch. At 0.5 mile, turn left on Brown Hill Loop and continue past a giant white oak tree that is more than 250 years old. Porcupines, wild turkeys, and white-tailed deer frequent the woods near the meadow edge. At the next junction, turn right on the south branch of Summit Trail and make a moderately steep 0.2-mile ascent along a stone wall to the top of 1,312-foot Brown Hill, where the open views include a portion of nearby Wachusett Mountain to the north, Little Wachusett Mountain to the east, and the Worcester Hills to the south. Brown Hill is an excellent hawk-watching destination in the spring and fall, as it is part of an active migratory corridor that includes Wachusett Mountain and Mount Watatic. Glaciers carved the grooves, known as striations, in the exposed rock as they passed over the hill during the last ice age.

Follow Summit Trail through a shrubby meadow of bayberry, sumac, and blueberry then turn left at a marked junction and follow the west branch of the trail past a ledge. Turn left again to rejoin Brown Hill Loop and descend the southwest slopes of the hill to a T junction at the trail's end. Turn right on Glacial Boulder Trail and pass another legacy of the ice age, a house-sized boulder deposited by glaciers some 12,000 to 15,000 years ago. At a four-way intersection, turn left on the combined Chapman Trail and Midstate Trail and descend to the junction with West Trail, an extension of Goodnow Road. (A left here will bring you back to the headquarters in about five minutes.)

Turn right and follow the combined West and Midstate trails past the east junction with Pasture Trail and a sign detailing a relocation of the Midstate Trail. Watch for American woodcocks foraging around the trail and field edges. Old sugar maples and stone walls line the road, which was once part of a stagecoach route to Templeton. At the next junction, turn left on the west end of Pasture Trail, which parallels the road before turning sharply left through the mixed forests in the southern portion of the sanctuary. Pass successive junctions with Hemlock Seep Trail and Fern Forest Trail. (The latter offers an optional short loop that extends the hike by 0.7 mile.)

At the second junction with Fern Forest Trail (at Fourth Pasture), Pasture Trail turns north and continues along an old farm road past Rock Fire Pond and Third Pasture, an excellent place to watch for butterflies, dragonflies, bluebirds, and other wildlife. In summer, check the milkweed at the trail edge for monarch caterpillars, easily identified by their white, yellow, and black coloring. At a posted junction at Second Pasture, turn right on Beaver Bend Trail and continue 0.5 mile along a narrow, rocky path to the northwest edge of the Wachusett Meadow wetland, which was the site of a large beaver pond that drained in 2010. Great blue herons abandoned a large rookery on the west side of the wetland after the pond emptied.

At a three-way junction at the base of South Meadow, turn right on South Meadow Trail and follow the grass path past an observation area on the north side of the wetland. A rare species that resides in the meadow is the Harris' checkerspot, a small orange-and-black butterfly that feeds on flat-topped asters in its larval stage. At the south end of the field, turn left and head uphill toward the photogenic sanctuary barn. A short side trail on the right leads to an observation blind at Wildlife Pond, a wetland on South Wachusett Brook. Watch for waterfowl and river otters in the pond and deer at the forest edge. Blue dashers and other dragonflies frequent the shrubby vegetation along the trail and pond edges in summer. Complete the loop at the parking area, which is to the left of the barn.

DID YOU KNOW?

The Goodnow family originally established a farm on the grounds in 1786. The Crocker family acquired the property in 1917 and donated it to Mass Audubon in 1956.

MORE INFORMATION

Open dawn to dusk year-round. Admission is $4 for adults, $3 for children; free for Mass Audubon members and Princeton residents. The sanctuary office hours are Tuesday to Friday, 10 A.M. to 2 P.M.; Saturday 10 A.M. to 4 P.M.; and Sunday, 12:30 to 4 P.M. The office is closed on Mondays except for Monday holidays, when it is open from 12:30 to 4 P.M. Maps and restrooms are available at the headquarters. Biking, dogs, and hunting are not allowed. For more information, visit massaudubon.org or call 978-464-2712.

WINTER ACTIVITIES

Skiing is allowed on West Trail, North Meadow Trail, and a portion of Pasture Trail. Skiers must sign in during office hours. Snowshoeing is allowed daily on all trails from dawn to dusk. Snowshoes are available for rent when the office is open. The sanctuary periodically offers snowshoe hike programs.

NEARBY

Wachusett Mountain State Reservation abuts the northern portion of the sanctuary. From the sanctuary boundary, the Midstate Trail reaches Wachusett Mountain's summit in 2.5 miles via Dickens Trail. Princeton House of Pizza is on MA 62 in Princeton town common; there are other restaurants in Leominster and Fitchburg.

MONARCH BUTTERFLIES AND POLLINATING INSECTS: A CONSERVATION CONCERN

The sight of colorful monarch butterflies in wildflower meadows was once a familiar sign of summer, but you may have noticed that monarchs have been rare in recent years. They have been gradually recovering from a significant population crash in 2013 and, like many other pollinating insects, are also in the midst of a long-term decline that is of considerable concern worldwide.

Monarchs have a dynamic but fragile life history. They are well known for their remarkable autumn migration, when individuals travel as far as 4,800 miles to wintering grounds in the mountains of Mexico and California. The butterflies that make this journey are part of a special generation that emerges in late summer and lives eight to nine months. The following spring, the next generations (which live three to five weeks) gradually make their way north across the continent, while at the same time, milkweed, the monarch's only host plant, emerges. Monarchs and milkweed have evolved a unique relationship: When caterpillars feed on milkweed leaves, they ingest toxins that deter birds and other predators. When food sources diminish and the days grow shorter in late summer, the fall migratory generation emerges and the cycle begins again.

Based on annual surveys of overwintering colonies, scientists have documented a clear long-term decline in monarch butterfly populations in recent decades. Pinpointing the reasons is a considerable challenge because there are many variables spread over thousands of miles. One of the most publicized and widely accepted theories is that the decline is related to a loss of milkweed due to development and modern agricultural practices, including the use of genetically modified, herbicide-resistant crops that allow farmers to easily eradicate other plants with pesticides. Species with limited adaptability and specific needs, such as the New England cottontail rabbit and the presumed-extinct ivory-billed woodpecker, are highly vulnerable to human-induced disruptions of their habitats and food sources. That said, some scientists, such as Dr. Anurag Agrawal of Cornell University, the author of the acclaimed book *Monarchs and Milkweed*, believe milkweed availability is not a limiting factor.

Another possible reason is an increase in unusual weather events in recent years, which many researchers believe may be linked to the changing global climate. Several severe storms in the Mexican mountain forests have caused significant mortality in overwintering monarch colonies. Although the wintering grounds have been protected as a World Heritage Biosphere Reserve since 1986, the forests have suffered from illegal logging, droughts, and outbreaks of bark beetles and parasitic plants.

The decline reached a critical point between 2012 and 2014, when the overwintering population dropped by 90 percent. Drought and excessive heat caused a poor breeding season in the South and Midwest in 2012, and unusually cold

Once a familiar sight in the Northeast, the monarch butterfly has rebounded quickly from a population crash in 2013, although their numbers remain concerning.

weather disrupted northbound migrants the following spring. The U.S. Fish and Wildlife Service began assessing monarchs for listing as an endangered species in 2014, a stunning development for arguably the country's most iconic butterfly. The crisis also attracted the attention of President Barack Obama, who commissioned a task force to investigate issues facing monarchs and other pollinators.

Fortunately, monarchs are usually able to rebound quickly from short-term disruptions when conditions are favorable, and there have been encouraging signs of a recovery. The two-year totals for the winters of 2015 to 2016 and 2016 to 2017 were up 600 percent from the height of the decline, even after a severe winter storm in 2017. During the summer of 2017, monarchs were reported with greater frequency than in previous years and were again a familiar sight in many areas of New England. Even so, the situation remains a concern.

Monarchs are not alone in their plight, as many other pollinating insects throughout the world have also suffered significant declines. According to a report released by the United Nations in 2016, 40 percent of invertebrate pollinators (mostly butterflies and bees) are potentially threatened with extinction. One phenomenon observed in many countries is colony collapse disorder, when bees abruptly abandon their hives. While research is ongoing, potential causes include the use of herbicides (with chemicals that cause neurological damage to insects) and human development of meadow and wildflower habitats.

The loss of pollinators is significant because they are responsible for the propagation of many food crops and flowers, thus playing a key role in the global agricultural economy. In turn, they are a food source for birds and other animals. Many ecologists consider butterflies to be "canaries in the coal mine," or early indicators of changes and potential problems in their environment. Identifying the causes of the declines is essential to preserve the many species affected and to ensure the overall health of our world.

43

LEOMINSTER STATE FOREST

A short loop provides outstanding views from the cliffs of Crow Hill, one of the region's most dramatic features. In the eastern portion of the forest, a longer circuit leads to rolling hills and scenic ponds.

DIRECTIONS

From MA 2 take Exit 28 in Leominster and follow MA 31 south 2.5 miles to the Gate 6/Crow Hill parking area on the right (west) side of the road for the Crow Hill trailhead, or 2.7 miles to the Gate 7/Rocky Pond parking area on the left (east) side for the Rocky Pond Road trailhead. *GPS coordinates:* 42° 30.934' N, 71° 51.410' W (Crow Hill), 42° 30.694' N, 71° 51.476' W (Rocky Pond Road).

TRAIL DESCRIPTION

Leominster State Forest protects more than 4,200 acres in portions of five towns, in the hills on the south side of MA 2. The extensive trail network, largely built by the Civilian Conservation Corps during the 1930s, offers many options for hikers and other recreational users. Described here are two loop hikes: a rugged but relatively short circuit over the dramatic ledges of Crow Hill and a longer outing through the forests and hills on the east side of MA 31. The trailheads are 0.2 mile apart on MA 31.

Crow Hill Loop

From the Gate 6/Crow Hill parking area, follow the blue-blazed dirt road, also used for emergency access to the ledges, on a moderately steep ascent through rocky woods and mountain laurels. Pass a stone wall and a large glacial boulder, partially covered with rock tripe lichens, on the left. At the road's end, at a turnout, follow the blue-blazed path uphill over rock steps. At 0.4 mile, continue straight

LOCATION
Westminster and Leominster, MA

CROW HILL LOOP
RATING
Moderate

DISTANCE
1.2 miles

ELEVATION GAIN
355 feet

ESTIMATED TIME
1 hour

ROCKY POND–BALL HILL LOOP
RATING
Moderate

DISTANCE
4.9 miles

ELEVATION GAIN
675 feet

ESTIMATED TIME
3 hours

MAPS
USGS Fitchburg; Massachusetts Department of Conservation and Recreation map: mass.gov/eea/docs/dcr/parks/trails/leominster.pdf

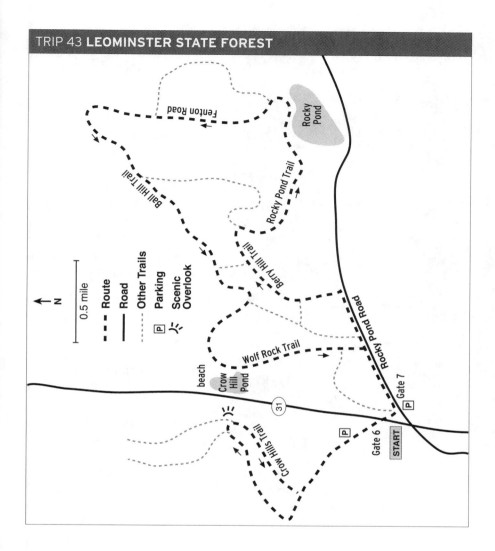

at a marked junction, following signs for the top of the ledges and picnic area. (The trail on the right leads to the base of the ledges.) In another 300 feet, reach the junction with the blue-blazed Crow Hill Trail at the picnic site at the south end of the ledges, where the loop begins.

Turn left and make a short climb to the junction with the yellow-blazed Midstate Trail then turn right and make a rocky scramble on the Midstate Trail to the top of the Crow Hill ledges. Continue along the ridge to overlooks with excellent views of Crow Hill Pond, the Monoosoc Hills, and the distant Boston skyline to the east, as well as Wachusett Mountain to the southwest. Fall foliage peaks in late October and lasts into early November most years. Use caution around the edge of the ledge and take care not to disturb rock climbers or their equipment.

Crow Hill's sheer, 500-foot-long cliff is a popular destination for rock climbers.

After enjoying the views, leave the Midstate Trail at the next junction and make a steep descent on stone steps to the junction with Crow Hill Trail. Turn right and continue along the base of the ledges, where you'll enjoy a different perspective of the dramatic cliffs. Again, use caution around rock climbers. At the end of the loop, at the picnic site, turn left and retrace your steps to the access road and parking area.

Rocky Pond–Ball Hill Loop

From the Gate 7/Rocky Pond parking area, follow Rocky Pond Road on an easy ascent past the junction with Paradise Road and Wolf Rock Road (your return route). At 0.4 mile, turn left on red-blazed Berry Hill Trail and make a moderately steep climb along a rocky woods road through groves of white pine and thickets of mountain laurel. When leaves are off the trees, Wachusett Mountain is visible to the southwest. In spring, listen for the trilling call of pine warblers, which favor open pine woods. Once common in Massachusetts, they have declined in places where pines have been succeeded by maturing oak-hickory forests.

At the crest of the climb, pass junctions with two trails on the left. (Both connect to Ball Hill Trail.) Following a sign for Rocky Pond Trail, continue on Berry Hill Trail on a moderately steep descent through forests of mixed hardwoods and pines. At the next junction, turn right on Rocky Pond Trail and descend the southeast slopes of the hill through more mountain laurel. Cross a creek and follow the narrow, rocky path past an outcropping and a giant boulder on the left. Rocky Pond soon comes into view through the trees.

At the base of the descent, turn left at an unmarked junction and continue to follow Rocky Pond Trail through old pine plantations on the north side of the pond. At 1.7 miles, reach the junction with Fenton Road. Although the loop continues to the left, a short detour to the right leads to an open view across the water to the upper slopes of Wachusett Mountain, about 3 miles to the southwest. The pond's outflow is the source of Mamouth Brook, which drains into Mamouth Swamp and Notown Reservoir at the state forest boundary.

Return to the junction and follow Fenton Road north along the east side of Ball Hill. Groves of paper birches, which thrive in sunlit openings and disturbed areas, line the road. Watch for tracks and signs of eastern coyotes, which are highly adaptable and have become widespread in Massachusetts since arriving during the 1970s. They often leave scat on rocks to mark their territories. At 0.6 mile from Rocky Pond, turn right at the road's end and follow a short connecting path to Ball Hill Trail. Turn left and follow the left branch of the loop, marked with light-blue blazes, on a narrow, winding route past mountain laurel and stone walls.

At the next junction, turn right and continue to follow Ball Hill Trail on a moderately steep ascent over the wooded summit of Ball Hill, which is shaded by more white pines. Then begin a moderately steep 0.8-mile descent to Crow Hill Pond. On clear days when the leaves have fallen, Mount Monadnock is visible through the bare trees. Continue on Ball Hill Trail past several junctions to the beach parking lot and a picnic area (a nice spot for a break) at Crow Hill Pond at 4.0 miles.

Walk to the left past the restrooms and follow yellow-blazed Wolf Rock Trail to a stone causeway that connects to the seasonal parking area on MA 31. Continue to follow Wolf Rock Trail on a pleasant, easy walk along the east side of Crow Hill Pond, with fine views of Crow Hill across the water. At the south end of the pond, cross several boardwalks and pass through a shady hemlock grove in a wet area. Complete the loop at the junction with Rocky Pond Road then turn right to return to the trailhead.

DID YOU KNOW?

After becoming a popular destination for Appalachian Mountain Club rock climbers during the 1920s, Crow Hill was used as a training site for U.S. Army troops from World War II through the 1970s. The 500-foot cliffs offer a number of climbing routes, ranging from easy to challenging.

MORE INFORMATION

Open year-round. A fee ($8 MA residents, $15 out of state) is charged at the Crow Hill Pond parking area in summer; other trailheads are free. The seasonal parking area on MA 31 at the Leominster–Westminster town line offers access to Crow Hill Trail and Wolf Rock Trail, but from Memorial Day to Labor Day it is available only for overflow beach parking. Biking and dogs are allowed. Hunting is allowed in accordance with state laws. Rock climbing requires a free permit available at the forest headquarters. For more information, visit mass.gov/locations/leominster-state-forest or call 978-874-2303. The Appalachian Mountain Club's Midstate Trail Committee maintains a website (midstatetrail.org) and a guide to the Midstate Trail.

WINTER ACTIVITIES

Snowshoeing is allowed on all trails. Skiing is allowed on multiuse trails and unpaved roads on the east side of MA 31, which are marked on the park map. The unpaved roads are also open to snowmobiles. The Gate 7/Rocky Pond Road parking area offers access to several ski trails.

NEARBY

Redemption Rock, a granite ledge and historical site where Colonial hostage Mary White Rowlandson was released from captivity during King Philip's War in 1676, is another potential starting point for a hike to Crow Hill or Wachusett Mountain. From the roadside entrance on MA 140 near the Princeton–Westminster town line (1.0 mile north of the junction with MA 31), the Midstate Trail reaches Crow Hill in 1.6 miles and Wachusett Mountain's summit in 3.2 miles.

44

MOUNT WATATIC

This moderately difficult but relatively short circuit, a fine low mountain hike for families, leads to long views from Mount Watatic's twin summits and a view of Wachusett Mountain from a lookout on adjacent Nutting Hill.

DIRECTIONS

From MA 2 take Exit 24A in Westminster and follow MA 140 north 1.9 miles to the junction with MA 101. Turn right on MA 101 north and continue 4.4 miles to the junction with MA 12 in Ashburnham. Turn left and continue 4.0 miles on MA 101 to the junction with MA 119. Turn left and follow MA 119 west 1.0 mile to the parking area on the north side of the highway. *GPS coordinates:* 42° 41.788′ N, 71° 54.272′ W.

TRAIL DESCRIPTION

Mount Watatic, at 1,832 feet, is the second-highest summit in Massachusetts east of the Berkshires. It is also the southern terminus of the Wapack Range, a chain of low summits that extends for more than 20 miles to North Pack Monadnock Mountain, near Peterborough, New Hampshire. The rocky, partially open top of Nutting Hill, Mount Watatic's northwest shoulder, offers views to Wachusett Mountain. This circuit combines State Line Trail (a former segment of the Midstate Trail) with the long-distance Midstate and Wapack trails, which overlap from the MA 119 parking area to the New Hampshire state line. Walking the loop clockwise as described allows for a more gradual ascent via Nutting Hill and a quick, steep descent to the trailhead.

From the parking area, follow the combined Midstate and Wapack trails along an old woods road to a beaver pond, part of a chain of wetlands at the base of Mount Watatic's west slopes. In summer, common green darners,

LOCATION
Ashburnham and Ashby, MA

RATING
Moderate

DISTANCE
2.8 miles

ELEVATION GAIN
700 feet

ESTIMATED TIME
2.25 hours

MAPS
USGS Ashburnham and USGS Ashby; Massachusetts Department of Conservation and Recreation map: mass.gov/eea/docs/dcr/stewardship/rmp/watatic/maps-mt-watatic.pdf

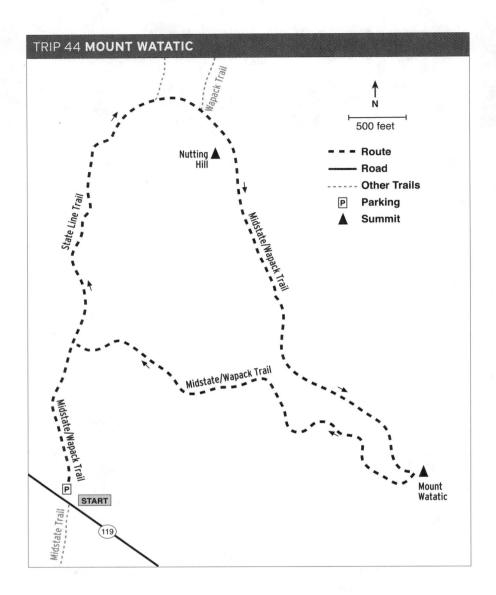

Nutting Hill ▲

Wapack Trail

State Line Trail

Midstate/Wapack Trail

Midstate/Wapack Trail

Midstate/Wapack Trail

Midstate Trail

P

START

119

N

500 feet

- - - Route
——— Road
------ Other Trails
P   Parking
▲   Summit

Mount Watatic ▲

blue dashers, and other dragonflies flit among the vegetation at the pond edge. The red maples start to change color at the onset of the fall foliage season in mid-September, and in early November the golden needles of tamarack trees (also known as larch) add a last splash of color.

At 0.2 mile, reach the start of the loop at a three-way junction where the Midstate and Wapack trails branch to the right for a direct, steep route to Mount Watatic's summit. To make the circuit via Nutting Hill, continue straight on blue-blazed State Line Trail for a moderately steep ascent along a rocky old cart road. White wood asters bloom along the trail edge in late summer. At 0.8 mile, stay straight at a marked junction where State Line Trail forks to the left (see "Nearby," below, for an optional extension to this hike) and continue for a few hundred feet to the upper junction with the Midstate and Wapack trails on the crest of the ridge. Turn right and follow the yellow-blazed Midstate and Wapack trails 0.1 mile to the 1,625-foot summit of Nutting Hill, where the partially exposed rock affords views of Wachusett Mountain to the south and Mount Watatic's upper slopes to the east. Butterflies and swarms of dragonflies frequent the sunlit opening in spring and summer.

After descending into the rocky gap between Nutting Hill and Mount Watatic, begin a moderately steep 0.8-mile ascent to Mount Watatic's summit. A network of stone walls offers ample evidence of the extent of historical land clearing, even on steep, rocky hills. Hard as it may be to believe today, these densely wooded slopes were once open pastures where herds of sheep grazed. The forests on the upper slopes include groves of spruce and fir, which occur on ridges at elevations between 1,000 and 2,500 feet in central New England. Northern birds in these woodlands include winter wrens, olive-sided fly-catchers, and ruby-crowned kinglets.

At the base of the summit, bear right and pass a gravel road that was built to provide access for a proposed communications tower and a portion of the for-mer Mount Watatic Ski Area, which operated on the north slopes from 1965 to 1984. Its closure has been attributed to the remote location and competition from the nearby Wachusett Mountain Ski Area. (A proposal to reopen it in 1988 was unsuccessful.) At 1.8 miles, reach Mount Watatic's 1,832-foot summit, where the sweeping views include Wachusett Mountain to the south, the tall buildings of downtown Boston across the coastal plain to the east, and a glimpse of Mount Monadnock through spruce trees to the north. Concrete supports mark the site of an old fire tower that was removed in 1997.

Even better views await at the open ledges on the east side of the summit, reached by a quick 450-foot walk on a rugged, unmarked path. There is plenty of space to enjoy a break or picnic and to take in the scenery, which includes Ward Pond, Lake Naukeag, Stodge Meadow Pond, and other lakes and ponds near the base of the mountain; Mount Hunger and the hills of the Midstate Trail corridor; and Mount Greylock and the Berkshire Hills on the western horizon. The northerly views feature the summits of the Wapack Range, capped by Pack Monadnock and North Pack Monadnock at the north end of the range; the hills of south-central New Hampshire; and the distant Sunapee Valley. Mount Watatic is an outstanding hawk-watching destination, thanks to its location in the heart of a migratory corridor, along with the nearby Wapack Range and Wachusett Mountain. Observers are often present counting birds during peak migration in late summer and early autumn.

After admiring the vistas, resume the loop on the Midstate and Wapack trails at the summit, following yellow blazes and signs for MA 119. Descend to another overlook with a partially southwesterly view to Wachusett Mountain. After a

At the north end of the Midstate Trail, Mount Watatic's rocky ledges offer spectacular views and the opportunity to see migrating hawks and monarch butterflies.

rocky segment along a stone wall, continue the steep descent through shady hemlock groves on the west slopes. (Use caution in winter, as this section may be icy.) Listen for the calls of migratory woodland songbirds, such as blackburnian and yellow-rumped warblers, in spring and summer.

At the base of the descent, pass through a large glacial boulder that was split in half by frost—a fun spot for a photo opportunity. Step across a seasonal stream and complete the loop at the lower junction with State Line Trail. Turn left and walk past the beaver pond to the parking area, 1.1 miles from the summit.

DID YOU KNOW?

After a proposal to build a communications tower at the summit met with considerable opposition, a collaborative including the Massachusetts Department of Conservation and Recreation, the Massachusetts Division of Fisheries and Wildlife, the towns of Ashby and Ashburnham, and the Mount Grace Land Conservation Trust purchased Mount Watatic in 2002 to protect it.

MORE INFORMATION

Open year-round, no fee, no restrooms. Hunting is prohibited in posted areas. The Midstate Trail Committee of the Appalachian Mountain Club maintains a website (midstatetrail.org) and a guide to the Midstate Trail, and the Friends of the Wapack (wapack.org) offers information and a guide to Wapack Trail.

WINTER ACTIVITIES

Skiing and snowshoeing are allowed. The portion of the combined Midstate and Wapack trails from MA 119 to Mount Watatic's summit is very steep and rocky. State Line Trail is wider, moderately steep, and rocky. The segment of Wapack Trail from Nutting Hill to Binney Pond in New Hampshire is fairly easy with gentle grades.

NEARBY

From the New Hampshire state line, Wapack Trail continues north past Emerson Hill to Binney Pond and Pratt Mountain, where outlooks offer outstanding views of the pond, Mount Watatic, and Mount Monadnock. This segment can be added as an extension to the Mount Watatic loop to make an 8-mile outing that takes about five hours to complete.

45

WILLARD BROOK STATE FOREST

This pleasant circuit passes through mountain laurel thickets and a rare pitch-pine forest on Fort Hill before concluding with a long, scenic segment along the banks of Willard Brook.

DIRECTIONS

From MA 2 take Exit 32 in Leominster and follow MA 13 north 10.6 miles to the junction with MA 119 in Townsend. Turn left and follow MA 119 west 5.0 miles to the Damon Pond entrance on the left. Parking is available at Damon Pond and along MA 119. *GPS coordinates:* 42° 39.723′ N, 71° 47.460′ W.

TRAIL DESCRIPTION

Willard Brook State Forest and adjacent Pearl Hill State Park protect a large expanse of land near the greater Fitchburg–Leominster area and the I-495 corridor. Willard Brook, the property's namesake, is a cold-water tributary of Nashua River that runs along MA 119 below the rocky slopes of Fort Hill. The trail network includes several blazed paths, named woods roads, and single-track routes often used by mountain bikers. The woods roads are ideal for cross-country skiing. This circuit, which begins at the Damon Pond entrance, follows Friends' Loop Trail over Fort Hill and Brook Trail along the banks of Willard Brook. Apart from a rocky section on Fort Hill, the walking is mostly easy. There are several junctions at the start of the loop, so follow directions and blazes carefully.

From the day-use parking area at Damon Pond (an artificial pond on Willard Brook), begin at the brown gate and a sign for Friends' Trail. The first segment follows three combined trails: orange-blazed Friends' Loop Trail, yellow-blazed Friends' Trail (a 4-mile, path that connects Damon Pond to Pearl Hill State Park), and blue-blazed

LOCATION
Ashby and Townsend, MA

RATING
Easy to Moderate

DISTANCE
3.3 miles

ELEVATION GAIN
325 feet

ESTIMATED TIME
2 hours

MAPS
USGS Ashby; Massachusetts Department of Conservation and Recreation map: mass.gov/eea/docs/dcr/parks/trails/willardbrook.pdf

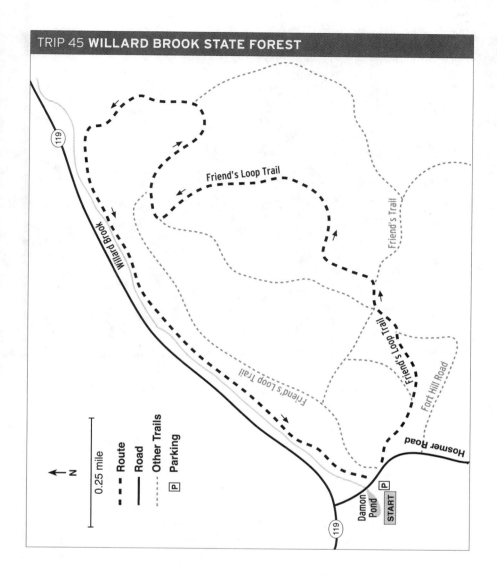

Family Friendly Loop Trail. Make an easy, gradual ascent of Fort Hill, heading past a small clearing and the first of several old red pine plantations. Although red pine is a nonnative species in most of Massachusetts, it was planted here during the 1930s when foresters feared the native white pines would be lost to blister rust disease. Another exotic species is Norway maple, which is native to Europe and was often planted along streets in eastern North America during the mid-twentieth century as a shade and ornamental tree.

After passing another clearing and a picnic area on the right, bear right at a Y junction, following the orange and yellow blazes. (The blue-blazed trail branches left here to loop back to the entrance.) Continue the ascent past groves of tall

From the covered bridge at the outlet of Damon Pond, Willard Brook meanders past small cascades.

pines and oaks and an old cabin at another field. Scan the clearings for wild turkeys, foxes, white-tailed deer, and other wildlife. Also watch for butterflies, including red-spotted purple, tiger swallowtail, and mourning cloak.

At the field edge, turn left at an unmarked T junction, pass a gate, and follow the blazed trails right at a Y junction. At the next junction, at 0.6 mile, turn left on orange-blazed Friends' Loop Trail, leaving Friends' Trail, which continues toward Pearl Hill State Park. Pass through a pine plantation and mountain laurel thickets on the slopes of Fort Hill, where the flutelike song of the hermit thrush is a familiar sound during spring and summer. Follow the blazed trail right near a woods road and then left at successive junctions with two single-track paths.

While the next segment is not overly difficult, the walking becomes a bit rougher as you traverse rolling terrain and needle-covered rocks on the north side of Fort Hill. Pass through an uncommon upland pitch pine forest, a rare natural community in interior Massachusetts. Pitch pine trees, distinguished by their ball-like needles, are well adapted to marginal growing conditions and harsh, acidic soils that other species can't tolerate. They are common on Cape Cod and in southeastern Massachusetts and also occur on inland ridges and sand plains. Reindeer lichen (also known as reindeer moss), which thrives in open environments, grows on the exposed rocks. A similar natural community can be found at Mass Audubon's Flat Rock Wildlife Sanctuary in Fitchburg.

Cross a brook on a footbridge and continue over Fort Hill's upper north slopes. Although there are no open views, you can glimpse portions of the surrounding valley hills through the trees, especially when leaves are off. After crossing another section of exposed rock, make a winding descent to the junction with Fort Hill Road, a blue-blazed woods road. Turn right on the road, leaving Friends' Loop Trail, which continues in the woods on the left. Continue 0.25 mile, past another pine plantation and a wetland on the left, to a Y junction with another woods road. Turn left, following blue blazes and a sign for the headquarters. (The road on the right leads to Pearl Hill State Park.)

Continue on the woods road another 0.3 mile then turn left on Brook Trail at a marked junction, beginning the return segment along Willard Brook. Although you'll occasionally see traffic on MA 119 above the opposite bank, this is a pleasant walk with many nice perspectives of the brook, including several small cascades and pools. As you head upstream toward the trailhead at Damon Pond, you'll gradually gain 175 feet in elevation. From headwaters west of the state forest, Willard Brook serves as a source for the Fitchburg and Ashby Reservoir. East of the state forest, it empties into Squannacook River, a major tributary of Nashua River, in West Townsend.

The mixed forests along the banks of the brook include eastern hemlock, a fire-sensitive species that thrives in moist ravines, as well as mountain laurel. Veeries, ovenbirds, and red-eyed vireos are among the common migratory songbirds that breed in these woods. You may even see a raccoon foraging along the muddy edges of the brook. After walking 1.3 miles on Brook Trail, complete the loop at the Damon Pond dam. The Willard Brook Covered Bridge spans the brook next to a picnic area below the dam, a fine spot to rest at the end of your hike.

DID YOU KNOW?

The Willard Brook Covered Bridge, also known as the Ashby Bridge, was built in 1988 as a replacement for the original bridge, erected in 1958, below Damon Pond. The current 37-foot wooden structure is one of several privately owned covered bridges in Massachusetts.

MORE INFORMATION

Open year-round. A parking fee ($8 MA residents, $15 out of state) is charged at the Damon Pond parking area on weekends after Memorial Day and in summer; access is free after 5 P.M. Biking and dogs are allowed. Hunting is allowed in accordance with state laws. Facilities at Damon Pond include a swimming beach, a picnic area, and a campground with 21 sites. For more information, visit mass.gov/locations/willard-brook-state-forest or call 978-597-8802.

WINTER ACTIVITIES

Skiing and snowshoeing are allowed at Willard Brook State Forest and Pearl Hill State Park. There are several wide woods roads, especially in the northern portion of the property, that can be reached via Fort Hill Road from the Damon Pond entrance. Portions of Friends' Loop Trail are rocky and moderately steep.

NEARBY

Trap Falls, where Trapfall Brook drops 12 feet in a distinctive triple cascade, is easily reached by a 0.1-mile walk from a parking area on the north side of MA 119, 1.0 mile east of the Damon Pond entrance. Pearl Hill State Park, on New Fitchburg Road in West Townsend, includes a seasonal day-use area with a swimming beach and 51 campsites. There are restaurants on MA 119 and MA 13 in Townsend.

46

MOORE STATE PARK

The many attractions of this popular and photogenic park include rhododendrons and azalea gardens, a restored sawmill and an old mill village on the banks of Turkey Hill Brook, Eames Pond, and woodland and meadow trails.

DIRECTIONS

From the Massachusetts Turnpike (I-90) take Exit 10 in Auburn and follow US 20 west to the junction with MA 56. Turn right and follow MA 56 north 9.7 miles through Leicester to the junction with MA 122. Turn left onto MA 122/MA 56 and continue 1.2 miles to the intersection with MA 31 in Paxton center. Turn left on MA 31 and continue 1.0 mile to the park entrance on Sawmill Road on the right. *GPS coordinates:* 42° 18.623′ N, 71° 57.281′ W.

TRAIL DESCRIPTION

Located just outside of Worcester, Moore State Park is home to a wealth of interesting natural and historical features. In the eighteenth and nineteenth centuries, several mills and an industrial village were established along the cascades of Turkey Hill Brook. After the mills went out of business in the early twentieth century, two prominent Worcester families purchased the land and planted the rhododendrons, azaleas, irises, and other flowers that attract many visitors today. Moore State Park was created in 1956, and portions of the park were added to the National Register of Historic Places in 2004. This hike combines popular trails to an old mill site and gardens with a less-traveled 1.4-mile loop through the forests in the northern section of the park. Although worth visiting in any season, the park is especially picturesque in mid to late spring when the floral blooms are at peak.

LOCATION
Paxton, MA

RATING
Easy

DISTANCE
2.1 miles

ELEVATION GAIN
200 feet

ESTIMATED TIME
1.25 hours

MAPS
USGS Paxton;
Massachusetts Department of Conservation and Recreation map: mass.gov/eea/docs/dcr/parks/trails/moore.pdf

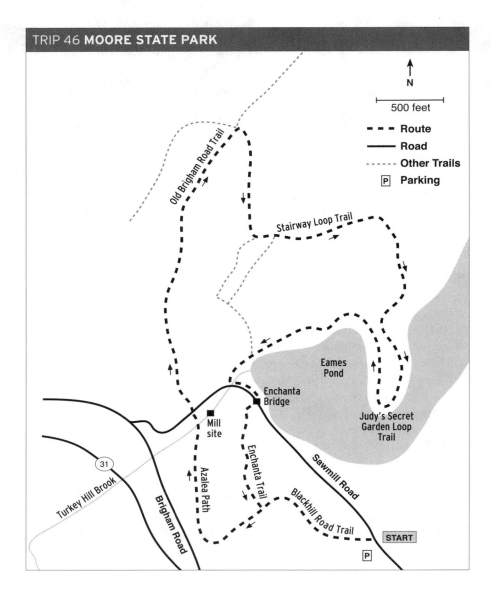

From the parking area, follow the grass path across the field to the left, heading away from Sawmill Road. The meadow was once used as a nursery to cultivate blight-resistant chestnut trees. Enter the woods on Blackhill Road Trail and continue past the junction with Enchanta Trail through oak-hardwood forest. At the next junction, near the park boundary, turn right on Azalea Path, an old carriage lane lined with planted azaleas and rhododendrons that make for a colorful spectacle in May and June. The rhododendrons are distinguished from the azaleas by their larger pink and magenta flowers and long, waxy, dark-green leaves. Tall oak and beech trees on the hillside provide a graceful backdrop.

At a sign for Artist Overlook, turn left and follow a short side trail to a picturesque perspective of one of the park's popular attractions, a restored sawmill on the banks of Turkey Hill Brook. The cascading brook, which drops nearly 100 feet as it flows through the park, provided plenty of hydropower for the former village's mills. After enjoying the scene, return to Azalea Path and continue to a footbridge adjacent to the sawmill, where there are good views of the original mill foundation and a waterfall at a stone dam. Rhododendrons are profuse along the sunlit banks of Turkey Hill Brook. In late spring and summer, blue flag irises and day lilies bloom near a small waterfall. Above the dam is Gristmill Pond, where yellow flag iris, a nonnative species that has naturalized in some wetlands after being introduced from Europe in the nineteenth century, blooms in abundance in late spring.

At the end of Azalea Path, cross the paved road (closed to public vehicles) near the sawmill and begin the next segment of the hike on Old Brigham Road. After passing a field and picnic area, enter the woods at a grove of tall pines and make a gentle ascent through hardwood forests of oak, maple, and birch and more planted rhododendrons and azaleas. Pink lady's slippers bloom along the trail edge in late May and early June.

After 0.4 mile on Old Brigham Road, at a gate near the park boundary, turn right at a sign for Stairway Trail and follow a winding path beneath tall oaks and pines. This less-traveled part of the park is a good place to look for white-tailed deer which feed on acorns provided by the abundant oak trees. From spring to midsummer, these woods come alive with the songs and calls of migratory songbirds, such as scarlet tanagers, chestnut-sided warblers, and red-eyed vireos. After crossing a stone wall, turn left on Stairway Loop Trail and descend past rocky ledges and a talus slope at an old quarry site. Pass another stone wall and follow the narrow path right and downhill to a junction on the wooded shores of Eames Pond, a large, fingerlike artificial pond formed by a dam on Turkey Hill Brook upstream from the sawmill.

Turn left on Judy's Secret Garden Loop Trail to make a 0.2-mile loop along the perimeter of a small peninsula that extends from the pond shore. Follow either fork of the loop, where more rhododendrons and azaleas grow amid the natural vegetation. At the end of the loop, turn left to rejoin Stairway Loop Trail and continue along the west side of Eames Pond on a narrow, rocky path lined with more rhododendrons. Next to the trail's end at the mill village is a wooden shelter that was built for a colony of brown bats in 1992. During the warm months, the bats emerge at dusk to feed on the many insects at Eames Pond. Researchers have used video equipment to monitor the size and health of the colony.

At the covered Enchanta Bridge, which spans the pond's outlet, several chairs offer the opportunity to relax and enjoy views across the water. Below the dam, Turkey Hill Brook cascades past more rhododendrons at a spot that makes for a fine photo opportunity. From the bridge, continue left on Sawmill Road for a few hundred feet to the junction with Enchanta Trail at a Healthy Heart Trail sign.

The trails of Moore State Park lead to colorful rhododendron gardens, waterfalls on Turkey Hill Brook, and the Enchanta Bridge.

Turn right and follow Enchanta Trail past more rhododendrons and tall pines to the junction with Blackhill Road Trail at the end of the loop. Turn left to return to the field and parking area.

If you have time to extend your outing, Davis Road Trail and Davis Hill Field Trails (a network of grass paths) lead through growths of mountain laurel and a series of large meadows in the eastern portion of the park. Watch for bobolinks and a variety of grassland birds, butterflies, dragonflies, deer, foxes, and other wildlife in and around the fields. The trailheads are on the north side of Sawmill Road opposite the parking area.

DID YOU KNOW?

While rhododendrons are common in the southern Appalachians, they are rare in natural settings in New England. Rhododendron State Park in Fitzwilliam, New Hampshire, protects the largest natural rhododendron population north of the Allegheny Mountains of Pennsylvania.

MORE INFORMATION

Open dawn to dusk year-round. A portable toilet is available at the parking area. For more information, visit mass.gov/locations/moore-state-park or call 508-792-3969.

WINTER ACTIVITIES

Skiing and snowshoeing are allowed. Old Brigham Road and the Davis Hill Field Trails meadow paths are ideal for beginners and intermediate skiers. The trails are also excellent for animal tracking, especially near field edges. Stairway Loop Trail is a narrow path with moderately steep sections above Eames Pond.

NEARBY

Tower Hill Botanic Garden, at 11 French Drive in Boylston, includes gardens, nature trails, and a visitor center, gift shop, and café. Open Tuesday to Sunday 10 A.M. to 5 P.M. (last admission at 4:30 P.M.) year-round; closed Mondays except for certain holidays. Admission fee: $15 adults, $10 seniors, $5 children 6–18, free for children 5 and under. For more information visit towerhillbg.org or call 508-869-6111. Food is available on MA 122 (Pleasant Street) in Paxton, and there are many places to eat in Worcester.

47

BROAD MEADOW BROOK WILDLIFE SANCTUARY

At New England's largest urban wildlife sanctuary, well-marked trails lead to interpretive stations, boardwalks, and fine views of Broad Meadow Brook and its habitats.

DIRECTIONS

From I-290 take Exit 14 and follow MA 122 (Grafton Street) south 0.5 mile. At the traffic circle, take the first exit and continue on MA 122/Grafton Street another 0.4 mile. Turn right on Massasoit Road and continue 1.6 miles to the sanctuary entrance at 414 Massasoit Road.

From the Massachusetts Turnpike (I-90) take Exit 11 and follow MA 122 north 0.7 mile to the junction with US 20. Turn left and follow US 20 west 1.0 mile then turn right on Massasoit Road and continue 0.5 mile to the entrance on the left. *GPS coordinates:* 42° 13.975′ N, 71° 45.856′ W.

TRAIL DESCRIPTION

In an oasis amid the development of the city of Worcester, Broad Meadow Brook Wildlife Sanctuary protects 430 acres of crucial habitats in the watershed of Broad Meadow Brook, a tributary of Blackstone River. The diverse natural communities include marshes, swamps, beaver ponds, vernal pools, hardwood forests, wildflower meadows, and a wildlife garden at the visitor center. This walk combines several of the trails as a 3.25-mile circuit with views of the various habitats. Along the way are interpretive stations, viewing areas, several universally accessible segments, and an outdoor playground.

At the visitor center, where maps and information are available, the various attractions include a bird blind, a shaded pavilion, a bee hotel, and a wildlife garden with planted shadbush, bayberry, and holly. Look for butterflies around the garden, such as tiger swallowtails and American ladies; also watch for Carolina wrens, house finches, and mockingbirds.

LOCATION
Worcester, MA

RATING
Easy to Moderate

DISTANCE
3.25 miles

ELEVATION GAIN
170 feet

ESTIMATED TIME
2.25 hours

MAPS
USGS Worcester South; Mass Audubon map: massaudubon.org/content/download/7960/144611/file/Broad-Meadow-Brook-Trail-Map.pdf

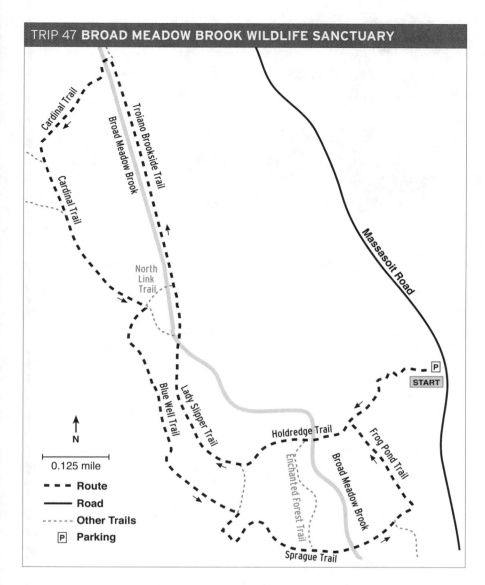

Begin by following the combined Holdredge Trail (orange blazes) and Sagatab-scot Ridge Trail (yellow blazes) on a winding descent via a universally accessible path past the playground and several interpretive signs. At a map kiosk, turn right and continue to follow the combined trails past a vernal pool, which offers breeding habitat for spotted salamanders, wood frogs, and other amphibians. The protected land around the sanctuary's vernal pools is especially important because the surrounding areas are heavily developed, with very few travel corridors.

Carefully step across Broad Meadow Brook then cross a short boardwalk and pass the junction with Enchanted Forest Trail at marker 2. The oak-hickory forests are characteristic of southeastern New England's mild, dry lowlands. At the

Amid the development of downtown Worcester, Broad Meadow Brook Wildlife Sanctuary provides crucial habitat for mallard ducks and other wildlife.

next junction, turn right on the combined Lady Slipper Trail (green blazes) and Sagatabscot Ridge Trail (yellow blazes), which lead through the woods above the west side of Cattail Marsh, one of several wetlands along Broad Meadow Brook. Broad-leaved cattails, which are native to New England, are an important component of freshwater marshes and pond edges. They offer food and cover for red-winged blackbirds, ducks, wading birds, and muskrats, which often use the leaves to build lodges. After 0.3 mile, turn right again at a junction near the wetland edge and follow Troiano Brookside Trail past several private residences at the sanctuary boundary.

At the junction with North Link Trail, featuring an information sign and a stone culvert, continue straight on Troiano Brookside Trail, heading north along the east side of a large wetland on Broad Meadow Brook. This portion of the trail is universally accessible via the Hampton Street trailhead at the sanctuary boundary. The city of Worcester had originally planned to build an artificial pond here to store stormwater runoff, but beavers moved in before the project started and created a larger wetland, saving the city money in the process. The increasing presence of aspen, birch, and willow trees in recent years indicates the beavers have abandoned the wetland, which is gradually transitioning to a wet meadow. In summer, yellow tansy, easily identified by its button-like yellow flowers, grows along the trail edge.

At the north end of the wetland, near the Hampton Street trailhead, turn left on red-blazed Cardinal Trail. Cross a footbridge and continue past a brushy wet meadow (watch for poison ivy along the trail edge), a paper birch grove, and an area of young regenerating forest. At the junction with a service road, turn left and continue on Cardinal Trail south through upland forests and past a brook crossing.

At a wide power-line corridor, Cardinal Trail joins a portion of Sagatabscot Ridge Trail. The clearing benefits a variety of wildlife and flora by providing habitat diversity, travel corridors, and edges that offer food and cover. One of the familiar wildflowers is black-eyed Susan (also often called black-eyed coneflower), a member of the aster family that has bright-yellow petals and often grows in large colonies. A wooden bench at Barbara's Meadow offers the opportunity to pause and watch for butterflies, dragonflies, and songbirds, such as prairie and blue-winged warblers.

Reenter the woods at another information kiosk and turn right at a four-way junction on Blue Well Trail, a narrow path marked with blue blazes. Continue 0.5 mile over gently rolling terrain in the woods, roughly parallel to the power line. A large vernal pool on the left often has water, even in dry years. Follow Blue Well Trail left at the junction with North Link Trail, near the power line. At the next junction, turn right on the west end of Holdredge Trail. After a few hundred feet, turn left on the purple-blazed Sprague Trail and descend the valley slope past a stone wall, a tall spreading oak, and a wooden bench. At the base of the descent, cross the outflow from Sedge Marsh, another wetland on Broad Meadow Brook. On the right is a bench with views of the edge of the marsh and a red maple swamp near the sanctuary boundary. From the swamp's outlet, Broad Meadow Brook flows south into nearby Dorothy Pond, which in turn drains into Blackstone River.

Continue along a universally accessible segment of Sprague Trail to a parking area and kiosk at Sprague Lane. Turn left and follow Frog Pond Trail north along a long boardwalk to a viewing area at Frog Pond, a small pool nestled at the sanctuary boundary, adjacent to a private residence. At the junction with Holdredge Trail, turn right and retrace your steps uphill to the trailhead and visitor center.

DID YOU KNOW?

The sanctuary began in 1989 as a 15-acre conservation project that linked land owned by the New England Power Company (now National Grid) and a conservation area managed by the city of Worcester. Other land acquisitions and donations have expanded this protected corridor to more than 400 acres.

MORE INFORMATION

Open dawn to dusk year-round. Admission is $4 for adults and $3 for children and seniors; free for Worcester residents and Mass Audubon and Greater Worcester Land Trust members. The visitor center, part of the Blackstone River Valley National Heritage Corridor, is open Tuesday to Saturday, 9 A.M. to 4 P.M., and Sunday, 12:30 to 4 P.M. Pets and hunting are not allowed. For more information, visit massaudubon.org or call 508-753-6087.

WINTER ACTIVITIES

Skiing is not allowed; snowshoeing is allowed. The trails are excellent for the latter, with gentle grades and the opportunity to see animal tracks in the various habitats.

NEARBY

The EcoTarium, at 222 Harrington Way in Worcester, offers interactive science and nature exhibits, including a tree canopy walkway, a planetarium, and animal enclosures. Visitors may also view native wildlife on the 55-acre grounds, which include forest, pond, meadow, and marsh habitats. Hours are Tuesday to Saturday, 10 A.M. to 5 P.M., and Sunday, noon to 5 P.M.; closed Mondays (ecotarium.org, 508-929-2700). There are many restaurants in downtown Worcester.

48

BLACKSTONE RIVER AND CANAL HERITAGE STATE PARK

Easy out-and-back trails lead to historical sites and natural habitats along Blackstone River, including the former Blackstone Canal and Lookout Rock on King Philip's Trail, which offers a fine view of the valley.

DIRECTIONS

From the east and west, on the Massachusetts Turnpike (I-90), take Exit 10A in Millbury and follow MA 146 south. (From the north on I-290 take Exit 12 in Worcester and follow MA 146 south.) Take Exit 3 and follow MA 16 east 2.0 miles then turn left on MA 122. In 1.2 miles, turn right on Hartford Avenue and continue 1.0 mile to the bridge over Blackstone River at Rice City Pond. Parking for King Philip's Trail is on the east side of the bridge. *GPS coordinates:* 42° 05.962′ N, 71° 37.197′ W.

The trailhead for the Goat Hill to Plummer's Landing hike is on the west side of the bridge. *GPS coordinates:* 42° 05.862′ N, 71° 37.415′ W.

TRAIL DESCRIPTION

Blackstone River, which flows 50 miles from Worcester to Providence, is one of America's most historically significant industrial waterways. After the nation's first textile mill was established at Pawtucket Falls in the late eighteenth century, the region rapidly developed into a national manufacturing center. The Blackstone Canal, which opened in 1828, was built to facilitate boat travel on the narrow, shallow river, which drops 450 feet along its course.

The two hikes described here both begin at the Hartford Avenue bridge at Rice City Pond. King Philip's Trail is a 1.2-mile walk along the east bank of the river to arguably the best scenic view of the valley. On the west bank, Goat Hill Trail, Canal Towpath, and Plummer's Trail collectively form a 2.4-mile route with close-up looks at the

LOCATION
Uxbridge, MA

KING PHILIP'S TRAIL RATING
Easy

DISTANCE
2.4 miles

ELEVATION GAIN
100 feet

ESTIMATED TIME
1.5 hours

GOAT HILL TO PLUMMER'S LANDING RATING
Easy

DISTANCE
5 miles

ELEVATION GAIN
65 feet

ESTIMATED TIME
2.5 hours

MAPS
USGS Blackstone; Massachusetts Department of Conservation and Recreation map: mass.gov/eea/docs/dcr/parks/trails/blackstone.pdf

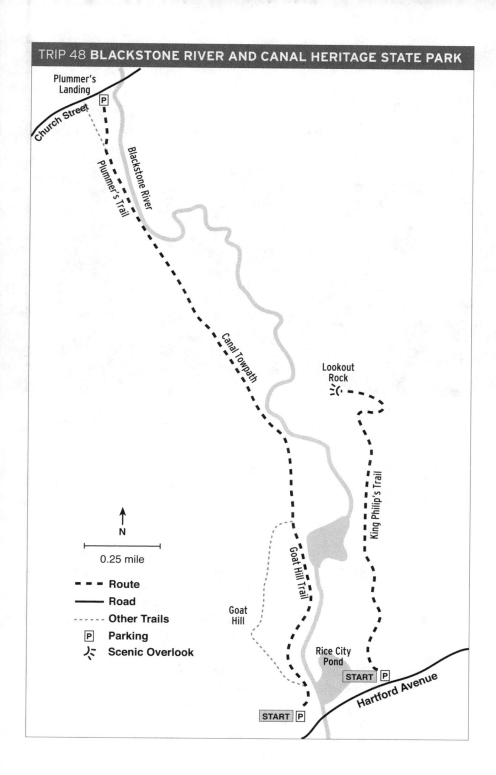

In fall, the colorful foliage of American beech trees brighten the trails along Blackstone River.

river, its associated floodplain, and a portion of the canal. It is possible to connect the trailheads by walking on the roads, but be aware of narrow shoulders and high traffic.

King Philip's Trail

From the parking area on the east side of the bridge, cross the grassy field and pass a rock outcropping on the right. The parklike setting provides a marked contrast to the past; the field was a 15-acre junkyard before the state purchased the land in 1981. At the edge of the field, follow the blue-blazed King Philip's Trail (the trail name is not posted) through a pine plantation and picnic area to a footbridge over a brook that feeds into wetlands on the north side of Rice City Pond.

Continue north along the base of the west slopes of Wolf Hill, one of the low, rocky hills of the Blackstone River valley. A short path on the left leads to a view of a marshy area at the wetland edge, where you can watch for waterfowl, wading birds, and muskrats, which benefit from the cover. One of the most elusive marsh birds is the American bittern, a shy species whose brown and white coloration allows it to blend almost perfectly with vegetation. On the right is a rocky talus slope at the base of Wolf Hill. Look for a house-sized boulder opposite another outcropping at a partial view of the river.

Continue over gently rolling terrain past the junction with an unmarked trail on the right, another brook crossing, and a red pine plantation. At 1 mile from the trailhead, follow the path as it bends right along the base of Lookout Rock, a steep outcropping. At the next junction, turn left and make a short climb past a cluster of boulders to the top of the outcropping, where there's a partially open view of the Blackstone Valley.

Following a sign for Lookout Rock, continue west along the ledge to King Philip's Overlook. Pass the junction with an unmarked trail on the right, which leads to a gate on Quaker Road. At the lookout, enjoy fine southerly views of the winding Blackstone River, its associated wetlands, and the valley hills. Fall foliage usually begins in late September, when the red maples in the wetlands start to change color, and continues into early November, when the oaks and beeches drop their leaves. The overlook marks the trail's end; retrace your steps to the parking area.

Goat Hill to Plummer's Landing

Start this walk from the parking area on the west side of the Hartford Avenue bridge (as detailed here) or at the trail's north end at Plummer's Landing on Church Street. Portions of the route may be wet during high water periods. From the interpretive sign, follow Goat Hill Trail north along the southwest corner of Rice City Pond. Watch for great blue herons, ducks, and other wildlife in the pond and along its marshy edges. The Rice City Dam, built for industrial use and flood control, was washed out by flooding in 1955.

At 0.1 mile, the trail forks into a short loop at a stone wall. The path on the left offers a short climb over Goat Hill, and the path on the right offers an easier walk along the river and through a field of glacial boulders. From the junction at the end of the loop, continue to a footbridge at Goat Hill Lock at 0.8 mile. Built in 1827, the lock was one of 48 established along the Blackstone Canal. Canal users paid a toll of one penny per mile per ton of cargo. The advent of the railroad made the canal obsolete by the mid-nineteenth century, and it closed in 1848. Near the footbridge is a beaver wetland.

At 1.2 miles, the trail follows a portion of the former canal towpath through Blackstone River's floodplain. Tall white oaks grow out of the well-watered soil, along with maples, birches, and pines. Cross a footbridge at the outlet of a large wetland that empties into Blackstone River. A nesting box offers shelter for wood ducks, which have made a strong recovery in recent decades as forests have matured. The river's course is constantly changing as it erodes new channels through the shallow floodplain. In several places, especially near the north end of the trail, the river approaches the canal, as evidenced by stones that have been placed to reinforce washed-out areas.

A brushy field near the wetland edge offers additional habitat diversity for a variety of wildlife, including red foxes, eastern coyotes, eastern bluebirds, tree swallows, indigo buntings, and birds of prey. Butterflies and other insects feed on asters, goldenrods, and other summer wildflowers. All of these species benefit from meadows and thickets, which are becoming increasingly uncommon as forests mature.

At 2.3 miles, bear right at a Y junction and continue 0.2 mile to the trail's northern terminus at Plummer's Landing and Church Street. (The canal path continues to the left to a bridge built out of an old lock.) The landing was once the site of Israel Plummer's store and inn, which served canal users and connected the valley with national and international markets. Present-day visitor facilities include a picnic area, a boat launch, and interpretive signs.

DID YOU KNOW?

The Heritage State Parks program was established in 1978 to preserve the history of Massachusetts's industrial areas. Other parks are located in former manufacturing centers, such as Lowell, Lawrence, Fall River, and Holyoke.

MORE INFORMATION

Open year-round, no fee. The River Bend Farm Visitor Center, at 287 Oak Street, is open during daylight hours year-round. Biking and dogs are allowed. Hunting is allowed in accordance with state laws. Several boat launches are available along Blackstone River; the paddling route from River Bend Farm to Plummer's Landing is 3.5 miles. For state park information, visit mass.gov/locations/blackstone-river-and-canal-heritage-state-park or call 508-278-7604. Additional information about the Blackstone River Valley National Heritage Corridor is available at nps.gov/blac and blackstoneheritagecorridor.org.

WINTER ACTIVITIES

Skiing and snowshoeing are allowed. The trail from Goat Hill to Plummer's Landing is mostly level and easy, with several short footbridges. Apart from a short segment at Lookout Rock, King Philip's Trail is mostly level and easy.

NEARBY

The former Stanley Woolen Mill, on Cross Street off MA 16 at the south end of the state park, produced military uniforms and garments for prestigious designers and was featured in the movies *The Great Gatsby* (1974) and *Oliver's Story* (1978). Millville Lock, the best-preserved lock of the Blackstone Canal, is at the junction of Hope and Central streets off MA 122 in Millville, 6.0 miles south of the park. Blackstone River Gorge can be viewed from County Street off MA 122 in Blackstone at the Rhode Island state line.

49

PURGATORY CHASM STATE RESERVATION

Two interconnected loop trails lead to a variety of perspectives of Purgatory Chasm, one of Massachusetts's most unique natural features, as well as Purgatory Brook and the surrounding rocky woods.

DIRECTIONS

From the east and west, on the Massachusetts Turnpike (I-90) take Exit 10A in Millbury and follow MA 146 south. (From the north on I-290 take Exit 12 in Worcester and follow MA 146 south.) Take Exit 6 in Sutton and follow Purgatory Road 0.2 mile to the reservation entrance. Parking is available at the visitor center and along Purgatory Road near the entrance to Purgatory Chasm. *GPS coordinates:* 42° 07.761′ N, 71° 42.824′ W.

TRAIL DESCRIPTION

Purgatory Chasm, a rocky quarter-mile-long granite canyon with 75-foot walls, is one of Massachusetts's best known and most unusual geologic features. It has been the subject of books, movies, poems, and American Indian and Colonial legends. Scientists continue to investigate its origins. Purgatory Chasm State Reservation, established in 1919, is a popular hiking and tourist destination.

This outing combines two loops. The first segment is a short but moderately rugged trek through the gorge on Chasm Loop Trail, which requires some minor scrambling over and around rocks. Hiking boots or other sturdy rubber-soled shoes are strongly recommended. Children will enjoy exploring the chasm and overlooks, but all visitors should use caution around high steps and steep dropoffs. The second segment is an outer loop through forests with a side trip detour along Purgatory Brook, which meanders through a narrow valley on the west side

LOCATION
Sutton, MA

RATING
Easy to Moderate

DISTANCE
2 miles

ELEVATION GAIN
245 feet

ESTIMATED TIME
2 hours

MAPS
USGS Grafton; Massachusetts Department of Conservation and Recreation map: mass.gov/files/documents/2016/12/wl/purgatory.pdf

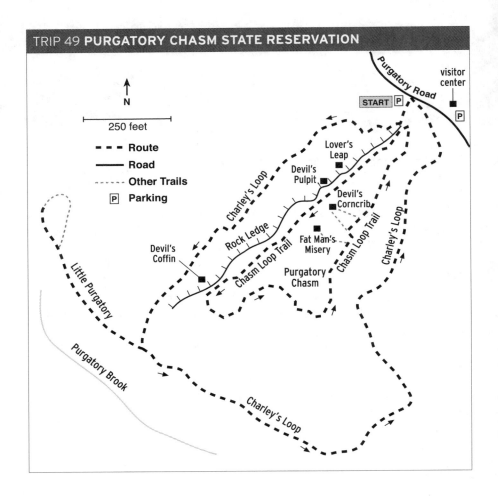

of Purgatory Chasm. (*Note:* Purgatory Chasm is closed when snow or ice is present, but the other trails in the reservation are open year-round.)

Begin at the main entrance to Purgatory Chasm on the west side of Purgatory Road, a few hundred feet north of the visitor center. From the picnic area, follow blue-blazed Chasm Loop Trail into the heart of the rocky gorge, where blue blazes indicate the easiest routes around and over the rocks. Prominent high points along the steep walls to the right include Lover's Leap (75 feet) and Devil's Pulpit (70 feet).

Unlike other gorges in New England, including Chesterfield Gorge (Trip 18), Purgatory Chasm is a dry ravine with no water flowing through it. The process by which it formed has long been a mystery for scientists. Some have theorized that the chasm was carved by the sudden release of glacial meltwater after an ice dam burst at the end of the last ice age more than 10,000 years ago. Others have noted that the chasm walls and boulders show no evidence of having been smoothed by water. Mauri Pelto, a professor of environmental sciences at Nichols College, proposes that glaciers carved the chasm through a large section of granite that had been weakened by a previous geologic fault.

Continue over rocks and beneath the high walls to a junction at the southwest end of the chasm. Turn left to continue on Chasm Loop Trail, which will lead you along the crest of the east rim. (The trail straight ahead connects to Charley's Loop Trail.) Several overlooks offer a perspective of the chasm from above. Short side paths on the left lead to Fat Man's Misery and Devil's Corncrib, two slotlike gaps in the rock that, according to Colonial lore, were made by the devil swinging a tomahawk. At 0.5 mile, reach the end of Chasm Loop Trail at the chasm entrance.

From the Healthy Heart Trail sign, begin the second segment by following yellow-blazed Charley's Loop uphill along the north side of the chasm, past outlooks at Lover's Leap and Devil's Pulpit. The forests are a mix of hardwoods and conifers, including oak, birch, maple, white pine, and hemlock. Some of the tall hemlocks that grow out of the chasm are more than 300 years old; they were never logged due to the rugged terrain.

From the crest of the climb, descend to the marked junction of Charley's Loop, Little Purgatory Trail, and Forest Road Trail at the southwest end of the chasm. Turn right on green-blazed Little Purgatory Trail and continue to a four-way junction with a woods road. A short detour to the left leads to a footbridge over Little Purgatory Brook, where you may see green frogs and red efts. Continue along the east bank of the brook, with the rocky valley slope to the right.

At 0.25 mile from the junction with Charley's Loop reach Little Purgatory, at a sharp bend in Purgatory Brook. The smooth rock and several geologic potholes (circular holes scoured by swirling water) are clear evidence that Little Purgatory has been formed and shaped by water. A stream cascades through a narrow gap in the rock, forming two small waterfalls. You can explore the cascades and mossy boulders by walking up the slope to the right; use caution around dropoffs.

To continue the hike, retrace your steps back to the junction at Purgatory Chasm. Turn right to resume the hike on yellow-blazed Charley's Loop, which follows an old woods road past a culvert and along the reservation boundary on the east side of Purgatory Brook. The land on the right is privately owned; please respect posted signs.

The mixed forests and rocky areas are ideal habitat for eastern chipmunks, which hibernate during winter but are a familiar sight during the warm months. They make dens in sheltered openings below rocks and logs, and you may even see one scampering around the base of Purgatory Chasm. All year long, look for resident birds, including golden-crowned kinglets, black-capped chickadees, red-breasted and white-breasted nuthatches, blue jays, and downy woodpeckers. In spring and summer, the pines and hemlocks host blue-eyed vireos, pine warblers, and other migratory songbirds. On mild early spring nights, vernal pools

Chasm Loop Trail passes through the heart of Purgatory Chasm, a popular hiking destination.

come alive with activity as wood frogs and salamanders congregate to breed. Black bears are occasionally seen at the park, especially around the picnic areas.

Turn left at the reservation boundary and make a short climb up the hill on the southeast side of Purgatory Chasm. Bear left near a large rock ledge then follow Charley's Loop as it bends north through the woods on the east side of the chasm. Shortly after passing several picnic tables, reach the end of the trail and the outer loop at Purgatory Road opposite the visitor center.

DID YOU KNOW?

Purgatory Chasm's unusual name is believed to derive from a Colonial legend demonizing the Algonquin god Hobomoko. Legend has it the god took on a devil-like form and flew an Algonquin criminal to Purgatory Chasm, where Hobomoko's violent actions formed the deep cuts and depressions in the rocks. Some historians believe the legend was created to encourage American Indians to convert from their own religions to Christianity.

MORE INFORMATION

Open sunrise to sunset year-round. There is a parking fee ($5 MA residents, $10 out of state). Leashed dogs are allowed; biking is not allowed. Rock climbing is allowed by permit only. Facilities include restrooms, picnic areas, and a playground at the visitor center. For more information, visit mass.gov/locations/purgatory-chasm-state-reservation or call 508-234-3733.

WINTER ACTIVITIES

Chasm Loop Trail is closed when snow or ice is present in Purgatory Chasm, but the park's other trails are open for skiing and snowshoeing. Charley's Loop Trail, Forest Road, and Little Purgatory Trail are good options for skiing, with gentle to moderate terrain.

NEARBY

The village of Manchaug, off Central Turnpike, includes a scenic waterfall and a paved walking trail with interpretive signs that detail the history of the local mills. The former Manchaug Mill is now home to shops featuring locally made crafts. There are restaurants on Main Street and Boston Road.

A rare Atlantic white cedar swamp, beaver ponds, historical sites, and scenic Wallum Lake are among the attractions of this circuit through the rocky woods and wetlands of Douglas State Forest.

DIRECTIONS

From I-395 take Exit 2 in Webster and follow MA 16 west 5.2 miles to Douglas. Turn right and follow Cedar Street 0.8 mile to a stop sign. Continue straight on Wallum Lake Road 0.9 mile then turn right and follow the access road to the contact station and parking areas. *GPS coordinates:* 42° 01.336′ N, 71° 46.094′ W.

TRAIL DESCRIPTION

At the south end of the Midstate Trail corridor, Douglas State Forest protects nearly 6,000 acres of wetlands and woods along the Massachusetts–Rhode Island state line. The diverse wetlands include a rare Atlantic white cedar swamp, vernal pools, freshwater marshes, shrub swamps, and a portion of 322-acre Wallum Lake, which extends across the state line to Burrillville, Rhode Island. Two abandoned railroads, an old mill site, and stone walls offer evidence of past land uses. This circuit, which begins at the Wallum Lake picnic area, combines the cedar swamp boardwalk and Coffeehouse Loop Trail with a segment along the Southern New England Trunkline Trail (SNETT), a rail trail. The walking is mostly easy, and the diverse habitats offer many wildlife viewing opportunities.

From the gate at the boat launch parking lot, walk to the nearby picnic area. At the trail sign next to the restrooms, turn right and follow the dirt road away from the lake, past the nature center and a junction at a Healthy Heart Trail sign. Continue to the start of Coffeehouse Loop Trail at a

LOCATION
Douglas, MA

RATING
Easy to Moderate

DISTANCE
4.2 miles

ELEVATION GAIN
200 feet

ESTIMATED TIME
2.5 hours

MAPS
USGS Oxford; Massachusetts Department of Conservation and Recreation map: mass.gov/eea/docs/dcr/parks/trails/douglas.pdf

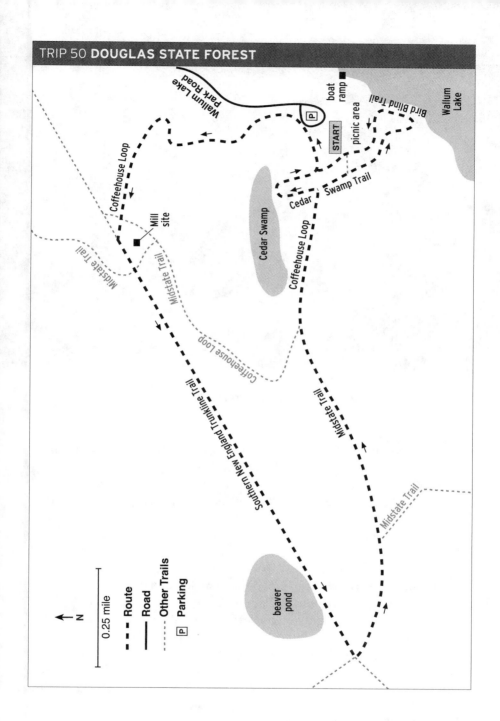

TRIP 50 **DOUGLAS STATE FOREST**

0.25 mile

← N

- – – Route
- —— Road
- ···· Other Trails
- P Parking

Boardwalks wind through the heart of a regionally rare Atlantic white cedar swamp.

small clearing, where an interpretive trail (part of the return route) enters from the cedar swamp. Turn right and follow Coffeehouse Loop Trail through a hemlock grove to a seasonal parking area. Walk to the left along the edge of the paved road for a few hundred feet then turn left at another trail sign and follow Coffeehouse Loop Trail left past a row of rocks at the edge of the parking lot. Enter an oak-hickory forest interspersed with mountain laurel, white pine, and hemlock.

Descend to a junction at a wetland, where the trail joins an old railroad bed that was originally built as a spur to a building that was used to store ice cut from Wallum Lake. Turn left and pass dense, marshy vegetation that offers cover for wading birds and waterfowl, including American black ducks, which have suffered a population decline in recent years due to habitat loss and competition from mallard ducks. After walking 0.25 mile on the railroad bed, turn left at the next junction and follow Coffeehouse Loop Trail for a few hundred feet to an old mill pond and the prominent stone remains of the former Aldrich sawmill and gristmill. Cross a footbridge over the pond's outlet then turn right at the pond edge and follow a short path back to the railroad bed. (You can shorten the walk 1.7 miles by continuing on Coffeehouse Loop Trail here.)

Turn left and continue along a portion of the SNETT, which merges with the spur line on the north side of the mill pond. The SNETT is a 21-mile-long recreational trail that links Douglas State Forest to Franklin State Forest in Norfolk County. The wide old railroad bed was part of the former New Haven Railroad Midland Division, which connected Boston with northeastern Connecticut. Now a rail trail lined with pines and oaks, it offers an easy, level passage between wetlands, including shrub swamps and vernal pools. At 1.0 mile from the mill site, reach open views of a large wetland, including several beaver lodges and a wood duck nesting box on the right.

At a four-way junction where there is a sign for the SNETT at the wetland edge, turn left and follow an unmarked woods road on a gentle ascent through the forest on the south side of the wetland. Shortly after passing a rocky cascading stream, the woods road merges with the yellow-blazed Midstate Trail, which enters from the right, from its southern terminus at the Rhode Island state line. In 0.5 mile, turn right at the next junction to rejoin Coffeehouse Loop Trail. (The Midstate Trail keeps going along the left fork of the loop.) Continue the easy climb through rocky woods and a large field of glacial boulders.

In 0.4 mile from the Midstate Trail junction, reach a four-way intersection with the interpretive trail at the edge of the Atlantic white cedar swamp. Turn left and follow the interpretive trail downhill to the start of the boardwalk, which offers close-up views of this rare and fragile natural community. Atlantic white cedar is a southern species that migrated into New England during a period of climate warming several thousand years ago. It has declined significantly throughout its range due to wetland development and timber harvesting. Watch for a tall black gum tree, another southern species that thrives in wetlands, near the start of the boardwalk on the right. At the end of the first boardwalk segment, follow the path through the woods at the perimeter of the wetland for a few hundred feet. Bear right on the second boardwalk and continue through a grove of trees that were blown down by a storm and continue past an observation area with benches.

From the end of the boardwalk, hike uphill to the clearing at the junction with Coffeehouse Loop Trail and the dirt road to Wallum Lake. You can retrace your steps along the road to the trailhead, but the interpretive trail offers a more interesting option. Turn right to go back to the four-way junction at the start of the cedar swamp loop then turn left and follow the red-blazed interpretive trail south to an old quarry site. At the next junction, turn right and follow Bird Blind Trail (orange triangle blazes) uphill to an observation deck in the woods above the lake. In spring and summer, watch for eastern kingbirds, which nest in trees near water and open areas. Follow the path down and to the left along the base of the hill, where a short boardwalk will lead you to a grassy field and picnic area on the shores of Wallum Lake—an excellent spot for a break.

DID YOU KNOW?

Wallum Lake, with a maximum depth of 75 feet, is home to ten species of fish, including largemouth bass, bluegill, and yellow perch. The lake has also been stocked with trout and salmon.

MORE INFORMATION

Open sunrise to sunset year-round. A seasonal fee ($9 MA residents, $15 out of state) is charged at the Wallum Lake entrance. Facilities include a boat launch, a swimming beach, a picnic area with two pavilions, and restrooms. Biking and dogs are allowed. Hunting is allowed in accordance with state laws. In summer, the parking lots at Lake Wallum may fill to capacity; visit on weekdays to avoid crowds. For more information, visit mass.gov/locations/douglas-state-forest or call 508-476-7872. For information on the Midstate Trail, visit midstatetrail.org.

WINTER ACTIVITIES

Skiing and snowshoeing are allowed. Douglas State Forest has an extensive network of foot trails and woods roads that are excellent for skiing. The old railroad beds are wide, level, and ideal for beginners and families, and the woods roads offer mostly easy grades.

NEARBY

Lake Manchaug Camping, at 76 Oak Street in Douglas, offers waterfront sites on 75 acres bordering Lake Manchaug (lakemanchaugcamping.com, 508-476-2471). The many attractions of the Blackstone River Valley Natural Heritage Corridor are a short drive east of Douglas State Forest. There are several places to eat on Main Street in Douglas.

APPENDIX A: LONG-DISTANCE TRAILS

NEW ENGLAND NATIONAL SCENIC TRAIL

From Long Island Sound to the hills and ridges of the Connecticut Valley, the New England National Scenic Trail, also known as the New England Trail (NET), traverses a variety of natural habitats, historical sites, and rural landscapes. The 233-mile route was designated as a National Scenic Trail in 2009, a distinction it shares with a few other fabled routes, including the Appalachian Trail and the Pacific Crest Trail.

The NET largely follows portions of three historical trails, one of which is the Metacomet-Monadnock (M-M) Trail in western Massachusetts. University of Massachusetts botany professor Walter Banfield and volunteers from the Appalachian Mountain Club (AMC) and other organizations created the M-M Trail during the 1950s as a hiking route from the Pioneer Valley to Mount Monadnock.

From the Connecticut state line, the NET follows the Metacomet Ridge, traversing Mount Tom and the Holyoke Range, through the central Connecticut River valley. It then bends northeast along the Pelham Hills and the west side of the Swift River valley and Quabbin Reservoir watershed. After traversing the ledges of Wendell State Forest and the Millers River valley, the NET continues through the remote, densely forested uplands of northeastern Franklin County, the Bald Hills of Northfield, and Mount Grace in Warwick (the trail's highest point at 1,621 feet), before ending near Royalston Falls at the New Hampshire state line. In southern New Hampshire, the M-M Trail continues without federal designation another 18 miles to the summit of Mount Monadnock.

Since the federal designation, the original M-M Trail has been relocated several times to accommodate the wishes of private landowners, especially north of the Holyoke Range. A 22-mile segment between Mount Lincoln in Pelham and Wendell State Forest was rerouted east, to state water supply land on the west side of Quabbin Reservoir. Although no longer part of the official route, portions of the bypassed M-M Trail, including segments at Holland Glen, Buffam Brook Conservation Area, and Mount Orient, are still open to the public. As of this writing, a few M-M Trail signs and markers are still present along the current NET and its original route.

A limited number of camping facilities are available along the NET in Massachusetts, including Mount Holyoke Outing Club's cabin at Mount Holyoke (seasonal, fee), AMC's Richardson-Zlogar Cabin at Stratton Mountain (reservations required, nominal fee), and primitive shelters at Wendell State Forest, Mount

Grace, and Royalston Falls Reservation (all free). Campers should visit the NET website to confirm availability and to post intent to stay.

The official NET website, newenglandtrail.org, includes maps, trail descriptions, updates and advisories, and camping information. AMC's *New England Trail Map & Guide,* a set of waterproof maps, includes suggested day hikes, as well as natural and historical information.

The following hikes in this book are on portions of the New England Trail:

- Mount Tom State Reservation
- Mount Holyoke
- Mount Norwottuck, the Horse Caves, and Rattlesnake Knob
- Mount Lincoln and Scarborough Brook Conservation Area
- Wendell State Forest
- Hermit Mountain and Hermit's Castle
- Stratton Mountain
- Mount Grace State Forest
- Royalston Falls Reservation

MAHICAN-MOHAWK TRAIL

Mahican-Mohawk Trail, originally conceived by Williams College students during the 1990s, is a partially completed long-distance trail that links the Connecticut River and Hudson River via historical American Indian travel corridors along the Deerfield and Hoosic rivers. As of this writing, roughly 40 miles of the planned 100-mile route are open, including a segment in Mohawk Trail State Forest and a 10-mile paddling trail on Deerfield River. Many organizations and agencies have been involved in the development of the trail, including the Appalachian Mountain Club, Massachusetts Department of Conservation and Recreation, and Deerfield River Watershed Association. Portions of the trail may be closed at times due to unsafe conditions or landowner restrictions. For more information, visit mass.gov/eea/agencies/dcr/services-and-assistance/grants-and-technical-assistance/the-mahican-mohawk-trail.html

MIDSTATE TRAIL

The Midstate Trail, established during the 1970s and 1980s, runs generally north and south 92 miles across the hills of central Massachusetts. It links many conservation areas and landmarks, including Mount Watatic, Crow Hill in Leominster State Forest, Redemption Rock, Wachusett Mountain, Wachusett Meadow Wildlife Sanctuary, Barre Falls Dam and Ware River, and Douglas State Forest. The Midstate Trail is the central link in a regional trail network that includes the 22-mile Wapack Trail in southern New Hampshire and the 77-mile North–South Trail in Rhode Island. Collectively, the three trails form a continuous 200-mile route and greenway corridor. The Appalachian Mountain Club's Midstate Trail Committee maintains a website (midstatetrail.org) and a guide to the trail.

POCUMTUCK RIDGE TRAIL

Pocumtuck Ridge Trail traverses the crest of the Pocumtuck Ridge, which extends 15 miles along the west side of the Connecticut River valley, from Mount Sugarloaf State Reservation in Deerfield to Rocky Mountain and Canada Hill in Greenfield. The trail, created by the Appalachian Mountain Club's Berkshire Chapter and other organizations in 2001, passes through a mosaic of public and private lands. There is currently one gap in the route, at a railroad crossing near the Deerfield River, but this can be bypassed by a road walk. The trail is marked with blue blazes that were updated in most sections in 2016 and 2017.

ROBERT FROST TRAIL

Robert Frost Trail, originally created during the 1980s to link conservation areas in the town of Amherst, now extends 47 miles along the east side of the Connecticut River valley, from Holyoke Range State Park to Wendell State Forest. The trail passes through a fine sampling of habitats, including the Holyoke Range and Mount Toby; Lawrence Swamp; the Mill and Fort rivers; numerous streams, brooks, and ponds; and protected farmland. This route connects with many other trails in the Pioneer Valley, including the New England Trail, the Amherst Conservation and Mount Toby trail networks, and portions of the former Metacomet-Monadnock Trail. A map and guide (2004) from the Amherst Conservation Department and the Amherst Area Trails Committee is available online at amherstma.gov/DocumentCenter/Home/View/610.

TULLY TRAIL

Tully Trail, a 21-mile circuit in the Tully River valley in north-central Massachusetts, was built in 2001 as part of the Tully Initiative and North Quabbin Bioreserve. The route links Tully Mountain, Tully Lake, Long Pond, Jacobs Hill, Spirit Falls, Royalston Falls, and other protected public and private lands. Overnight camping is available at Tully Lake Campground (open seasonally) and at Royalston Falls Reservation (a group shelter at Falls Brook). Tully Trail coincides with a portion of the New England Trail in Royalston. For more information, visit thetrustees.org.

WAPACK TRAIL

Wapack Trail, created during the 1920s, offers outstanding low mountain hiking along the crest of the Wapack Range, including Mount Watatic; Pratt, Barrett, Kidder, and Temple mountains; Pack Monadnock; and North Pack Monadnock. Along the way are many fine views of Mount Monadnock and the surrounding countryside. The 21-mile route overlaps with the north end of the Midstate Trail, from the Mount Watatic Reservation entrance on MA 119 to the New Hampshire state line. Friends of the Wapack maintains a website (wapack.org) and a guide to the trail.

APPENDIX B: CAMPING

From secluded backcountry shelters to full-service facilities, central Massachusetts offers a variety of options for campers. A few primitive shelters are located on the New England Trail and other trails. Public campgrounds generally offer basic amenities, including restrooms, showers, swimming beaches, boat launches, and picnic areas. In addition to the public sites listed below, there are many privately owned campgrounds that offer extra features, such as playgrounds, family activities and events, and RV hookups.

The camping season generally runs from May to September or mid-October; specific dates vary annually by location. Reservations for Massachusetts state forest and park campgrounds can be made anytime from six months to one day in advance through Reserve America (reserveamerica.com). For all campgrounds, public or private, be sure to contact the management ahead of time to confirm availability and amenities.

FRANKLIN COUNTY

Monroe State Forest, Tilda Hill Road and River Road, Florida (413-339-5504, mass.gov/locations/monroe-state-forest); three primitive shelters at Dunbar Brook, Ridge, and Smith Hollow, no facilities

Mohawk Trail State Forest, Cold River Road, Charlemont (413-339-5504, mass.gov/locations/mohawk-trail-state-forest); 47 seasonal sites, six log cabins available year-round near Cold River and Mahican-Mohawk Trail

Kenneth Dubuque Memorial State Forest, 466 West Hawley Road, Plainfield (413-339-5504, mass.gov/locations/kenneth-dubuque-memorial-state-forest); two primitive shelters at Basin Brook and Moody Spring, no facilities

Wendell State Forest, 392 Wendell Road, Millers Falls (413-659-3797, newenglandtrail.org/facilities/wendell-state-forest-shelter); one primitive shelter on New England Trail near Ruggles Pond day-use area, no facilities

Stratton Mountain, Northfield (newenglandtrail.org/facilities/richardson-zlogar-cabin); Appalachian Mountain Club's enclosed Richardson-Zlogar Cabin on the New England Trail, available by reservation for a donation of $3 per person, two-night limit, great views

Mount Grace State Forest, 78 Winchester Road, Warwick (978-544-3939, newenglandtrail.org/facilities/mt-grace-shelter); one primitive shelter on the New England Trail, north of summit near MA 78 crossing, no facilities

Erving State Forest, 200 East Main Street, Erving (978-544-7745 for campground, seasonal from late May through Labor Day weekend; 978-544-3939 for recreational area, year-round; mass.gov/locations/erving-state-forest); 27 sites near Laurel Lake, swimming beach, boat launch, nature trails

HAMPSHIRE AND HAMPDEN COUNTIES

Granville State Forest, 323 West Hartland Road, Granville (413-357-6611, mass.gov/locations/granville-state-forest); 22 sites on Halfway Brook near Hubbard River

Tolland State Forest, 410 Tolland Road, East Otis (413-269-6002, mass.gov/locations/tolland-state-forest); 92 sites near Otis Reservoir, boat launch, swimming beach

Daughters of the American Revolution State Forest, 78 Cape Street, Goshen (413-268-7098, mass.gov/locations/daughters-of-the-american -revolution-dar-state-forest); 51 sites near Highland Lake, beach, boat launch, universally accessible trail

WORCESTER COUNTY

Federated Women's Club State Forest, State Forest Road, Petersham (978-544-3939, mass.gov/locations/federated-womens-club-state-forest); fifteen primitive sites near Soapstone Hill and Quabbin Reservoir, unstaffed, access via Erving State Forest (see above)

Bearsden Conservation Area, Bearsden Road, Athol (978-413-1772, athol-ma.gov/parks-trails/pages/bearsden-conservation-area); two primitive shelters on Millers River at Duck Pond and Buckman Brook, cabin near main entrance, no facilities, reservations required

Tully Lake Campground, 25 Doane Hill Road, Royalston (978-249-4957, tullylakecampground.org); 35 sites (seventeen waterfront) on Tully Lake near Doane's Falls and Long Pond, boat rentals and launches, hiking and mountain bike trails

Royalston Falls Reservation, MA 32, Royalston (978-249-4957, newenglandtrail.org/facilities/ttor-shelter-royalston-falls); one primitive shelter on New England Trail and Tully Trail near Royalston Falls, no facilities

Lake Dennison Recreation Area, 86 Winchendon Road (US 202), Baldwinville (978-297-1609 seasonal, 978-939-8962 year-round, mass.gov/locations/lake-dennison-recreation-area); 150 sites on Lake Dennison, beach, boat launch, access to 50 miles of trails

Otter River State Forest, 86 Winchendon Road, (US 202), Baldwinville (978-939-8962, mass.gov/locations/otter-river-state-forest); 75 sites, six yurts, beach at Beaman Pond, nature trail to Lake Dennison

Willard Brook State Forest, 10 Townsend Road (MA 119), Ashby (978-597-8802, mass.gov/locations/willard-brook-state-park); nineteen sites, one group yurt, beach at Damon Pond

Pearl Hill State Park, 105 New Fitchburg Road, West Townsend (978-597-2850 for campground office from Memorial Day weekend through Labor Day weekend, 978-597-8802 year-round, mass.gov/locations/pearl-hill-state-park); 50 sites, beach at Pearl Hill Brook Pond, trails to Willard Brook State Forest

Wells State Park, 159 Walker Pond Road, Sturbridge (877-422-6762 reservations, 508-347-9257 park headquarters, mass.gov/locations/wells-state-park); 60 sites at Walker Pond, trails, boat launch

INDEX

ABOUT THE AUTHOR

John S. Burk is an outdoor writer, photographer, and historian from central Massachusetts. He has authored or edited more than a dozen books and guides, including AMC's *Massachusetts Trail Guide*, *New England National Scenic Trail Map and Guide*, and *Bay Circuit Trail Map and Guide*. He has also contributed to *AMC Outdoors*, *Northern Woodlands*, *Natural New England*, *Sanctuary*, and other publications. To see more of his work, visit johnburk.zenfolio.com.

AMC BOOK UPDATES

At AMC Books, we keep our guidebooks as up-to-date as possible to help you plan safe and enjoyable adventures. After publishing a book, if we learn that trails have been relocated, or that route or contact information has changed, we will post an update online. Before you hit the trail, check outdoors.org/bookupdates.

While hiking, if you notice discrepancies with a trip description or map, or if you find any other errors in the book, please submit them by email to amcbookupdates@outdoors.org or by letter to Books Editor, c/o AMC, 10 City Square, Boston, MA 02129. We will verify all submissions and post key updates each month. We are dedicated to making AMC Books a recognized leader in outdoor publishing. Thank you for your participation.

ABOUT AMC IN CENTRAL MASSACHUSETTS

Established in 1918 as one of AMC's very first chapters, the Worcester Chapter has approximately 3,000 members and offers hundreds of trips each year. Trained and dedicated leaders guide hiking, backpacking, bicycling, paddling, skiing, and climbing excursions, in addition to family activities. The chapter's 20s and 30s group has been very successful in attracting young members and often hosts social events, in addition to outdoor activities. In partnership with land managers, AMC's Worcester Chapter is the lead trail maintainer of Mount Wachusett State Reservation and the Midstate Trail.

Learn more at amcworcester.org and read about all twelve of AMC's regional chapters at outdoors.org/chapters. Browse a complete list of upcoming AMC activities in central Massachusetts and elsewhere in the Northeast at outdoors.org/activities.

APPALACHIAN MOUNTAIN CLUB

At AMC, connecting you to the freedom and exhilaration of the outdoors is our calling. We help people of all ages and abilities to explore and develop a deep appreciation of the natural world.

AMC helps you get outdoors on your own, with family and friends, and through activities close to home and beyond. With chapters from Maine to Washington, D.C., including groups in Boston, New York City, and Philadelphia, you can enjoy activities like hiking, paddling, cycling, and skiing, and learn new outdoor skills. We offer advice, guidebooks, maps, and unique lodges and huts to inspire your next outing. You will also have the opportunity to support conservation advocacy and research, youth programming, and caring for 1,800 miles of trails.

We invite you to join us in the outdoors.

YOUR CONNECTION TO THE OUTDOORS

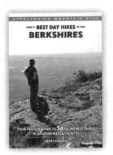